I Also Ran
by
Mike Who?

MIKE FLEET

'Oh, to be at Motspur Park
with the sun in its heaven
and the half-mile about to begin!'

Bob Phillips

Cover Photos

Centre
"Mike Who" in mermaid mode post Commonwealth Games, in Perth,
Western Australia, 1962.

The photo is © Pathe News and reproduced with their permission. It was
previously unknown to the author until discovered by Martin Rowe (Croydon
Harriers technical wizard).

Top
Mature Mike (Top left No. 5) chases a youthful Steve Ovett, the race winner (far
right No. 1)

Left
Peter Snell (No. 28) wins 1962 Commonwealth 880yds, with Mike fifth.

Bottom Right
Chris Chataway wins 1956 Croydon 800m, with Mike (L) third.

This book has been very carefully researched and sources checked as fully
as possible.

Acknowledgement is given to all known sources.

Published June 2011

© Speedy Publications of Purley
2 Ridge Park, Purley, Surrey, CR8 3PN

ISBN 978-0-9566471-0-8

Designed and printed by CDS.

I Also Ran
by
Mike Who?

MIKE FLEET

SPP
Speedy
Publications
of Purley

*I dedicate my book to all the
wonderful people whom,
thanks to athletics, I have been
privileged to meet.*

Contents

Foreword

by The Right Honourable Sir Christopher Chataway

This is a book, as the author says, about an almost lifelong involvement in the great sport of athletics. To those with a love of the sport it will be a source of interest, amusement, surprise and, I think, inspiration.

I first met Mike Fleet on a track in Croydon in 1956. I was a few months away from the end of my athletics career preparing for the Melbourne Olympics 5000 metres. Mike was just 18 at the start of what would be a much longer athletic journey.

It was during an 800 metres and, with a last minute burst, I just managed to inch past a boy, of whom of course I had never heard. The time inside 1:54.0 was good enough for me and in those days very good indeed for a lad of Mike's age.

My pride must have been injured to have to struggle so hard to beat somebody so much younger and I am relieved to read from this book that I was good humoured and encouraging. I am not always pleased by the later recollections of those who remember me in my aggressive, competitive youth!

Mike went on to run the 800 metres as fast or faster no less than a hundred times in a career that won him many titles and international representation. He ran inside 1:49.0, which put him in the leading cohort of his generation. And yet his potential was never quite fulfilled.

Perhaps more than in most sports ultimate success in athletics depends upon the luck of being fit and injury free upon a particular day and luck was not always a lady to Mike Fleet. His assault on the ultimate peaks was thwarted by illness. But he did not let disappointment fester. He turned out to be one of those for whom it is a spur.

Over more than half a century his contribution to the sport he loves, despite its occasional unkindnesses to him, has been remarkable. Croydon Harriers owes him a huge debt for almost four decades as its Honorary Secretary, and he has served in many a committee room as one of sport's indefatigable administrators.

There is very little he does not know about the arcane skills required of a starter or a timekeeper. He has branched out from the middle distance races to the very different world of the field events. But perhaps his biggest contribution of all has been as a coach.

Quite apart from his professional contribution as a PE teacher and lecturer, he calculates that he has given some 12,000 hours of unpaid coaching. He has coached to the highest level and he has had the disappointment of seeing early promise discarded.

He has coached many who had no very particular talents and no illusions of greatness but to whom their personal goals were of real importance. He says that he has had the huge privilege of helping hundreds of athletes to achieve successes. He writes also that there is nothing to match sharing the uninhibited joy of a boy or girl setting a personal best.

The sport of athletics has taken Mike around the world and placed him in a host of unlikely situations. It has given him much and he has given it even more. Here the reader gets an account of one man's athletics career but also amusing interesting insights into the history of the sport and into its nooks and crannies. Also some, I hope, will find in these pages an inspiration to follow Mike into coaching.

Mike and Chris have post race chat 1956.

1

The Story of a Non-Olympian...

...dedicated to the many hundreds of people from whom I have derived inspiration.

Three in particular stand out, Alf Tupper, Tommy Jover and Gordon Pirie.

The fictional fish-and-chip-eating Alf Tupper, the athletics star of the Rover comic; Tommy Jover, the mercurial, dashing Dulwich Hamlet FC winger of the 1950s and the late great legend of British athletics, the enigmatic Gordon Pirie.

...Alf Tupper, boyhood hero, the totally inspirational "Tough of the Track", whose world beating athletic exploits thousands of boys avidly consumed in the Rover comic, was the weekly target of my limited teenage literary attention. No challenge was beyond him. How many of today's finely honed athletes could match his 5 miles in 26 minutes? I believe I am right in recalling that he beat Roger Bannister in running a mile in less than 4 minutes while eluding the police for an alleged lorry high-jack!

See Figure 1 – Alf Tupper

In one notable mile race which featured the conniving Greystone committee man Marchant, Tupper had to overcome an unfair handicap, plus nineteen other men, to win. Nearing the end of the race, Tupper muttered "This is where I bounce him" and cut loose. If his judgment was wrong and his energy faded before he reached the tape he would finish as an "also ran". Alf ran elbow to elbow with him. He heard the captain's harsh gasping breath. Marchant fell back. Alf hurled out his arms and broke the tape. He always viewed blazer clad university "Toffs" with disdain, "ran 'em all" and feared no one other than his redoubtable Aunt Amy! A welder by day, he lived rough, and flourished on an outrageous diet of fish and chips and lard sandwiches. He was certainly not averse to a pint or two of the best, in those distant times when it was often claimed that beer was the only drug readily available to assist athletes. Nowadays when I succumb to the excesses of an "Alf Tupper supper" I can relate to the need of his metabolism to persuade him to run it off. Alas, having succumbed to the effects of the passage of time, I have to rely on the fat-destroying benefits of a glass of good red wine.

I cannot remember you ever having been beaten, Alf. What a man. Good health!

Elsewhere in real sporting life, Tommy Jover caught my youthful attention as a dynamic footballer at many Dulwich Hamlet F.C. home matches to which I was taken by my father in the 1950s. From the moment the Champion Hill public address blared its "Entry of the Gladiators" welcome to the teams, out would come the pink-and-blue-clad combatants, invariably led by the trotting Tommy. When the music stopped, most of the players did too, but not so my hero!

He seemed never to stop running, exuding the joy of fitness even when way out of the action. More often than not he used his impressive speed to reach an "impossible ball" and then wreak havoc among off-guard defenders. At the final whistle Tommy would pause to shake nearby hands before jogging off, one assumes for the traditional soothing team bath, followed by a well deserved "cuppa"!

More than fifty years elapsed before I was to discover that Tommy had enjoyed a significant second sporting life, as an athlete. He was a 9.9sec Herne Hill Harriers 100 yards man, who had represented Great Britain with distinction in the 1946 European Championships in Oslo. He was lead runner in the 4x100m relay team which finished 5th in the final in 42.4sec, the team having run 0.1 sec faster in the semi-final. No wonder he could so easily outrun his opponents on the football field!

It was with great delight in the summer of 2008 that I discovered he was still alive and President of his beloved Dulwich Hamlet FC. I made several fruitless telephone calls, attempting to contact him via the club before I resorted to thumbing the pages of an old telephone directory. Thankfully the search did not take long for there was just one Jover in the book and significantly, preceding the initial T. I immediately picked up the phone and dialled. To my relief a man's voice answered.

"Hello?"
"Oh, hello, I am Mike Fleet, you don't know me. I am very much hoping to talk to Tommy Jover."
"It's me!" said the man, *"How can I help you – I was 91 in July you know?"*

See Figure 2 – Tommy Jover (left), the speedy Dulwich Hamlet winger

In the very friendly conversation which followed, Tommy told me that he had only been out of hospital for a short while, but was feeling better. Then I explained briefly the reason for my call. He seemed surprised that he had been instrumental in inspiring me at the formative stage of my modest but rewarding athletics career. I expressed the hope that we would be able to meet soon, but that I would shortly be off to China to watch the Beijing Olympics and that I was going in particular to support my Loughborough-based protégé Martyn Rooney and other Team GB athletes in pursuit of Olympic glory. Tommy understood, and we agreed that our meeting would have to be postponed.

"As soon as you're back you must come round for a cup of tea and a chat," Tommy kindly invited.

On August 19th Rooney ran himself into the Olympic 400m final at the tender age of 21 with Britain's 8th fastest 400m run, a fantastic 44.60sec clocking. I would like to think that Tommy, the former international Herne Hill Harriers sprinter, watched and enjoyed that run as much as I did, for very sadly he passed away just six days later.

Like thousands of other South London schoolboys, I was genuinely inspired too, in truly athletics terms, by a local hero, the hugely admired, controversial Coulsdon athlete, Gordon "Puff Puff" Pirie. He was affectionately known as "Dagwood" after his initials D.A.G. and not by any unlikely association with comic character Dagwood Bumstead. The only tenuous connection, might have been Bumstead's huge appetite and the fact that he appeared in what is described as a long running comic strip "Blondie". The fictional Dagwood only ran when he was late for work and was always frantic to catch his lift. Pirie, in direct contrast, trained regularly at lunchtimes on my old school playing field, which was then a rare green oasis in central Croydon, remaining so until the mid 1960s.

Gordon was the first star athlete whom I saw close up in captivating action. His Herculean lunchtime training sessions thrilled throngs of boys who would otherwise have been engaged in playground football. He would sprint and stride interminably, seemingly without effort, and would further enthral his youthful admirers when at well chosen moments he used his huge lung power to expel refreshing mouthfuls of water impressive distances in their direction.

See Figure 3 – Gordon Pirie, characteristically in the lead

Always attacking world records or the sub 4 minute mile barrier, he regularly attracted crowds of 5,000 or more to witness his efforts at the Croydon Arena in the 1950s, where he also trained impressively, often using numerous awestruck club athletes as training fodder. The World 3000m record he set in 1956 stood for 6 years. His Croydon Arena 10,000m ground record of 29:17.2 achieved in the same year remains intact. I confess to having been sucked into small sections of several mind boggling sessions, some of which featured so much mileage that we mere mortals were obliged to run in relays in order to provide him with realistic support!

Gordon ran many hundreds of miles too, in army boots, over the nearby Farthing Downs. No respecter of humbling officialdom as he saw it, he would cut his competitors numbers down to lighten his load when racing. He was a constant critic of poorly prepared cinder tracks which were all too often encountered in those distant days. No respecter of reputations either, he always believed and more often than not proved, that he could beat rivals over distances as short as the mile, not really considered to be within his range.

One fine autumnal day in 2008, after his tragically early death, I arranged to meet up with Dick Booth, fellow Pirie admirer and author of "The Impossible Hero", the definitive biography of the great runner. We made our "Pilgrimage" to the Gordon Pirie memorial seat on his beloved Farthing Downs in Coulsdon and while we reminisced that mild November morning it was easy to imagine the gaunt figure of triple Olympian Gordon ghosting by.

Cheeks puffing out characteristically with effort, his feet willingly burdened with army boots, mercilessly pounding the ground in pursuit of eternal perfection, he was certainly an awesome, inspirational, unforgettable rebel. One of two inquisitive passing dog walkers, previously unaware of the achievements of the man immortalised by the bench, kindly took photos which record the occasion for posterity.

See Figure 4 – Mike and Pirie biographer Dick Booth on Gordon's memorial seat, Farthing Downs

After Tupper, Jover and Pirie, there has been a myriad of men and women who, either wittingly or unwittingly, have also been hugely inspirational to me, whether setting examples to follow or sharing their own fascinating "Memory Lanes".

My aim, fellow enthusiast, and you must be an enthusiast to be reading this story, is to share with you the joys, delights, and perhaps some of the disappointments, of an athlete who ALSO RAN!

2

At the Start

I always jokingly refer to my place of birth as having been "within the sound of the Streatham Ice Rink" in South London, not the traditional Bow Bells which would certainly have been more romantic. The chosen nursing home in nearby Albemarle Road, where family and fate decided I should arrive, was a significant 880 yards away, so that the delighted screams of any Valentine's Day revellers who might have been romanticising on the ice, could not have been heard.

The very nature of my feet-first arrival on 14th February 1938, St. Valentine's Day, suggested, I am told, that it was thought even then that I might become an athlete of some kind, possibly even a pole-vaulter. In those days, before foam modules, vaulters chose, more often than not, to land feet first on the heaped-up available sand. Those personally blank days of babyhood and early infancy were, I was reliably informed by my parents, athletically barren. From time to time I am still reminded that my lungs gave every indication that I was an extremely healthy baby!

See Figure 5 – In the footsteps of Milo de Cretona

I was the first child of modestly sporting parents: mother had won a gym badge at school and father had collapsed during a cross-country race and played family tennis before World War II, my future as a serious athlete would indeed have been a long shot flutter for a rash gambler.

Recent research has however discovered thatany true athletic ability I might have had could have been helped along the gene pathway by a possible distant relative, one John Fleet (1845-84), known as "Young Fleet". He was a good-looking Victorian gentleman, according to my mother on seeing his picture, and came from Manchester, city of my father's birth in 1908. He is described in Warren Roe's book "Front Runners" as a pedestrian star who, in 1867, despite his "game and strenuous efforts" succumbed in a thrilling 880 yards race won by James Nuttall in 1 minutes 55¾ seconds by a mere 2 yards. In the same year he set a British Record of 6 minutes 50 seconds for the mile and a half, and ran his best mile in 4 minutes 23½ seconds. Any genealogical connection has yet to be proved!

See Figure 6 – John Fleet

According to the most reliable of witnesses, namely my 99-year-old mother Beryl, affectionately known as the "The Old Bat", I had to be reined in very soon after learning to walk. Any need for more precise detail was promptly forgotten as she asked whether I had remembered something far more important, namely her minimal weekly meat order from Parkers the Butchers!

So far as I can recall, my first encounter with anything mildly approaching the adrenalin buzz of our beloved sport came during infants' school mid-day break on the smallest of playing fields. It was in reality a small undulating, unattractive, much child-worn back garden, of what is today the detached "des. res" at the junction of Florida Road and Brickfield Road in Thornton Heath. In those distant days just after the war, it was the best that the austere sounding and looking Mrs Coffin, the Principal of Aberdeen House Private Infants School, could provide.

The favourite playtime activity of the decidedly noisy little throng there was a brutally basic version of "Chain He". With their hands linked, the fortunate dashed headlong at other contestants and "Refuseniks" alike until all were caught. The terrorised minority were more often than not forced to retreat scratched and breathless into the relatively safe haven of the gooseberry bushes at the bottom of the garden. Even there they were at further risk, both externally from the gooseberry bushes' prickly defences and internally from the tempting but more often than not unripe fruit.

See Figure 7 – "Chain He"

The late summer-term lunch-times were the safest, with the hairy green berries just emerging from their earlier, near lethal marble-like state. Whatever the ripeness of these spoils, they were definitely incompatible with the warm government-issued milk which most young post-war children were forced to drink at the start of each day! Any serious running was certainly not inspired by athletic ambition then. It was merely a matter of self preservation ahead of the masses.

I definitely didn't like being caught and it was that hate, plus the fact that my father was for much of his life a Midlander, which maybe later led me to unofficially adopt the Birchfield Harriers motto of "Fleet and Free". Or perhaps in those distant days it would more appropriately have been "Fleet and Flee!" Thanks to the "generosity" and sense of humour of one of their officials, I am now the somewhat embarrassed owner of a miniscule crop-top which does at least have the relevance of bearing their badge and the motto. I do wonder, however, if there is a hidden message which I have missed!

Apart from a wonderful press photo, which I discovered at about that time under a bedroom carpet, of a magnificent looking athlete executing a perfect sprint start at the 1936 Berlin Olympic Games, who I was later to learn was the legendary Jesse Owens, post war 1946 saw me blissfully unaware of serious competitive athletics.

See Figure 8 – The legendary Jesse Owens blasts out of blocks in Berlin

On one memorable occasion a little later, my father, a National Fire Serviceman during World War II, who had been based at a commandeered house beside Tooting Bec Common, took me to see the action on the nearby athletics track. There, wide eyed and fascinated, I witnessed sprinters trowelling start holes in the cinders, and splendid sateen-shorted demi-gods striding and sprinting in enthralling competition before my sport-starved wide young eyes, among them star miler, the lilac-shorted Bill Nankeville of Walton AC, Herne Hill Harrier Terence Higgins and David Rawe, plus otherwise unidentified Belgrave Harriers sporting their maroon and gold vests. I must then have been watching my first athletics match, since I clearly remember the distinctive vests, the red and black hooped ones of Herne Hill Harriers too. I am surprised however that I do not remember a starting pistol being fired. Perhaps gunpowder was at a premium so soon after the war!

Despite that exciting experience, I was however understandably oblivious, at the time, of the best British 800m performance and world record set in 1938 by Sydney Wooderson. The legendary little Blackheath Harrier had run 1:48.4[1] when I was just six months old. There were clearly no Olympic aspirations yet so far as I was concerned! Little could I have imagined sixteen years later that I would better his time, yet when I did, a new world record would have moved significantly beyond my reach! It would be even longer before I had the privilege of actually meeting the very modest little man with the towering reputation, who was amazingly only 5 feet 4 inches tall!

That brief but memorable encounter came much later in 1978, when

---

[1] Sydney crossed the line in 'second' place behind his brother Stanley who had started off 85 yards, with five others spread strategically behind him for Sydney's benefit.

Blackheath Harriers celebrated their Centenary by staging a 100x1mile relay at the Croydon Sports Arena. Wooderson, some 24 years my senior and with feet wisely bandaged for support, ran beautifully for a man in his late sixties, setting a standard which didn't permit any of us upstarts to dare contemplate an easy day.

Clearly with the benefit of hindsight, my athletic future had already begun to take shape. Throughout infancy, primary and secondary schools, National Service, student life, and during my career as a physical education and geography teacher, athletics coach and long-time Croydon Harriers Secretary, and most recently into retirement, I ALSO RAN, retrogressively I must add, with less speed and less frequency!

The inevitable evolution of my athletics was possibly due in part to my "headless chicken" approach to the many scouting wide games in which I took part which were tackled with very little thought, but considerable tactical application. I was not deterred by my grandfather Fred Gann who was a voluble sceptic:

"All that running about must put a strain on your heart, m'boy", he would often proclaim.

Perhaps the passage of time from the early 1900s had dulled his memory, for several people credited his robust health to an active life which featured rowing and tennis but also included, maybe most significantly for me, "Goal Running". This was a grandiose game of chase popular in East Kent in his youth. It was a form of handicap athletics and they even employed a starter! Its bequest might well also be in the genes. However, despite his doubts, he did many years later, I guess, approvingly inform the Whitstable Times and Tankerton Press of my first major success, details of which sneaked in after the opening paragraph...

Only a split Second
Behind Chataway

"Eighteen-years-old Michael
Fleet, the only grandson of Mr.
and Mrs. F. S. Gann of 5
Saddleton Road, Whitstable, and
the son of Mr. and Mrs. (Beryl)
Fleet, of Thornton Heath, is
hoping to become a sports and
languages master..."

The idea of becoming a languages master was new to me, but the other information apart from the reduced margin of my defeat was true enough. The old chap's account went on to add 0.1 sec to Chataway's time, but it was clear from the feature that any doubts he had held earlier about the benefits of athletics had been allayed!

In scouting wide games I conspicuously ignored the clues, following the leaders at a discreet distance until the final check. I would then sprint home first, often without any idea of the academically generated solutions to be sought! Any concession by me to unravel their hidden information was the threat of ego-deflating delay. One simply had to be back at base first! Perhaps I should have been suspended from Baden Powell's fine movement for such behaviour well before I was actually removed for a different reason, namely "fouling the nest", as the troop leader so succinctly put it! All that I did, after having been dropped from their soccer team, very unfairly I hasten to add, was to pour a generous dose of hydrogen sulphide onto the 61st Croydon Scout Troop football shirts! Even I was surprised at the speed I was able to call on, when I was disturbed midway through the dread deed. Once again my competitive nature had dropped me into deep water, and I was only saved from immediate detection by applying my pace to escape discovery. I hasten to add that after a telling off from my father and a good laundry job by my mother, I was reinstated.

At about the same time my grandfather, who lived by the sea at Whitstable in Kent, unwittingly contributed to my latent athletics career when he made me a mid-sized shrimping net. This stroke of luck led me to spend many happy hours during my early summer holidays, trudging at low tide through the shallow therapeutic water covering the mud flats off nearby Tankerton. The hand-made net was optimistically pushed ahead, in patient pursuit of supper. I am sure that this significantly contributed to strengthening of my then somewhat spindly lower limbs. Their transition from the "Sparrows Legs" inherited from my mother, to "the thigh development and tapering lower leg of a great middle-distance runner", referred to in my favourite caption in "Tackle Athletics This Way", price 12s 6d by National Coach Dennis Watts ten years later, must surely be a link to those far off shrimp catching summer days at the seaside. How kind it was of that popular and observant expert to have been so complimentary.

See Figure 9 – "The Shrimping Boy"

A short time later whilst camping on Daphne Du Maurier's estate at

Menabilly Barton in Cornwall, I came pretty close to endangering my then unanticipated athletic career. Oblivious of any athletics potential and the rule applying then against winning prize money, I very nearly entered the boys 100 yards sprint in the Par Carnival Sports. Had there been a half mile, I would almost certainly have had a go, doubtless with a good chance of going back to camp with a pound or two. As it was, our scout leader, a suitably tall fellow in full uniform but with the sporting concession of plimsolls, entered and easily won the high jump, earning sufficient cash to buy us all ice creams and put his amateur status at risk!

Once into my mid-teens, I became more aware of the need to train regularly. Often on weekdays after completing my Whitgift Middle School homework, I would trot out of the house in T shirt, thick navy-blue rugby shorts and best Bata plimsolls ready for my routine half hour run. The self-created breeze, especially welcome on my cheeks on warm summer evenings, was beginning to become one of the great free pleasures of life. That refreshing stint from Virginia Road in Thornton Heath to the Streatham end of Green Lane and back which has now been swallowed into the anonymity of South London, was in those days a realistic and relatively safe challenge.

Yes boys and girls, mums and dads, it can be done! I did my homework and I also ran! My record for the distance, a time which now eludes me, can be traced directly to the unwelcome attention of a surprisingly quick and tenacious corgi dog. That highly competitive canine creature "sportingly accompanied" me at greatly increasing speed for the final five hundred yards of my memorable barrier-breaking, or was it a front door breaking, run up my road to the safe haven of the family home. I do recall chopping a huge chunk off my previous best which ensured that the "dear little dog" physically failed to do likewise to either or both my legs!

See Figure 10 – "Corgi Record Chase"

There was one other occasion when unplanned speed training had to be incorporated. On other more relaxed occasions it was by choice. A very rare, threatening group of cycle chain-wielding youths swaggered along the pavement towards me but being drunk and uncoordinated, they seemed far less of a danger than the aforementioned hound. I did however deem it prudent to inject a good 300 yard precautionary surge, which incorporated a detour to the other side of the road. This had a doubly desired effect, for not only did I achieve another very quick run, but I also improved my powers of acceleration. I must concede that

I would nowadays, were my body to permit, think twice about running there alone at night. There are far too many unruly youngsters at large, plus a prevalence of dogs seeming to have been specifically trained to pursue athletes.

In moments of wishful thinking, I have sometimes tried to imagine that I could match the motorised speed of 1950 ace racing driver Stirling Moss who surely set, and may still hold, the "Green Lane Grand Prix record" over the unmeasured mile! That must have been achieved when he was "gonged down" by a police patrol while blissfully unaware of exceeding the 30mph limit. Rumour had it that he got off lightly in return for some autographed photographs!

On a more artistic note, stimulated by ambition, I would imagine replicating In my running the grace and rhythm of a gazelle, racing at full speed, bounding over and between imaginary hills and valleys. Exhilarating pieces of music too, like the Litolf Scherzo in D, or the finale of Saint Saens' Piano Concerto No.2, would often inspire me to go for unscheduled runs and would accompany me in my head. I would speed, Impossibly fast in my mind, over challenging routes and then quickly return to reality. Clearly I was pre-empting the present day trend of iPod use but at least in my musical reverie there was no exclusion of the sounds of danger.

Sharing the roads of my area at about that time and clearly endowed with short legs better suited to climbing hills than mine was an enthusiastic little fellow whom I judged offered no challenge to my competitive career. David Cocksedge was later to become as dedicated to athletics as I was but in the totally different field of statistics, as a key member of the National Union of Track Statisticians. I did subsequently become a NUT, however only peripherally, as self-appointed custodian of the stadium records for the Crystal Palace National Recreation Centre.

Such were, and happily still are, the distractions of an almost incurable running enthusiast's body and mind. Cast almost in the near addictive Ron Hill mode of a daily run for a fix of adrenaline, regardless of illness, broken limbs or foul weather, I had trotted along regularly until a few complaints from my body decreed discretion and subsequently rewarding rest days.

Nowadays my exercise is restricted by wear and tear. A 20 minute maximum swim, a gentle gym workout, a two or three hour walk or umpiring a hockey match are still possible at 70+, and preferable to clutching at the remnants of a damaging run which would surely also generate ridicule.

Fortunately I did not go down the path of an elderly female fitness fanatic whom I still see plodding round Croydon at snail's pace, in her velvet tracksuit and piratical headscarf! How the athletic fraternity misguidedly mocked, as she is known more sympathetically near where she lives as "the lady who runs everywhere". Joan Pick, a 60+-year-old "Energy economist", has only used motorised transport once since 1973 and that was when she was taken to hospital by ambulance. She has only made a few train trips, justified by the need to attend her mother's funeral.

See Figure 11 – Joan Pick beats the bus

Far from being a "fruitcake" in the colloquial sense, this lady is more simply a person adhering to strongly held principles. While these are in many ways laudable, I do at least think that she deserves the "luxury" to which I have recently treated myself to aid continuing exercise, and that is a bicycle!

3

Baptisms of Fire

The Kensington Avenue Primary School Sports Day loomed large for those of us who, during break, regularly tested our "Segs and Blakeys", and ultimately shoes to the point of destruction, by running continuous laps around the tarmac playground. This was a much more popular activity than talking to silly girls, or even to swapping rare cigarette cards.

Sadly for any embryonic half milers or more, events in the sports day programme did not extend beyond 75 yards. Even over that limited distance there was the seemingly impenetrable barrier to success in the form of the apparently invincible Anthony Botten. Already unfairly boosted by a pristine pair of gleaming white Bata plimsolls, he had clearly been rendered unbeatable by the mysterious additional benefit of his uncle's "sprint grips[2]". The nervously waiting, cross-legged ranks of competitors didn't really know what was in store for them. After our enforced, seated, one hour "warm-up", or was it a "public barbecuing" beneath the relentless rays of the summer sun, we were all ready to race, or should that have read, ".. we were already roasted"? Maybe that experience subconsciously planted the seeds of my Loughborough thesis entitled, "A Study of the Physiological Effects of Warm-up on Explosive Performance" which was to emerge thirteen years later.

Predictably the grip-boosted Botten won with ease, while we who "Also Ran" struggled sweatily for the minor scraps of pre-teenage glory. My own smart new Bata plimsolls surely helped narrow the gap, but I had no answer to those grips! Afterwards, I was stupid enough to indulge in an overly histrionic attempt to alleviate my admiring mother's imagined disappointment. I put on a whirling dervish-like display of contrived anguish. This was a truly immature departure from Baron Pierre De Coubertin's famous ethic of sporting participation, of which at the time I was sadly unaware, and which in part I loosely translate here.

"The important thing (in the Olympics) is not so much winning but taking part; the important thing in life is not the triumph but the struggle; the essential thing is not to have conquered, but to have fought well".

---

[2] Wooden cigar-like grips believed to be beneficial in the 1920s

Rather unsportingly, I secretly wished that "Golden Boy Botten" might be taken down a peg or two by being pitted against our fleet-footed neighbour, the dashing "Auntie Fuller", convincing winner of the parents' race…! It was not to be and I got the public telling off which I deserved. I really should have been less demonstrative since my "reward" for drawing attention to myself was my first ever representative selection for, as you might imagine, the high jump, a then completely alien event for me! It seemed that my shrewd teacher, Mr Sibley, had used his talent-spotting of any innate athletic ability or perhaps it was simply his forte to find the perfect punishment to fit the crime? Whichever it was, I discovered that I had been chosen to appear at the District Sports the following week… in the dreaded event!

I claim that I was understandably nervous because I had no idea of the technique required, but was nonetheless excited by the selection. My misguided delight at having been chosen to represent the school was clearly tempered by my lack of experience. The challenge of the event itself, for which I had about as much interest as any self-respecting pot-holer, was for me indeed short-lived. It was further dampened by the daunting prospect of having to make only my second ever solo bus ride without the reassuring back-up of a parent, as had been the case a year or two earlier, while making my debut aboard a vintage London Transport LT vehicle complete with external stairs. Then only the hot pursuit of my frantically pedalling fireman father prevented me from contemplating my debut as a bus-assisted, record breaking backwards long jumper!

Once at the venue, Woodside Junior School in Addiscombe, I recall that I did manage to get off the ground, but in so doing became almost inextricably entwined in the weighted rope over which we were supposed to soar. If my memory serves me correctly, my almost self-asphyxiating performance, led to the premature conclusion of the event on grounds of health and safety or whatever preceded such adventure-restricting measures in those far off days!

Humbled and embarrassed, I secretly hoped that my mishaps might have led to the invention of something more user-friendly. Had "The Fleet Flexi Non-Knotting High Jump Lath" evolved as a result, my name might have gone down in athletic history. Well, perhaps not! Little could I realise then, that more than sixty years later, I would return to that very same field with six of my training group to coach athletics-hungry youngsters

Today's cognoscenti are, however, only too well aware that the major honour in the context of high jump, deservedly went to that "most backward" of its exponents, Dick Fosbury, who pioneered his unique reverse technique[3] in 1968 with a 2.24m triumph in the Mexico Olympics. Although highly successful, this became confusingly known as the "Fosbury Flop", acknowledging the movement of the athlete appearing to flop from a single foot take off backwards over the bar. Far from being a failure, the technique has triumphantly stood the test of time with all top jumpers still employing it.

See Figure 12 – Dick Fosbury pioneering the successful "Flop"

In 1949, at 11+, it was my good fortune to gain a scholarship place at the Whitgift Middle School in central Croydon which, with a name change became Trinity School of John Whitgift five years later. Today the school is only a memory there in name, with the huge Whitgift Shopping Centre having replaced it in 1966. Trinity School was then re-established on the site of the former Shirley Park Hotel two miles away. I soon discovered that I had arrived in the "awesome after-glow" of the seemingly "jet powered" A. D. Sexton, highly respected holder of a string of school athletics records, and school head boy the previous year and whom I am now extremely fortunate to consider a personal friend. I was also lucky to find myself in the presence of two other older and very talented athletes, John De'ath and Alan Hine, both of whom trained impressively on the North End field, often in the famous black and red hooped vests of the Herne Hill Harriers. One other early memory from about that time, hardly a figment of my vivid imagination, is of a "City Gent's 220 yard Sprint". It was, I thought, achieved in sub 25sec on the Whitgift Middle School track, in the appropriate garb, bowler hat, black jacket, pinstripe trousers and briefcase with the one concession of a pair of spikes by one Colin Buchanan who would later become Bishop of Aston and then of Woolwich, who, from retirement in Leeds, admits to having trained on the hallowed turf, but denies all knowledge of any such eccentricity. Should another "City Gent" read this and identify himself, I will publicly exonerate the Right Reverend Bishop Buchanan of all involvement!

See Figure 13 – Aerial view of Whitgift Middle School

In these inspirational sporting surroundings, it was all too easy to forget why one was attending such a fine seat of schoolboy learning. Enthusiastic young runners like me found distractions aplenty in dream

---

[3] The "Fosbury Flop" evolved at about the same time as, and was similar to, the "Brill Bend" developed by Debbie Brill of Canada.

land! After each PE lesson there was an optional 500yd "Big Side Path Run", prescribed by purple-blazered sports master Arthur Mapp, which was endured by the majority and eagerly undertaken by the enthusiasts who more often than not energetically raced it. For me it soon became THE event of the week. Other more challenging educational "tit-bits", like Latin, physics, French or even the fromologists[4] and philatelic society meetings, paled into insignificance!

My earliest serious racing memory is of a 2:44.0 half mile win in 1950 as a 12 year old against, among others, a boy called Fleming, who challenged tenaciously. The summer 1951 edition of the Mid-Whitgiftian records that on one of the three days over which "Sports Day" was held, April 30th and May 2nd and 5th, a certain young Fleet finished second in the U15 440 behind an unrecalled rival by the name of A.D.K. Currie who clocked 69.6sec. It sounds as though he had been just a bit too hot for me to handle!

At fourteen there was an unwelcome "aerial" experience for me when travelling with my grandfather in his car. We were en route to a football match in Folkestone when the accident occurred. The old fellow somewhat rashly tried to overtake the coach carrying his beloved Whitstable Town FC, and on cutting in front of it he encountered a motor cycle and side car. Braking on instinct he gave the unfortunate coach driver no chance and we were unceremoniously flipped into the air. Luckily for all concerned, the Gods were smiling that day and we survived relatively unscathed. I only sustained a severe shaking up and bruising, a small cut on the head and a cracked watch glass. The unfortunate car was a write-off and to add insult to minor injury we had to endure watching the "Oystermen" lose 1-7 to the now extinct Folkestone Town FC.

See Figure 14 – "Did I get out of that?!" Upside down on Barham Down.
Young Mike R

In 1952, star British distance runner Chris Chataway fell dramatically when leading the Helsinki Olympic 5000m with 150m to go. Czech Emil Zatopek surged by to win one of his three sensational gold medals, with Alain Mimoun of France and Herbert Schade of West Germany in hot pursuit. The press photo went into my scrap book, to enshrine some more inspiration there and more importantly in my memory bank. Little did I know then that, four years later, I would be challenging the very same Chataway in an 800m race at the Croydon Sports Arena.

---

4   Collectors of cheese labels.

Serious athletics apart, my friends and I were often competitively innovative, if at times somewhat lacking in foresight. I recall one "fruitful" autumn Sunday afternoon enjoying the thrill of a steeplechase with a difference round my friend Roger Bing's back garden. The provision of deckchairs as obstacles, was straightforward enough, while the steepness of the typical suburban plot made up for the lack in size of our "track", but the absence of a pond meant that we had to find something to replace the water jump...a pile of apples near the compost heap caught our eye as an alternative throwing challenge. Three throws to the left, three to the right and three ahead on each of the ten laps, we calculated would account for nearly all the apples, while leaving the Bing's house unthreatened by the flying fruit. Clearly our steeplechase provided the potential for a productive interface between things academic and things sporting. Three components, mental arithmetic, running and throwing appeared to be fully justified. Naïvely, what we had not envisaged, was the need to assess the impact of projectiles on a nearby glasshouse! The great event had hardly gone beyond the halfway point before the sound of breaking glass and almost simultaneous shouts of anger from a garden, which appeared to be much too close for comfort, brought our innovative event to a premature close. At that point we called a halt, deeming it prudent to hurry indoors for an alternative activity and refreshments. Seemingly within seconds, two heavily breathing young lads could be seen innocently reading the previous day's football results in the lounge.

My first representative run for the school was on a hot June afternoon in 1953 competing as an intermediate over the half-mile, on a bone-hard, crisp, worm-strewn sloping field at Shooters Hill. The school magazine blandly reported the result as a winning run for me in 2:20.2. The immediate "inspirational" post-race analysis from my purple-blazered PE master Arthur Mapp, a man of eagle eye and few words, lives on!

"*Well done, Fleet*", it was always surnames in those days.
"*You strode out strongly down the back straight*", he said encouragingly.
I had little option, for "down" indeed it very much was! I remember my rugby shorts felt decidedly restrictive, especially during that unavoidable long striding section of the race.

In 1954, the school magazine blandly recorded that my two lap time had been trimmed to 2:14.0. By then my self motivation was pretty good, but the added "bait" of a school athletics All Round Badge, requiring a good performance in each of the three disciplines, was a challenge not to be missed. With the running module already solved and long jumping fairly successful I turned my attention to the demands of javelin throwing. Way back then, with Health and Safety restrictions unheard of, with a few fellow "savages" I spent many an exciting, unsupervised summer term lunch break hurling spears on the lower field near St. Michael's Church, West Croydon. There were no accidents, but the high incidence of "tennis elbow" among the participants suggests with hindsight that the presence of Wilf Paish, National Coach of the 1950s, might have alleviated our pain and advanced the distances achieved.

Years later, the wider value of Arthur Mapp's Athletics All Round Badge scheme was evidenced on the national stage when it was successfully used as the template for the very popular and now late lamented AAA Star Award Scheme, born of the national Organisation and Development Committee of which for two years I was the frustrated non-voting secretary. Failure to win the Mrs Howard Houlder Junior Athletics Cup that year was a great disappointment, and focused my sights further ahead to the challenges of senior athletics and the burning ambition to win the school's coveted top athletics trophy, the Dux Ludorum Cup.

Elsewhere on a far more elevated stage, on Thursday 6th May, Roger Bannister ran himself into history on the Iffley Road Track, Oxford, by breaking the four minute mile barrier with a time of 3:59.4.

In June, I was led to believe that I had been selected to represent Croydon Schools in the long jump at Motspur Park. I didn't smell a rat when a prefect rather than PE master Mr Mapp told me of my selection and that I was to meet at the school at a time quite different from that notified to the others selected. It was only when senior prefect David Marshall roared up on his motor-bike and instructed me to hop on and hang on, that I began to have serious doubts. In the interest of survival I hung onto Marshall. We stopped somewhere just short of Motspur Park, and it was there that I learned the truth.

"*Listen to me*" instructed the prefect, "*You're Derek Cooper from now on. He was selected for the senior long jump but he wants to play cricket for the school...DEREK COOPER, senior long jump, remember!*"
I was almost too terrified to react.
"*But, but, but,... I'm an intermediate!*"
"No BUTS about it", snapped Marshall, "Remember, you're Derek Cooper, senior long jump."

An hour or so later my active ordeal was over...well almost. The public address clicked and boomed, "Here is the result of the senior boys long jump... and in third place D. Cooper, Croydon, 18' 7½". Those three competitors should report to the selection stewards table with suitable identification". I deemed that it would be prudent to give the opportunity a miss and hastily sought out my motor bike ride home. A relieved Marshall smilingly congratulated me.

"*Well done, Fleet*", he said, extending a hand.
"*Derek Cooper!*", I responded cheekily.

He put his foot down, and I almost didn't get the lift. The following week our kind art master, Mr Renouf, of World War II mini-submarine fame, amended the Surrey Schools, third place certificate for me. The hard earned document was then buried deeply out of public view in my divan drawer.

See Figure 15 – Surrey Schools' Long Jump Certificate
See Figure 16 – Art master to be, Sub Lt Tony Renouf emerging from
below decks
See Figure 17 – Scene of subterfuge revisited. Mike and Derek Cooper at
Motspur Park 56 years later

Later in the same year there was more Roger Bannister magic to inspire me. Word of his epic Vancouver Commonwealth Games victory over arch Australian rival John Landy somehow reached a riverside field near the Thames at Wallingford where I was on scout's camp. It might have been in a letter from my parents, or possibly from a sneaked look at the sports page of Skipper's newspaper, but who cares, Bannister had won a true epic.

Sadly I can only share in words my amused recall of the Chaplinesque 1955 school film, and more specifically the sports day section with its hilariously fast viewing time of about 4 minutes. It showed sprints, jumps and throws, some presentations, a shot of genteel spectators eating cream teas and strawberries, and my 2:05.0 half-mile win, the latter crammed into an incredible world record breaking slot. My non-featured wins in the 220 yards (25.7), 440 yards (56.0), and long jump (18' 5"), clinched the coveted Dux Ludorum cup at the first attempt.

See Figure 18 – School quarter-mile champion
See Figure 19 – School long-jump champion

I was the proud wearer of my first pair of running spikes, purchased from the still-trading family business, Hewitt's of Croydon. No more racing in trainers for me. A fine pair of Sandy Law calf shoes trimmed with snakeskin, the tongues of which (not the dead animal's) flapped audibly as I ran, adorned my apprentice feet. I just had to stay ahead because rivals could otherwise hear me closing in! The days of rugby shorts too had been superseded and I somewhat self-consciously wore black sateen ones with a rather revealing slit up the side. Decency was maintained thanks to Fred Hurtley and one of his world famous "Jockstraps" which I had timorously bought after a considerable delay from Eric Filby Sports at East Croydon, having naturally reassured myself that the lady assistant was at lunch. Eric, a rare Wimbledon tennis finalist and table tennis international, the epitome of discretion, quietly completed the delicate transaction and even supplied a plain brown paper bag to avoid my blushes.

The following spring, we Trinity boys were inspired by the much revered and loved local athletics hero, the great Gordon Pirie, who suddenly appeared, training regularly at lunchtime on the school's central Croydon field. His use of the facility, which was conveniently situated within a quarter of a mile of the bank where he worked (yes world class athletes had to work too in those distant days), was regularly watched by many open-mouthed admiring lads, who could hardly comprehend the quality and quantity of the seemingly interminable "quarters" which he regularly reeled off.

The quixotic Pirie's tenure there was sadly terminated by Horace Clayton, the affronted headmaster, as abruptly as it began. He had taken exception when Gordon foolishly described his training venue in a radio interview as "A rough old field in central Croydon!" How we missed watching him stride seemingly without effort, at speeds we could not have matched even as a relay team. Importantly however, many precious seeds of ambition had been sown. Several of us were determined to emulate him as athletes, while others harboured more conspiratorial ambitions to blow unwanted water as far as he had been seen to do.

That autumn, thanks to the spread of television, many more people than ever before, something in the region of 12 million it was reported, had the opportunity to witness one of the most gripping athletic battles of modern times. That was when Britain's Olympic Championship faller of 1952, Chris Chataway, took on and beat the Soviet Union's world record holder "Iron Man" Vladimir Kuts over 5000m at the White City Stadium in north-west

London. With no television in our family home, the hint was dropped to our suitably equipped friends "Baron and Baroness" Bradbury two doors away. Arthur and Lorna, as they were more normally known, extended the desired invitation by return. It was eagerly accepted. I ran up the road, intent on missing nothing, while my parents and sister followed at a more rational pace.

About twelve people and the dog crowded round the 12" black and white set, and none was disappointed as the laps unravelled, with the leading Russian mercilessly injecting surges of pace in the vain hope of throwing off the attentions of our red-haired pale-faced hero. As Chataway broke the tape one crucial foot clear in a new world record of 13:51.6, everyone jumped up, cheered and hugged each other... the memory is as clear as if it was yesterday!

See Figure 20 – Inspired Chris Chataway beats Vladimir Kuts

An illicitly obtained Whitgift Middle School maths exercise book with tables on the back featuring "dinosaurs" like the rod, pole and perch, dutifully retains my early results in fine detail from 15th March 1955. On that day I ran a 2:08.5 school standard. It continued right through the testing National Service times and exciting student days at Loughborough in the late 50s, to the International thrills of the early 1960s. I would like to imagine that the late lamented school secretary Miss Loveridge, the severest custodian of exercise books (missing pages from returns were her speciality) would at once have been both appalled and delighted! She would have been appalled that one of her precious items of stationery had fallen into irregular use, and yet, I hope, delighted that this flimsy item had survived into the New Millennium, preserving most of my competitive athletics career in fine detail.

See Figure 21 – Personal race records 1962

Among the high and low lights listed in 1955 was my first experience of the crunch of running on a cinder track and a winning senior debut in 2:01.2 as a senior boy at the Alleyn's School Townley Road track. The triangular match also featured the now non-existent Selhurst Grammar School, where in the unforeseen future I would become a member of staff. A similar time in the Surrey Schools Championships five weeks later earned selection for the All England Schools Championships on the very dusty Belle Vue speedway track in Manchester, where my inexperience saw me ignominiously bundled out in the heats. My father who had driven up to the place of his birth to see me run, at least had the splendid Olympic Games-style parade of athletes to remember!

On reflection, the highlight of that season was the tea which followed the Alleyn's School match, with not only sandwiches but also exotic cakes topped with desiccated coconut!

Fig. 1 – The Inspirational Alf Tupper every boys athletics idol. Image D C Thompson.

Fig. 2 – Tommy Jover (left), the speedy Dulwich Hamlet winger.

Fig. 4 – Mike and Dick Booth, Gordon's biographer on Gordon's memorial seat, Farthing Downs.

Fig. 3 – Gordon Pirie, characteristically in the lead. Photo Gerry Cranhan.

Fig. 5 – Mike in the footsteps of Milo de Cretona.

Fig. 6 – John Fleet.

Fig. 8 – The Legendary Jesse Owens blasts out of blocks in Berlin. Photo Courtesy of the Library of Congress.

Fig. 7 – "Chain He at Aberdeen House School".
Illustration by Daisy Collingridge.

Fig. 7a – Mike with Russell Coffin, 92, son of the late head mistress, at the Aberdeen house school entrance 2011.

Fig. 9 – "The Shrimping Boy".
Illustration by Daisy Collingridge.

Fig. 10 – "Corgi Record Chase".
Illustration by Daisy Collingridge.

Fig. 11 – Joan Pick beats the bus. Paul Matyniuk photo.

Fig. 12 – Dick Fosbury pioneering the successful "Flop" Mexico 1968 Mark Shearman photo.

Fig. 13 – Aerial view of Whitgift Middle School.

Fig. 14 – "Did I get out of that?!" Upside down on Barham Down. Young Mike R.

SURREY SCHOOLS ATHLETIC ASSOCIATION

Certificate of Merit

awarded at the

SURREY SCHOOLS COUNTY CHAMPIONSHIPS

held at

Motspur Park 26th June, 1954

to

Fleet

of Whitgift Middle School

Event Senior Boys Long Jump

Position 3rd.

Chas. F. Peach
Chairman

John H. Masters
Hon. Secretary

Fig. 15 – Surrey School's Long Jump Certificate.

Fig. 16 – Art master to be, Sub Lt Tony Renouf emerging from below decks.

Fig. 17 – Scene of subterfuge revisited. Mike and Derek Cooper at Motspur Park 56 years later. Nicola Photo Courtesy Fulham FC.

Fig. 18 – School quarter-mile champion.

Fig. 19 – School long-jump champion.

Fig. 20 – Inspired Chris Chataway beats Vladimir Kuts.

Fig. 21 – The start of Mike's schoolboy records

Fig. 22 – LAC Schools at White City Brian Linke leading.

Fig. 23 – White City Stadium panorama Senior boys 880yds.

Fig. 24 – It's not WHAT you know, but WHO you know. Jack Crump business card.

Fig. 25 – Penultimate School Half Mile. Phil Collins 2nd L, Mike 3rd L. Gilbert Collins photo.

Fig. 26 – "It's Fun being Trinity School Athletics Captain!" Mike front row 3rd from left next to master i/c Arthur Mapp.

Fig. 27 – 1956 Croydon Arena mid straight 880yds start in London Inter Old boys Match.

Fig. 28 – Programme for Croydon International.

Fig. 29 – Chris Chataway (R) wins thrilling 800m with Mike (L) a very close 3rd.

PETER HILDRETH and JACK PARKER *taking the last hurdle in the 120 yards Hurdles event, Great Britain v. Czechoslovakia match. They finished in the same order in 14.3 sec.*

Sat. 2.30 p.m.   **110 Metres Hurdles—(Men)**   Event 3
Бег с барьерами на 110 метров (мужчины)
(Match Event)

Amateur Records :

WORLD'S RECORD: 13.5 sec.—R. H. Attlesey (U.S.A.), at Helsinki, 10th July, 1950. (Subject to ratification) 13.4 sec.—J. Davis (U.S.A.), at Bakersfield, U.S.A., 22nd June, 1956.
EUROPEAN RECORD: 14.0 sec.—H. H. Lidman (Sweden), at Milan, 22nd September, 1940.
UNITED KINGDOM BEST PERFORMANCE: 14.3 sec.—D. O. Finlay, at Paris, 4th September, 1938.
U.S.S.R. RECORD: 14.1 sec.—Y. Bulanchik, at Stalingrad, 21st September, 1952.

U.S.S.R.	GREAT BRITAIN
1 **Vasily Kuznetsov** *(Best Performance 1956 14.4 sec.)*	2 **P. B. Hildreth** *(Polytechnic H.) (Best Performance 14.4 sec.)*
3 **B. Stoljarov** *(Best Performance 1956 14.4 sec.)*	4 **F. J. Parker** *(South London H.) (Best Performance 14.3 sec.)*
	Reserve :
	6 **R. D. Shaw** *(Achilles Club) (Best Performance 14.7 sec.)*

Lane 1; (3) 2; (2) 3; (1) 4; (4).

26

110 Metres Hurdles

Result   —   Результат

1st .... TIME : ....sec.
2nd .... TIME : ....sec.
3rd .... TIME : ....sec.
4th .... TIME : ....sec.

Points   —   Очки

U.S.S.R.................... Great Britain....................

Sat. 2.30 p.m.   **Throwing the Discus—(Women)**   Event 4
Метание диска (женщины)
(Match Event)

Amateur Records :

WORLD'S, EUROPEAN AND U.S.S.R. RECORDS: 187 ft. 1½ in.—N. Dumbadze (U.S.S.R.), at Tbilisi, U.S.S.R., 18th October, 1953.
BRITISH (ALL-COMERS') RECORD: 162 ft. 5 in.—N. Ponomaryeva (U.S.S.R.), at White City, 13th October, 1954. (Subject to ratification) 165 ft. 4½ in.—O. Fikotova (Czechoslovakia), at White City, 6th August, 1956.
BRITISH (NATIONAL AND ENGLISH NATIVE) RECORDS: 148 ft. 5½ in.—S. Allday (Great Britain), 2nd June, 1952; (Subject to ratification) 148 ft. 5½ in.—S. Allday, 23rd June, 1956; 154 ft. 3 in.—S. Allday, at White City, 11th August, 1956.
WHITE CITY RECORD: 165 ft. 4½ in.—O. Fikotova (Czechoslovakia), 6th August, 1956.

U.S.S.R.	GREAT BRITAIN
1 **I. Begljakova** *(Best Performance 1956 172 ft. 8½ in.)*	2 **S. Allday** *(Spartan L.A.C.) (Best Performance 154 ft. 3 in.)*
3 **N. Ponomareva** *(Best Performance 1956 179 ft. 8 in.)*	4 **S. Needham** *(Spartan L.A.C.) (Best Performance 137 ft. 3 in.)*
	Reserve :
	6 **M. Giri** *(Phoenix A.C.) (Best Performance 144 ft. 2 in.)*

Order of competition: 4, 1, 2, 3.

Result   —   Результат

1st ....ft........in. (................) metres
2nd ....ft........in. (................) metres
3rd ....ft........in. (................) metres
4th ....ft........iii. (................) metres

Points   —   Очки

U.S.S.R.................... Great Britain....................

27

Fig. 30 – "The event the never was!" Ponomareva discus details from "the match that never was" programme.

Fig. 31 – Friends for life. (From left to right) Jean Luc and Chantal Cescina, Marty and Henk Boersbroek, Mike Fleet, Yvonne and Ferdi Koch.

Fig. 32 – The start of over 50 years plus as a Croydon Harrier.

Fig. 33 – Friends of influence in the fifties – Austin Fox, Frank Turk and Ken Fuller. MF photo.

Fig. 34 – Coach Bill Coyne on wind gauge duty.

Fig. 35 – Mike wins RAF Jever 800m from Frank Di Rienzo.

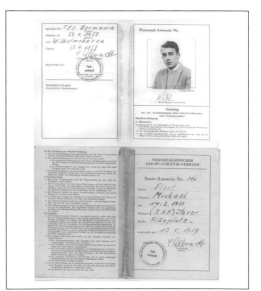

Fig. 36 – Start Ausweiss TSV Germania, Wilhelmshaven.

Fig. 37 – Winning RAF Jever Team HQ 2TAF Munchen Gladbach. Team captain Mike, centre, with trophy.

Fig. 38 – What Health and Safety? Loughborough XC. Hurdling a stile in style. Glynne Jenkins photo.

Fig. 39 – Mike L 21st Birthday Southern Cross Country Championship XC Aylesford, cheered on by Frank Turk R.

Fig. 40 – Disputed Loughborough dead heat Mike (L) and Wynne Oliver.

Fig. 41 – Anchoring Barker's and Derry and Toms to historic victory over Harrods at Wimbledon.

Fig. 42 – First Athletics Weekly cover appearance and first AAA vest partnering winner Mike Rawson (3).

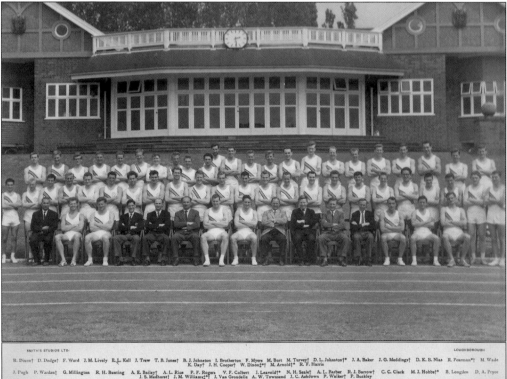

Fig. 43 – Loughborough Athletics Team 1959/60.

Fig. 44 – "Not bad after a swim" First Sub 1:50.0 800m Mike (1) leading Peter Snell.

Fig. 45 – International Debut GB v Hungary. A disappointed third. Gerry Cranham photo.

Fig. 46 – World Student Games 1961 Fisu I/D.

Fig. 47 – GB Athletics Team Sofia. John Holt (End right, second row) later to become Secretary General of the IAA. Menzies Campbell (Top left) later to become leader of the Leberal Party. Mike (third row, centre).

Fig. 48 – "Cross-sport inspiration" Olympic diver, Liz Ferris' MF photo. Inset – Gerry Cranham photo.

Fig. 49 – Ron Delany wins World Student Games 800m Mike 5th second from right.

Fig. 50 – Leaving our trusty Viking behind at Gatwick. Mike and trilby-hutted Menzies Campbell with others.

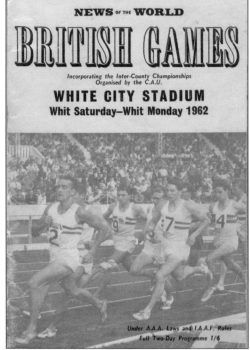

Fig. 51 – White City Whitsun Games. Cover Boy Mike in the lead!

Fig. 52 – 1962 "Welsh distraction" Janice Catt in action.

Fig. 53 – 1962 AAA Championships 4th, 3rd English. Mike behind 10 and 17.

Fig. 54 – 1962 Happy Harriers Quartet White City, Mike Fleet, Bob Harvey, Michael Soubry, Doug Webb.

"Old Pound"
Partridge Green
HORSHAM
Sussex,

8:9:62,

Dear Mike,

I hope you have recovered from running 1:48.9,
which put you 7th=equal on the UK all-time
performer list.

viz :- (* - 800m + 0.7s)

D.J.N. JOHNSON.	1:47.3 *	Oslo	7:8:57
B.S. HEWSON	1:47.7 *	Colombes	13:9:58
M.A. RAWSON	1:47.7 *	Colombes	13:9:58
J.V. PATERSON	1:48.2 *	Bordeaux 82m	29:6:57
P.F.P. KILFORD	1:48.6 *	Warsaw	7:9:61
T.S. FARRELL	1:48.7 *	Billingham	2:7:60
R. PIERCY	1:48.7 *	Warsaw	1:9:61
M.A. FLEET	1:48.9	Brighton	1:9:62
A.J. HARRIS	1:49.0	Motspur Pk.	24:6:61
T.A. SCHOFIELD (10)	1:49.0	Welwyn GC	28:7:62

PLEASE ASCERTAIN IF POSSIBLE (1) Exact Date of P.T. Glossop 440" 48.9 at L'hh in 7.61
(2) From Gordon Pirie, his brother, Peter's
date of birth.

Yours Patrick Mackenzie;

Fig. 55 – 1962 Welcome information from fellow
NUT. Updated UK All-Time Rankings.

Fig. 58 – Peter Snell holds off George Kerr for Perth
Gold. Mike 5th. 1962.

Fig. 56 – East African Airways Comet 4B.

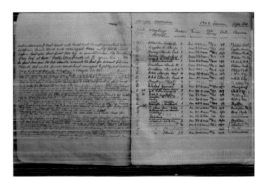

Fig. 59 – Personal best page from the record book
MF photo.

Fig. 57 – 1962 Commonwealth final. Mike
unusually chasing Kenyan with Peter Snell waiting
to strike.

Fig. 60 – Southern 880yds title winner Welwyn.

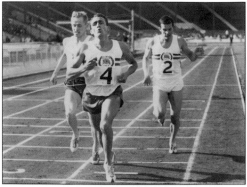

Fig. 61 – Win in controversial shorts v Sweden White City.

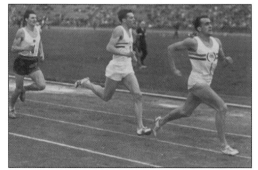

Fig. 62 – Volgograd "World Record" in lane three. Soviet Sport Photo.

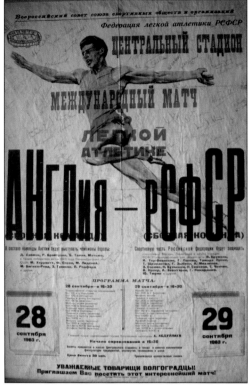

Fig. 64 – Russian poster exchanged for a bar of Cadbury's Dairy Milk chocolate! MF photo.

Союз спортивных
обществ и организаций СССР
и ВЦСПС

ИЗДАТЕЛЬСТВО ГАЗЕТЫ

Советский Спорт

Москва, К-62, ул. Архипова, 8
Телефон К 4-05-06

№ ______ 27 April 1964 г.

Mr. Michael FLEET,
2I Redford Avenue,
Wallington, Surrey,
ENGLAND

Dear Sir,

Enclosed are two pictures of the mens 800 m event taken by our photographer in Volgograd last September. I hope you'll like them.

With best wishes,
sincerely yours

Alexei GRIGORIEV,
assistant foreign editor

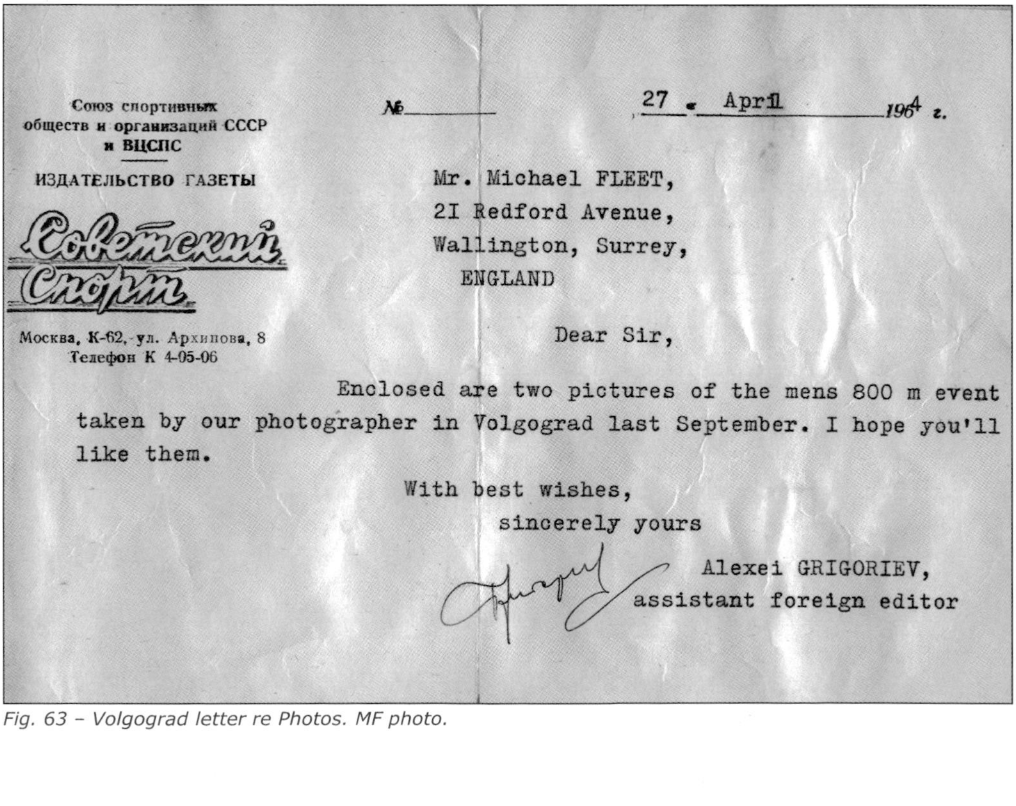

Fig. 63 – Volgograd letter re Photos. MF photo.

Fig. 65 – Selhurst Grammar School Team.

Fig. 66 – Brightwell Inter Counties "Bombshell." Robbie Brightwell, 40, Mike, 30 and John Boulter, 7. Gerry Cranham photo.

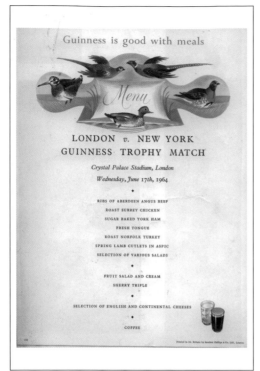

Fig. 67 – London v New Crystal Palace match York Menu. MF photo.

Fig. 68 – John Le Masurier's dreaded "Kiss of non selection" list.

Fig. 69 – 1964 Olympic Gold Medallist Lynn Davies. Welcome home poster donated by Stan Levenson of the Daily Worker.

Fig. 70 – In the bag!... The oh so elusive Surrey title 1967. Photo Ron Linstead.

Fig. 71 – Nicola in ESAA 200m Championship. Nicola timekeeping (blue cap) at Olympic Trials with "Stan the Man" Burton (top right). MF photos.

Fig. 72 – Sydney Wooderson setting new world record of 4:06.4 at Motspur Park in 1937. Corbis Photo.

Fig. 73 – Mike with sister Judy. Photo Croydon Advertiser.

Fig. 75 – 1974 AAA silver in 4x400 Mike to Roy Fox.

Fig. 74 – Something tells me it's all over. MF looking back down track.

Fig. 76 – Mike with Fritz and Gudrun Emmert at the rain-soaked Munich European Championships 2002. NF photo.

Fig. 76c – The Indestructible Jahlman Singh with admiring sympathisers, at UK Veterans Multi-event. MF photo.

Fig. 76a – Tanja Granig Croydon Harriers' Austrian hurdler visitor.

Fig. 76d – Mike presenting Wilfried Spronk the Munich Olympic Stadium director with a Croydon Harriers tour T Shirt, 1986. NF photo.

Fig. 76b – Decathlete Lloyd Maloney javelin throwing in Aden.

Fig. 76e – Janko Stamoff guide to GB team during 1961 World Student Games, on holiday 40 years later.

4

The Big Break-through

The School's annual inter-house cross-country championship, traditionally run in early spring, was run from the games field in Sandilands, east into the level half-mile Grimwade Avenue and onwards around Lloyd Park, for a two-mile lap before returning along the reverse to the school field. This was a compulsory character-building challenge event for a growing throng of perspiring, predominantly reluctant boys. I was one of the minority who welcomed it!

Our team training runs were led by the visually non-inspirational and clearly academic rather than sporting, but none the less devoted duo of Messrs Blandford and Robbins. Appearing in kit more akin to Abrahams and Liddell immortalised in the inspirational film "Chariots of Fire", these two gentlemen introduced me to cross country running. The neglect of this in recent times has, in my opinion, led to the demise of Britain as a leading force in middle distance running. Steve Ovett did it, Seb Coe did it, Steve Cram did it and we did, it but in recent times participation levels have dropped dramatically. Warm weather training, the popular late winter activity encompassing venues like the Algarve, Cyprus, Lanzarote and further afield to South Africa and California for the more privileged, is in my opinion no substitute for wintertime hills, mud, sweat and tears.

The two academics regularly shepherded us round the school course which incorporated Lloyd Park and the adjacent Oaks Farm. The latter was then all too clearly a working establishment. We seemed to be deliberately routed to run the gauntlet of the stinking pig sties and horned threat of the resident herd of cows, or were they bulls? Present day runners there only have to be on the lookout for frisky dogs and possibly the wayward frisbee. Our cunning brown-plimsolled, long-shorted leaders had a soothing stroke of motivational genius up their sleeves too; the free steaming hot post-run mug of blackcurrant cordial. That was certainly the clincher! Very welcome though it was then, I can't abide the stuff now!

I had never really shone in the junior school run, but in the senior race of 1956, my final school year, I managed to close in as an exhausted runner-up behind the seemingly invincible Robin Hatton. This feat was achieved thanks only to the placebo effect of my smart new red Adidas trainers which were otherwise wholly unsuited to the task. Their newness and flat soles certainly took a toll on my feet as I toiled over the unforgiving ground. I reckoned that I looked pretty professional in the plantar division but finished decidedly sore and was glad the shoes' red leather blended in with my bloodstained socks. It was a lesson well learned. Never again did I run in new, wholly unsuitable footwear! Despite my suffering, that run earned me selection for the Trinity's inter-school cross-country programme of three or so matches, the clearest memory of which remains parting a herd of deer, Red Sea style, in Richmond Park. The result of that race is lost in a fading memory and in the mists of time.

I opened what was to become a landmark season in March 1956 by winning the coveted Trinity School Dux Ludorum trophy for the second time on an almost hot sports day, so much for global warming! My winning performances were, 220yds 24.3sec, 440 yards 53.6sec, 880 yards 2:06.0, long jump 19' 7". For me the die had truly been cast. The season evolved excitingly to the prestigious London Athletic Club Schools meeting at the awe-inspiring White City Stadium. Thanks to my father who drove me there through very heavy traffic I arrived in good time and reasonably relaxed to begin what would become a twelve-year affinity with the iconic venue.

See Figure 22 – LAC Schools at White City, Brian Linke leading
See Figure 23 – White City Stadium panorama, Senior boys 880yds

In the ensuing years my father's support coupled to "The Knowledge" which he acquired during the tough World War II years as a London fireman, prepared me well for many of my most memorable two-lap tests. On this occasion my pre-event excitement offset the daunting subterranean march which competitors had to make from changing room to trackside beneath the stand, the dog track AND the running track. The sun, initially a distant spot of brightness way ahead at the top of the stairs grew brighter and more welcoming with every step. In the heats my half-mile time improved from 2:01.2 to 2:00.8 for me to qualify for the keenly contested final.

After taking third in the final just 0.2sec slower on that April Saturday, a gaunt rather serious looking elderly gentleman approached me on the infield of the famous track.

"Good run, young man," he murmured, *"if you need help at any time you're welcome to telephone me,"* he said handing me a business card.

"Thanks very much," I gasped in exhaustion rather than awe, for I was totally unaware of the importance of my new mystery contact. Jack C.G.Crump, Secretary of the British Amateur Athletic Board, walked quietly away. At that time it was he, together with 1924 Olympian Harold Abrahams, who shared control of athletics in *"our green and pleasant land"*. Little did I then realise the value of that contact.

See Figure 24 – It's not WHAT you know, but WHO you know. Jack Crump's business card

One spring over 50 years later, while discussing athletics through the hedge, new neighbour Sue Burgess mentioned that her father had run for Wallington Grammar School when he was a boy. I had many a strong recall of my friendly rivalry with another Old Walcountian, Phil Collins, but also remembered some testing encounters with a strong round faced, curly haired team mate of his. Could it have been her father?

"What's your maiden name, Sue?" I queried through the accommodatingly thin privet.
"Ray," came the response.
"I reckon I ran against him at the L.A.C. Schools Meeting at the famous old White City Stadium," I exclaimed.
Sue's father Cliff Ray, had finished just behind me in fourth place, rather too close for comfort I guess, as the evidence from my precious exercise book revealed:
"Chased hard, but couldn't hold Blythe or Linke...nearly 4th!"

One can only guess at what might have happened to my career, had what transpired to be a crucial result been reversed by the athlete who was later to be revealed as my new neighbour's father.

My first taste of "International" competition took me to Paris that May as a member of a London Schools team which took on the Paris University Club at the Stade Sebastian Charlety. I was a surprise winner, running scared from the front in an unfamiliar 600m race in 81.5secs, which earned me the "Best Track Performance of the Match Award" a fine classical looking boxed medal. The result clearly suggested that something better over 2 laps could well be in store.

Memories linger of the post match "Vin d'Honneur", of swarthy little men outside our downtown Hotel Mattle trying to sell us risqué post cards, while our fertile young imaginations tried to take us through the forbidden portals of the nearby Follies' Bergère. I also recall foolhardy athletes whom I secretly envied for their nerve trying to go up and down the Metro escalators the wrong way. One of my team mates then was long jumper David Littlewood, now Britain's top track official and IAAF representative, but he was not one of the daredevils.

Cycling back to school for the final term of exams, with the shining new medal in my blazer pocket, I was about to pass a pretty girl who lived nearby. I immediately saw the opportunity to impress, braked somewhat squeakily, probably making her jump out of her skin, and called out, *"Look what I've got here!",* proudly producing my unexplained medal.

"Oh that's nice, but sorry I'm late... can't stop," she said leaving me no time to even précis my best achievement to date. Deflated, I pedalled on to central Croydon and into school to seek out my kindly, purple-blazered, Scottish P.E. master Arthur Mapp, who did just the right thing.

"May I?" he queried, before taking out, at my assenting nod, the golden treasure from its silk-lined case. *"That's wonderful, Fleet, did you break two minutes?"*

I explained that I had won a 600m race in 81.5sec, which in the impossible circumstance of me completing two laps at the same pace, would have been the equivalent of something under 1:50.0 for 880 yards. *"Indeed, very well done,"* said the Scot, a man of few words. He had paid me the compliment of an appreciative sentence and restored my damaged ego.

One sunny evening 55 years later at a post-tennis match party on the Hampshire coast, two of the players were discussing education as might reasonably have been expected, for one was Chris Tarrant, recently retired as headmaster of my beloved Trinity School; the other a former Croydon schoolgirl...

"I went to the now disappeared Selhurst Grammar School" said Valerie Smith.
"Amazing coincidence, so did my mother" Chris replied.

The conversation moved on to Chris's Headmastership, and to the good old Croydon schools of the 1950s and 1960s. The late lamented Selhurst Grammar schools' for Boys and for Girls, John Ruskin Grammar School for Boys and St Ann's School for Girls. Not surprisingly too, the Whitgift

Middle School for Boys, which was renamed Trinity School of John Whitgift in the 1950s, to ensure that fellow Whitgift Foundation School, Whitgift did not corner all the academic kudos.

Inevitably sport came up, and somehow the name Mike Fleet was mentioned, and it was Valerie's turn to be astounded.

"There's a former international athlete MIKE FLEET who works at Trinity" said Chris.
"I used to partner him at badminton when we were at school!" she gasped.

As yet unaware of this scenario, I wondered why I had been called in to see Sandra Rimell, secretary to the current Trinity Headmaster Mark Bishop, in early September 2010.

Mark certainly generates respect and even at 70 plus I address the Headmaster, "Headmaster!"
Had I blotted my copybook, or maybe I was in for a pay rise?

"Come in" Sandra responded to my tap on her door, *"I've got a discreet message for you from Chris Tarrant"* she said adding to my relief but increasing my curiosity. Very odd I almost thought aloud.

"He plays tennis with a lady called Valerie Smith who remembers you from schooldays. Would it be alright with you for her to make contact? Do you remember her?"

"Valerie...Valerie..." I searched deep in the mists of memory.

"I guess she could be Val Byatt with whom I once lost heavily in the Surrey Junior Badminton Championships" I recalled

She was the first girl towards whom my young head turned, and the very one who had paid scant attention when I proudly showed her my best track performance medal, awarded in Paris way back.

"Certainly, no problem, it would be fun to make contact again. Yes tell Chris that's fine with me."

I thanked Sandra, and heaved a sigh of relief, I hadn't been in trouble, a pay rise would have been nice, but an interesting door had been opened!

A few days later a letter arrived from the lady in question, who was indeed the same Valerie, Valerie Byatt, when she and I were youthful badminton partners.

Since then, having recounted the saga of the medal on the telephone, I have been given a welcome but unnecessary apology for the scant regard she paid to my prize.

The incredulous Valerie could not believe how dismissive she had been.

"Well, I was young, and I was late for school, but how awful," she murmered.

Then we both laughed. Times move on and there was no harm done.

Maybe when we meet again, I will risk taking the medal along in the hope of a better reaction!

My landmark first sub 2 minute "half mile" followed at the end of that month, in what was to prove my last two-lap run for the school at North End. The old exercise book records that, *"I ran hard all the way,"* and that the bell time was 58.5 seconds. Seeking inspiration en route, I aimed for a similar time to Brasher's opener in that much more significant battle against the clock at Oxford over twice the distance, two years earlier. The result, in central Croydon, a 1:59.6 clocking against Colfe's School was indeed one of my greatest thrills.

See Figure 25 – Penultimate School Half Mile with Phil Collins

The sub 1:59.0 transition advanced that June with a welcome 1:58.5 win in the Surrey Schools Championships at Motspur Park, another Trinity School record which stood the test of some 20 years. My final run in school colours on 4th July was against Caterham School in a quarter mile run in 51.2sec, on the friendly central Croydon grass. It was another record which survived for a similar length of time.

See Figure 26 – "It's Fun being Captain" Mike front row third from left next to master i/c Arthur Mapp

A big and pleasant surprise came at the end of August in my first serious encounter against senior men, an inter-city match at the Croydon Arena. So much for present day "pioneering" inter-city encounters which, although commendable, are not quite as innovative as they are claimed to be! Thanks to my kind-hearted father, our family hosted Nigerian high jumper, Prince Ima Igiehon for the weekend. He proved to be a delightful guest but one particularly difficult to understand with his Afro-Mancunian accent! I proudly ran for Croydon Borough, then classed as a city for competition purposes, against Bristol, Cardiff and Manchester. I clocked 1:54.8 in 5th place of nine and went home content. This caused more than a few raised eyebrows in high places, but luckily for me it didn't stop there.

See Figure 27 – 1956 Croydon Arena mid straight 880yds start in London Inter Old boys match

Soon after that, my progress encountered a slight hiccup! Frank Turk, my friend and scout leader, who had shrewdly nudged me towards serious athletics, long harboured the ambition to run a sub 2 minute 880yds. He asked me to help.

Despite my policy of running a good bit faster, I readily agreed to assist him in his serious attempt in a suitably low-profile match. It was a week after my big break through at the Croydon Arena, when we lined up there for an inter-club race. Since he hadn't fancied my suggested 58sec opener, a 60sec first lap was the intermediate target. He had agreed to stick to me like a limpet, and at the bell I felt reassured by the heavy breathing close behind. In the event, I had got it wrong by producing an inadequate 61sec lap, so I gently accelerated, aiming to ease my friend towards his target.

Unfortunately this obviously suited everyone else, especially Ray Harper of Deptford Park who couldn't believe his luck and promptly sabotaged the script. Believing the heavy breathing to be that of Frank, I allowed him through to win! The frantic screams of the, by then, spectating Frank, who had succumbed to the pace and dropped out before the bell, could not save me from the ignominy of self-inflicted defeat. Clearly Frank had not been destined to experience the double buzz of winning and of running under the "Magic Two". The "wrong winner" Harper and I shared the modest 2:00.0 minute clocking as I fought back to an inches margin at the tape. Frank bought me fish and chips on the way home, and we discussed the merits of such a meal, which had been the staple diet of my childhood comic hero, Alf Tupper.

Over 40 years on, Brian Proctor, then Croydon middle and long distance coach, clearly remembers the debacle. Unaware at the time of my "race plan", he was far from impressed by my seemingly naïve and more than courteous wide move off the final turn, which allowed the grateful, amazed and heavily breathing Harper through to win!

Soon afterwards in August, the Jack Crump "Trump Card" came into play, with an invitation for this recent schoolboy to run in the 800m, in a Croydon and Commonwealth Team, managed by the great man, to meet an Amateur Athletic Association Team at the Albert Road Arena. Many big names were lined up for the meeting, among them Gordon Pirie, Chris Brasher and Chris Chataway, the two successful first sub four-minute mile "musketeers" who had paced the third, Roger Bannister, to his barrier breaking sub four minute mile triumph two years before, top hurdler Peter Hildreth, Pakistani hammer record holder Abdul Khaliq, et al. This was the cast for a night to be remembered. A crowd of some 5000 turned up. In those days, Croydon was second only to the White City as an athletics magnet in London.

Now three months later, at 8.10pm on a balmy autumn evening in 1956, I found myself lined up for an 800m, alongside one of those legendary international first sub 4minute mile musketeers, Chris Chataway. He had chosen to run below distance as a sharpener for his forthcoming return encounter with Vladimir Kuts at the White City Stadium. The relaxed Chataway took off his cable-knit university sweater, calmly removed his wrist watch and requested that the marksman take care of them for him. A bundle of nerves, I watched in awe and had to be reminded to take off my tracksuit top.

"*On your marks,*" …we stepped forward to the no longer used mid-home straight starting line… A bang, a blur, and we were off.

The frenzy of men's racing pace was new, but exhilarating. A 55sec or so lap called at the bell, it was certainly new territory for me. No time to think about it, I just had to hang in. 1:53.6 after the gun, I had crossed the line in third place, just 0.3sec adrift of the "Great Man" who had burst through late to hit the two-ply strand of white botany wool stretched above the finishing line. A little further back still came Michael Blagrove of Ealing, who to this day can honestly claim to be the only man ever to run a four minute mile! No, not better than 4 minutes, that unique performance belongs to Bannister. Blagrove clocked exactly 4:00.0 to run his name into quiz question books. It remains his best ever time set in 1958 behind Derek Ibbotson, a one time world mile record holder.

Amazed, I found myself the centre of attention, having been catapulted to the top of the 1956 British Junior Men's 800m (874.6 yards) rankings with a personal improvement of about 0.5sec. Unknown to me then, my time was the second fastest known two-lap run by an eighteen-year old Briton. I later discovered that way back in July 1935, one Ralph Scott of Ashby-de-la-Zouch Grammar School had clocked 1:53.9 for the half mile in Junior A.A.A Championships. For comparison, my time rounded up to 1:54.3. On occasions 0.4sec can seem like an eternity! Chataway having retrieved his wrist watch from the custodial marksman, kindly congratulated me.

"Extremely well run," he complimented, *"I understand that you are only eighteen, quite amazing! Thanks for helping to give me the hard race I needed."*
He further thoughtfully advised me:
"Don't overdo it, you've got plenty of time!"

See Figure 28 Programme for Croydon International Meeting Arena Big Match
See Figure 29 – Big Break Through. Chris Chataway Race Finish

With that and a firm friendly handshake, he was off, disappearing through the throng of frantically enquiring pressmen, to change and then depart allegedly for a well earned beer.

Another outstanding Pirie performance followed, a solo 2 miles in 8:42.6, which was celebrated in characteristic rebel fashion by the expulsion of two large mouths full of water on unwitting spectators as they made their way past the changing rooms. Shades of his similarly ostentatious displays for wide-eyed schoolboys a few months earlier! Regrettably the opportunity for Chataway to try out his new-found speed never took place, due to the "Nina Ponomareva hat-stealing affair" in Marks and Spencer, Oxford Street, and to the legal and diplomatic furore which followed. The Soviet team withdrew amid much acrimony and flew home. The English speaking Chief Coach of the USSR team Gavriel Korobkov, was held in high regard by British boss Jack Crump who wrote in his book: *"He shook my hand warmly on departure. He said little but I fancy we both understood a great deal."*

See Figure 30 – "The event that never was!" Ponomareva from match programme

Meanwhile Mrs Ponomareva remained holed up in the Russian Embassy. She was ultimately found guilty at the Great Marlborough Magistrates Court, of attempting to steal five hats and was fined £3! She went straight from the court to the London Docks where she boarded a Russian ship which took her home to a heroine's welcome.

Two weeks later, my second representative trip abroad and my first as a senior athlete, was to represent Croydon Borough in Holland. I was to take part in the athletic aspect of the Croydon-Arnhem Sports and Cultural exchange. My first race on that trip was on a track in tranquil woodland near the Hartenstein Hotel, Oosterbeek, made famous during Operation Market Garden in World War II. The hotel had served as the Parachute Division's command post defended so bravely by Lt Col Frost and his men. It later became the Divisional HQ of Major General Urquhart while the surrounding German Panzers were being held at bay. During the battle of Arnhem and the astonishing allied parachute drop the British suffered 1,300 fatalities and the Poles 378. The toll of the entire battle of Arnhem is recorded as 7,167 killed, missing or wounded.

Thankfully those awful times had been confined to history and twelve years on, one could not have asked for a more relaxing environment in which to compete. There I was participating in a sporting battle where so many less fortunate men of my age had tragically lost their lives.

During this memorable trip, I had the very good fortune to meet two young Dutch athletes, Henk and Marti who would later become Mr and Mrs Boersbroek and firm friends, through whom many more rewarding exchanges were arranged for our respective clubs.

See Figure 31 – Friends for life – Henk and Marty Boersbroek, Jean Luc and Chantal Cescina, Ferdi and Yvonne Koch

The euphoria of the Chataway experience was still with me and I was able to lead throughout to register 1:55.4, my best winning time at that point. The competition ended in gathering gloom way after the relays in unusually spectacular fashion, with the pole vault, finishing by the light of car headlights. To this day I admire the fearless winner, bespectacled Mike Nugent, recalled as he disappeared into the night sky and returned to terra firma leaving the bar aloft. One assumed the judges could see well enough to confirm that he did actually clear it!

Two days later our otherwise delightful Dutch hosts then played their master card. They "treated" us to a cultural tour of the huge, very hot and steamy paper works at Renkum. One can only liken the experience to a prolonged Turkish bath which featured much climbing and clambering along cat walks over steaming cauldrons of dubious porridge-like material along its path to becoming paper. OK, Don Thompson, the diminutive 1960 golden Olympian who walked miles on the spot in his steam filled bathroom in training, would surely have revelled in the alien environment, but we lesser mortals positively wilted in it... and my good friend Don Turner of Durban to Pietermaritzburg fame would surely agree.

Reality then chose a timely moment to return, and brought me back down to earth in more ways than one. On an improvised 300m grass track, taped out on the Vitesse Stadium soccer pitch, Keith Marsden, a modest standard Achilles Club athlete, but much more experienced than me, comfortably showed that my season was then one race too far in the city of "The Bridge Too Far". I trailed home dejectedly outside 2 minutes, an undistinguished second behind the guest.

Cupid's arrow struck positively on the long return ferry trip, but not in my direction! The very attractive Heather Stevens, already on the radar of many young bloods in the team, drew further attention to herself by careering hair-raisingly out of control through the city centre on a Vespa[5]. The lads were full of admiration, but not so the Arnhem police who took a dim view of her unlicensed antics, and marched her off to the station. She was eventually released for the journey home only to fall foul of sea sickness, but as luck would have it the young Croydon Harrier's plight was spotted by the attentive Alan Sexton, my schoolboy athletics hero, who studiously nursed her alongside the ship's rail throughout the voyage. The rest is history, with the now 50 years married Mrs and Mrs Sexton very good friends of mine to this day! Athletics, they clearly found, sooner than I did, has much more to offer than might at first appear.

I have to thank George Pallett, the Surrey County Junior Team manager at the time, for further bringing me back down a peg or two! Having failed to select me for his team for a match against Hampshire and Sussex in Croydon, he was quizzed by Bill Ward, the "Advertiser Sports Man" as to why he had omitted me from his selections.
"*Fleet,*" he exclaimed, "*I'd just never heard of him!*"
Who would ever want to be a team manager?

---

[5]   Vespa – Iconic Italian post World War II motor scooter which emerged phoenix-like from the flattened Piaggio aeronautical factory. One wonders whether Heather's unco-operative "steed" was one of the legendary 150GS models of 1950?

I remember receiving several letters in quick succession, from local clubs extolling their virtues in efforts to gain my membership. Three of them, from Blackheath Harriers, Herne Hill Harriers and South London Harriers, were long and effusive. The fourth from Croydon Harriers was short and to the point and went something like this:

Croydon Harriers
Wiltshire Road
Thornton Heath
THO 8516
August 1956

Dear Michael

Well done in your races at the Croydon Arena.

Croydon Harriers needs lads like you. Mr Phil James, you know him from Croydon and Surrey Schools, would like to meet with you and me at the track on Tuesday at 6.30pm.

Please telephone me to let me know if you can come.

Yours sincerely

J. R. Lisney

The local press confidently speculated that I would not join either of the two most local clubs – South London Harriers or Croydon Harriers. With just a little persuasion from my friends, next-door neighbour Ken Fuller, a fine young sprinter, and scout leader Frank Turk, both established Croydon Harriers, I filled in my form at the back of the Croydon Arena Grandstand on the decreed evening, paid my five shillings, and have been a happy Croydon Harrier ever since!

See Fig 32 – The start of over 50 years plus as a Croydon Harrier

In the meantime I had decided to defer my teacher training for which my application to the specialist Physical Education College at Loughborough had been submitted. I then had to face up to the fact that my athletics career would be going on virtual hold, while I served Queen and country as a national serviceman in the Royal Air Force.

See Figure 33 – Friends of influence in the fifties – Austin Fox, Frank Turk and Ken Fuller

5

Per Ardua Ad Astra

"Per Ardua Ad Astra" can be translated as *"Through struggle to the stars"* and that interpretation does reflect, at my non-combative level as a young National Serviceman, the pursuit of my athletics ambition whilst serving Queen and country from 1956 to 1958. I spent much of my duty time watching a potential enemy on radar screens, and working with fighter control.

According to the Croydon Advertiser on 8th September 1956, my club career had just been born:

"Here's a snip for Croydon Harriers: Michael Fleet, highly promising young half miler, has joined them. He has just left Trinity School and has started his National Service in the RAF. Fleet's home is in Virginia Road, Thornton Heath."

Up to that time I had been self-coached, but picking the brains of experts and respected athletes. Then, thanks to an introduction from my Uncle Arthur to Bill Coyne, a colleague of his and top Polytechnic Harriers coach, I had the chance of knowledgeable support and motivation. I enthusiastically welcomed his offer of help, and he was duly invited round to develop the contact. When the great day arrived, I guess I set a PB when I ran to the nearby house of a bemused young lady, whom I naïvely thought would be impressed by this momentous news, and who would surely want to meet him, this being the same girl who had lacked interest in my schoolboy medal when I tried to catch her attention some time before. Now I thought a meeting with my new coach would do the trick; how misguided I was!

See Fig 34 – Coach Bill Coyne on wind-gauge duty

From then on for three years, Bill stuck to his task and helped me on my way very constructively, especially when I was abroad. After all too few sessions with Bill and his talented group in Regents Park, which certainly set me on the right path, my call-up to the RAF materialised. Regrettably, I would never again have the polar bears on Mappin Terrace to motivate me at the end of each run. Later he kept in touch by post and his advice and encouragement proved invaluable.

Having taken the precaution of what I considered to be a severe haircut, I headed out of Paddington en route to RAF Cardington to be kitted out in readiness for the next two years. Three days and as many haircuts later, I was a somewhat subdued and very shiny above the ears National Serviceman, travelling nervously in a locked and guarded train heading for "Square bashing" at RAF Bridgnorth in Shropshire. On arrival at Bridgnorth station a real bully of a sergeant forced everyone to run up and over the footbridge to the awaiting transport, a task which even I found a bit of a challenge. Several of the less fit who fell, were exhorted to "get up and get a move on", while others who just about managed the task were mercilessly mocked by the red faced brute. His "performance" was so outrageously extreme that the appalled railway stationmaster called in the civilian police to establish some reason. Over the gate I thought I saw a sign "Welcome to RAF Bridgnorth", or was it my imagination?

"So does anyone here think that he's an athlete?" screamed the shaven-headed drill sergeant on the daunting parade ground.
"We've got a cross-country team here, and we need more decent runners," he barked
"I'm an athlete," stammered the newly crowned British U20 800m number one.
"So, what do you do then, airman?" he queried with obvious disbelief.
"I run halves and quarters," I proffered with a little more confidence.
"Oh yeah, you don't look as if you could walk that far, let alone run it," he sneered. *"But... but, sergeant, I ran 1:53.6 for the 800m in August, and I'm top British Junior."*
"Who are you trying to kid, airman; we've got the AAA Under 20 Champion, Derek Haith of Thames Valley Harriers here, and he's number one at 1:53.8! So, what's your name then, airman?" he queried.
"I'm Aircraftman Fleet, sergeant," I mumbled, almost completely disarmed.
"Never heard of you, son. If that's the case, then I'm Roger Bannister!"

Tears welled up in my eyes. I had effectively been shot down in flames, and maybe needed them to drown my distress. It took an urgent letter home, and a surreptitiously snatched telephone call, followed by a nervous week of waiting, before my press cuttings arrived to confirm my claims in black and white.

"Hell, you've really done it, ain't you?" exclaimed our highly embarrassed sergeant.

Not quite an apology, but at least an acceptance, which allayed the worst of my fears that our drill sergeant wouldn't be able to read!

For the following few weeks, I was more than happily integrated in the station cross-country squad which featured several serious bent-nosed pugilists, who habitually slowed down to shadow box every few hundred yards. With us too was the well known Derek Haith, Britain's number two U20 800m runner, and of course our delightful drill sergeant, a Highgate Harrier, who in fairness will in perpetuity remain unidentified...! Some years later I met his son, who assured me a reunion would be welcomed by his father, but maybe he was fearful of retribution, for nothing has been heard since. Don't worry "Sarge", all is forgiven...

We RAF sportsmen trained together enthusiastically in readiness for the next inter-station race, which it transpired was unfortunately scheduled to take place a week after many of us had been posted elsewhere! On more than one occasion during that period we were obliged to sharpen our speed ahead of an inquisitive herd of cows. They seemed to display a distorted bovine sense of humour which regularly involved an unnerving run behind us along the banks of the Severn. With the river immediately to our left we knew that in the worst case scenario of their apparently threatening horny extensions getting too close for comfort, we had the option of a watery escape route. Shame, one imagined, about the non-swimming sergeant!

A day pass was issued to enable me to attend Loughborough College for an interview and a practical test. Dressed in RAF best blue and clutching a small pack containing my PE kit, I entered the sporting "Holy of Holies" and waited my turn for interview in the Martin Hall.

"So why Mr Fleet, did you only put our college down as a choice?" queried Clint Sayer, Head of the Physical Education Department.
"Sir, because its reputation is the best, and I do not wish to train for teaching anywhere else."
"I note that you are a highly ranked runner," he added, smiling.

Next was the practical test, orchestrated and overseen by the inimitable Anglo-Greek athletics lecturer Basil Stamatakis, who explained in ornate English what he wanted us to do.

"The basketball to be used speedily, gentlemen, as of a rugby ball," he instructed.

My impetuous partner immediately hurled the "rugby/basketball far too quickly for me to react with an unexpected face-high pass, the target of which was promptly confirmed by my bloodied nose and watering eyes! Seemingly unaware of my discomfort, the almost incomprehensible Stamatakis sought "arching crabwise for back mobility showing."

It was almost a relief to attempt a previously unachieved "crab-arch", but as luck would have it I was the third in line or else I would not have known what to do. Adrenalin-assisted success provided an opportunity to let the accumulating blood drip to the floor!

Despite my sore nose and strained back, the encouraging words...

"We note that you are a highly ranked runner," were repeating encouragingly in my head. I was confident that I would be offered one of the coveted places at Loughborough.

Having learnt to keep my "nose clean", to burnish "them" brasses and to put the beds of troublesome colleagues on roofs, I felt ready to move on to face the challenge of trade training elsewhere. My next posting was to RAF Middle Wallop in Hampshire, where the throaty roar of an aged flight of Boulton Paul Balliols all too often drowned any conversation. There, we newcomers received a far more friendly welcome than had been previously experienced, if somewhat bizarrely delivered by incumbent billet Sergeant Ian Swindale. He leapt out of an upstairs window, intelligently feet first, landing with the poise of a paratrooper, before calling us awe-inspired "sprogs" to order! He looked really fit and strong. It turned out that he was a nationally ranked Top Ten discus thrower and more than useful shot putter. For me it seemed there was some potential in our sporting common denominator. I could only assume that the eccentricity of the Lozells Harriers' leap from aloft was to impress us and to additionally strengthen his leg muscles. A fine demonstration of extreme plyometrics in their infancy!

I experienced an even more friendly personal welcome when I encountered the already well-established and amiable Geoff Meddings of Woodford Green AC. He introduced me to authorised athletic freedom from the camp confines and to the hidden "delights" of an innocent looking hill way beyond the station boundary. The tree-topped mound, at a distance evocative of a Paul Nash painting, proved to be much further away and very much steeper than had been at first imagined! Had it been a sand dune, Percy Cerutt – the enigmatic coach of great Australian athlete Herb Elliott, would surely have applauded our strenuous endeavours on its testing slopes.

With time at Middle Wallop fast coming to an end and I successfully opened an unwanted career path as a fighter plotter, my unmet choices having been languages, map work and photography. I felt sure that, even in my sleep, I could accurately push a small numbered brick around a table-top map with a stick! Confidently clutching letters from Jack Crump, plus one from Wing Commander Davies, Officer i/c RAF athletics in the UK, I was almost in eager anticipation of my next posting, which I naively imagined would be one of the mainland's top athletically oriented RAF stations.

The posting notice arrived with a military travel pass to Holland and onwards to Germany. My dismay deepened further by the prospect of the mandatory North Sea crossing aboard the notorious SS Empire Wansbeck[6], the folklore surrounding her falsely leading us to believe that she had been salvaged from the seabed for her trooping role. A far from ideal pre North Sea crossing meal of greasy fish, chips and processed peas at Harwich put paid to the prospect of a comfortable voyage. We soon to be 2nd Tactical Air Force men were then unceremoniously battened down in the bowels of the notorious ship, cheek by jowl with a decidedly drunken group of Green Howards. Thoughts of setting foot in Europe as soon as possible suddenly seemed to be attractive, but did not entirely ease my doubts and disappointment.

My abject arrival, one grey and damp evening via a north European transit camp attractively named RAF Goch, at the far distant RAF outpost of Borgentreich, hidden away in decidedly rural Germany, was hardly worthy of recall. A threatening gaggle of muddy looking, distinctly Teutonic geese near the guardhouse hissed an ominous welcome. Feeling very depressed and virtually alone in the world, I flopped heavily down to the solace of my recently acquired bed, and promptly finished up, or more specifically down, on the concrete floor below... There was only one thing to do apart

---

[6] The ship in fact had a previous life as "The Linz", a German vessel of 3,508 tons built in 1943 and subsequently captured by the allies in a Norwegian Fjord in 1946. She then regularly plied the all too often turbulent waters between Harwich and the Hook of Holland as a troop carrier under the British Merchant flag. After that she was sold to the Greek shipping brothers Kavounides, renamed the Esperos, finally being broken up in Spain in 1980.

from laughing at my predicament and that was to find the station running track. That was the obvious reason for this privileged posting. I could soon be running a few therapeutic laps round it and then my world would become a happier place! The gym staff would surely be delighted to note my enthusiasm and direct me to the track.

On reaching the station gym, not much more than a Nissen hut, I sought directions to my imagined track.

"Evening corporal, how do I get to the running track?" I asked the large, football-shirted individual languishing behind the counter.
"What running track, airman? We've only got a football pitch here. You do play soccer, don't you? We're men short in the squad, what position do you play?"
"I'll think about it and let you know," I mumbled disappointedly and jogged on to the football pitch to start training.
"Hey you, airman, you can't run there, that's the football pitch!" yelled the PTI corporal.

Sadly similar sentiments are still regularly expressed at shared facilities in England, especially when throwers are endeavouring to hone their skills prior to the athletics season or wanting to continue in August as the football season approaches. In mid-summer, with the London 2012 Olympic Games looming, we in Croydon discovered to our dismay that our new throwing cage was under threat of closure due to the refurbishment of the soccer pitch in readiness for "top class tussles of the Kent League".

A few minutes later I had run the gauntlet of the military police and the hissing geese beyond the gate and started on what turned out to be one of my most inspirational runs ever. My mile-hungry legs simply ate up the ground and the cheek-cooling chill of the central German evening breeze rapidly revitalised my jaded spirits. I determined to start to put matters right the very next morning. A huge herd of hungry pigs foraging purposefully in an adjacent field grunted, seemingly in unison and porcine understanding and approval of my resolve. They certainly didn't want their peaceful country life disturbed by this poor imitation of Gordon Pirie, the word's greatest cheek-puffing exponent, some of whose athletic brilliance I was privately trying to emulate. Neither did the frightened fox, which raced ahead of me back through the daunting Borgentreich station gate at world record pace!

Mysteriously, not long after that, Doug Wilson the News of the World athletics reporter wrote…

*"What has happened to Mike Fleet
the 18 year old Croydon Harrier
who astonished everyone last Summer
when he ran Chris Chataway to a yard
in a 1min 53.2sec half mile?*

*Fleet who is now on National Service
with the RAF in Germany
is stationed miles away from a track
and it seems unlikely that we shall hear
much of him this season.
The big danger, of course is that
when a youngster loses touch
with the sport at this age
he may well lose interest completely"*

Newly acquired coach Bill Coyne and old friend Frank Turk certainly made sure that I didn't lose interest by sending a regular supply of training activities and athletics snippets to whet my sporting appetite. The young airman nurtured with Athletics Weekly articles and copies of L'Equipe soon began to appreciate the benefits of "O" level French. Some suitably phrased blighty-bound letters, and hey presto a few weeks later, I was summoned to Station Headquarters. I was told of my posting with immediate effect to RAF Jever near the port of Wilhelmshaven in Friesland, Lower Saxony. In the preceding weeks, with nothing like the wartime heroism of RAF prisoners in Colditz Castle, I had learned to escape, not by running but by the determination to run.

Travelling alone across Northern Germany in 1956 carrying "all one's worldly belongings" in a huge brown non-issue kit bag was indeed daunting for a non German-speaking British serviceman, even if there was a running track at the end of the journey. Word had spread of my pending arrival and where I would be billeted. The welcoming party was led by Geoff Hann, whom it turned out was a fellow Surrey athlete from Kingston. He soon made me feel comfortable and happy about the new set-up.

Short of being at home in Britain, RAF Jever turned out to be as near a perfect posting for an aspiring athlete as one could imagine. The station was a flying base for fighter jets, Hawker Hunters and Supermarine Swifts and boasted all the facilities to be expected of such an important base. There was the 400m red shale running track, a gymnasium, a weights room, an athletics team and perhaps most importantly Flight Lieutenant Ken Saw the highly competitive Physical Fitness Officer... Oh yes and extra fried eggs for sportsmen coming off night duty! Ken Saw as it turned out, proved to have acquired a pretty strong team of athletes, most impressive of them being Lloyd Maloney a 6' 3" tall multi-eventer from Montserrat. A "Rat" according to the man himself, as applied to West Indian islanders by the neighbouring Antiguans, Lloyd by dint of amazing talent, rather than Daley Thompson or Dean Macey-like application, had actually won the AAA Decathlon Championship bronze medal in 1957. Also prominent in the squad were Thames Valley Harrier Frank Di Rienzo a strong, middle-distance runner, and sprinter Brian Sawyer who had played for Rotherham United against the Arsenal in the FA Cup in a marathon series of replays. Another key player was circus stunt man Johnny Morgan, who by dint of his ability to hop round on one hand had been talent-spotted as a shot putter. Morgan was also something of a legend for having hit a certain Cpl Gordon Pirie with a 16lb shot! Fortunately Gordon was made of stern stuff and went on, as history records, to become one of Britain's greatest ever distance runners.

I learnt many invaluable life skills at RAF Jever.... For example how to drive a diesel track roller, how to accept graciously large crusty loaves thrust down my pyjamas at midnight and how to identify lost private biplanes flying obliviously towards the East German border and us!

That May the 101 Signals Unit Jever Sports Day provided me with an ideal low key competitive RAF track debut. Such was the standard of athletics in the 2nd Tactical Air Force and in British Army of the Rhine then that I only lost to one Forces' athlete throughout my tour, and then only in my number two event the 400m.

See Figure 35 – RAF Friends and Rivals. 800m with Frank Di Rienzo

On both occasions in 1958 it was Javelin fighter pilot Flt Lt. David Brown, a Thames Valley Harrier, who provided me with high class friendly rivalry, to show that I still had some way to go. The blow was softened somewhat in the second of these encounters, when I was pulled round in 49.4sec, the first of my sub 50sec runs. Tragically two years later, David met his untimely death in a flying accident in Cyprus. Rumour had it that my two treasured encounters with him caused a flurry of illegal betting in Officer's Messes throughout the command.

See Figure 36 – Start Ausweiss TSV Germania, Wilhelmshaven

Another rare defeat came at the hands of Metz, the local middle distance star and friendly rival in my adopted German Club, TSV Wilhelmshaven.

North German winters can by extremely cold, and my first experience of one was just that, with plenty of frozen ground, several bouts of snow and a seemingly non-stop Easterly wind which had been clearly generated by the Russians to weaken our resolve! One inhospitable grey evening I got a harsh lesson in the severity of the weather there. Exhilarated after a solo run in the nearby forest, having overcome fears generated by my vivid imagination of hungry wolves padding silently in the snow waiting for me to drop, and steaming healthily in just vest and shorts, I re-entered camp. Without thinking, I foolishly drew more attention to myself by jauntily greeting a miserable looking military policeman on gate duty.

"Halt, airman," he shouted, *"Where's your 1250[7]?"*
Naturally in the interest of security I had left my identity pass locked in my room!
"Sorry sergeant it's in my billet. I didn't want to lose it in the forest," I replied.
"Stand to attention by the barrier, airman, you're not going anywhere until you're identified," he snapped.

Clearly the fact that I was wearing RAF Jever kit, complete with badge would not suffice! I suppose his vivid imagination might have turned me into a Russian in disguise! I was forced to comply, rapidly losing my exercise generated body heat and very soon wished for arrest and the warmth of the guardroom cell. But it was not to be. I've heard of humans freezing to death in extreme conditions and I think that after some ten minutes of shivering, had I not heard Flight Lieutenant Saw's incredulous enquiry and the positive response in my favour which ensued, I might even have started to suffer from frost bite.

"What the devil are you playing at, Fleet?"
"Duty sergeant won't let me in sir, I haven't brought my 1250," I spluttered.
"Leave it to me Fleet. Get off to a shower and come round to my place in an hour for supper, the wife and I want to talk about baby-sitting."
"Thank you sir," I mumbled gratefully.

---

[7]   1250 RAF identity pass.

Immediate release ensued and needing no second invitation, I was off leaving the red faced sergeant with the angry PFO.

During that winter, the RAF Jever cross-country team regularly trundled through north Germany in a venerable Magirus Deutz coach, and it was on one of those low level sorties that Teutonic geese once again reared their ugly heads.

We had run in the snowy 2nd Tactical Air Force cross-country championship at a bleak RAF Wildenrath, and during the return journey a unanimous call of nature found the team happily relieving the problem at the side of a "quiet country lane".

As the steam rose, so too did a crescendo of angry hisses from the gaggle of previously slumbering geese, unceremoniously shocked from their slumbers by the dousing. Almost simultaneously lights blazed on in a previously unnoticed farmhouse just a few metres away. Never have exhausted cross country runners moved as quickly as we sought sanctuary on the old coach, which in collaboration with the compassionate driver, hastily departed the scene, belching out a black exhaust screen of darkest diesel fumes. The fork-wielding farmer stood no chance of revenge!

My 1958 400m win in the Internationales Sportfest in Wilhelmshaven, is memorable in that, schoolboy and RAF medals apart, it produced my first "Real" prize, a book predictably all in German. That fine tome entitled "Gelbe Wand am Grunnen See" remains a treasured "trophy", and now 50 years later, thanks to adult German classes, I can get the gist of some of its contents! Of course I had no inkling then that the book would be valued many years later on something called the internet, at £85.

When I recorded a modest season's 800m best of 1:55.6 in the traditional inter-services encounter against the British Army of the Rhine in Monchengladbach, I could then hardly have imagined that the army runner-up, Lt. Chris Garrett, would preside over my marriage 44 years later, as the Rev. Chris Garrett.

Following RAF Jever's second successive title win in the 2TAF team Championship, our generous Commanding Officer, Group Captain Rochford Hughes arranged a champagne celebration in the officer's mess lounge. After welcoming and congratulating us, a happy blend of officers and other ranks, with myself as the fortunate team captain, the CO cracked a celebratory bottle of champagne, the cork from which flew missile-like through the parchment sail of a handsome model galleon mounted on the mantelshelf. The ensuing spontaneous round of laughter and applause was calmly accepted by the involuntary gunner, as only a highly ranked officer could. Had we wide-eyed youngsters only known our leader's service pedigree, the admiration for his accuracy at disabling the ship's small fore-sail, the applause and the laughter might have lasted even longer.

See Figure 37 – Winning RAF Jever Team HQ 2TAF Munchen Gladbach

Much later I learned that in 1941 the then Flight Lieutenant Hughes, piloting a Sunderland flying boat was attacked by two Bf110s and with injured men on board and both engines shot up "landed safely" off Benghazi. In an ensuing march in Italian occupied territory, he and his men reached allied lines with 130 prisoners in tow. My now even more respected badminton rival, Air Marshall Sir Rochford Hughes OBE died on 17th September 1996.

The 400m proved to be more fruitful territory time-wise and I was thrilled to break the "magic 50" twice with 49.4sec clockings, especially in the match against the Deutsche Luftwaffe which, as an international military first, was an historic post-war encounter.

Home from Germany one Saturday on pre-demob leave, I called in to the Tooting Bec track in South London, and foolishly succumbed to the temptation to race. To my embarrassment I found my travel-weary legs up to no better than a 1:58.2 run and I trailed in a distant second, leaving the winner Paul Rutter of Oxford City AC with the dubious distinction of being the only Brit, to beat me over two laps that year. It was a salutary experience; a race which certainly brought me down a necessary peg or two.

Then it was off to RAF Innsworth and the final pay parade. Endeavouring to elicit favour with my military superiors for one final time, I marched up to the paying officers' table far too fast. Much to everyone else's amusement I slid on the highly polished floor before disappearing at the salute, under the table and into the bemused man's feet.

"5030685 Sir," I spluttered from my supine situation.
"Are you all right, airman?" he enquired from above.
"If so you had better try again," he kindly advised, smothering a smile as

I clambered embarrassed to my feet.

Our intake's "Demob" was delayed for a day or two more to allow special release for the unfortunates who had been guinea pigs in the Christmas Island "atomic adventure". We didn't begrudge them that small token of understanding. Happily clutching our final free military rail passes, members of my National Service intake from autumn 1956 eagerly returned to civvy street. With the unpredictable Russians still up to their tricks we were retained on the reserve and accordingly my uniform was bagged up, complete with moth balls, and stored in the loft.

I was an adult civilian for the very first time, no longer a schoolboy or a National Serviceman, but a young man keen to become a Loughborough student.

6

Loughborough – The Athletes' Mecca

Throughout its history, Loughborough, first College and now University, has been the Mecca for many of Britain's most ambitious athletes. The "Mecca thought" had certainly been behind my rather presumptuous sole listing of that seat of learning, when some months before the two years, nine days, six hours and five minutes earlier I had gone to serve Queen and country.

The Grove, a stylish converted Victorian house in Ashby Road, Loughborough became my student residence in September 1958. I then settled into a life of study and sport which was to become my rewarding routine for the following three years. Attendance at the Fresher's Fayre in the Victory Hall had been recommended in order to make oneself known to the student leaders of Loughborough sport. An enthusiastic chap manning the athletics stand surprisingly seemed keen to know what my best long jump was, but when he heard that it was only 18"6", wasn't too excited; but Derek Hayward, later to become Secretary of the Kangaroo Club and key English Schools official, was in fairness pretty interested when informed of my running pedigree! I was easily persuaded to take part in the Fresher's Sports that October, when I got my first taste of the competitiveness of the place, far later than in any previous season. I won the half mile in a modest, but virtually unchallenged 2:01.7, my slowest time of the year. The eight man Inter-Hall relay however turned out to be a real nightmare for, as number one man and with my proud parents among the spectators, I committed the cardinal sin of breaking twice and "earned" disqualification for my team from the Grove. The sense of having nine pairs of eyes keenly focused on this hugely embarrassed defaulter was beyond any description... not surprisingly, I never false-started again.

Behind the cross-country stand there was a tall bespectacled fellow who spoke enthusiastically of the College's challenging course in and around Charnwood Forest. Another tall curly headed fellow, clearly with an interest in steeplechasing, sang the praises of barriers to be cleared and a stream to be crossed. A couple of Saturday afternoons on, an inquisitive squad of Freshers eagerly followed Clive Plumpton, the bespectacled Portsmouth A.C. star and British Universities Champion and tall Technical College student Brian Knott from Blackpool, off the campus and up Outwoods Drive en route to savour the challenges of the Colleges' Course with its rocky Charnian climbs, wooded trail, stile and fast road finish. Naturally with Loughborough being Loughborough, that run wasn't quite so simple and incorporated a demanding number of repetitions over 150 yards on one of the steepest hills en route. That proved to be the precursor of several similar "extra miles" which contributed to the sporting excellence of the place.

See Figure 38 – What Health and Safety? Loughborough XC. Hurdling a stile in style

Two hours later an ever extending skein of muddied, steaming and sweating, but confirmed cross-country club recruits, took their first shower at the famous Stadium alongside the Ashby Road, where legions of Loughborough athletes had eased their weary limbs before them. Among the group was an unobtrusive David Saul who was later destined to become Premier of Bermuda, complete with luxury yacht. He is now The Right Honourable Dr David J. Saul, Ph.D., M.Ed., B.A., Dip.Ed. J.P.; what more can I say?!

During the evolving autumn and on into the winter I learned, in common with a large majority of the young sportsmen there, just how lacking we freshers were in overall fitness. Whereas in the past we had been training hard for our specific disciplines alongside studying at school or serving in the forces, we now found ourselves in a totally new and widely demanding environment. Clearly the academic side was in parallel with the physical; we were programmed for swimming, gymnastics and getting into the intricacies of basketball, golf and volleyball too.

Fellow students way back then included Robbie Brightwell and John Cooper who both went on to win Olympic medals in Tokyo in 1964, triple AAA hammer champion Mike Ellis, and John Sheldrick, my discus thrower room mate, who later won Commonwealth bronze in 1962. Lecturers Don Anthony, Jack Archer and Ian Boyd all had Olympic credentials. Archer had run at Wembley in 1948 while Anthony and Boyd had both represented Great Britain in Melbourne in 1956. Curiously the Loughborough of those days bore little resemblance to the well-staffed and structured unit which is envied by so many these days. We had no coaches attached to the team, so self-help groups evolved around a common denominator and it was my great good fortune that I found myself training alongside the stars. I may be doing athletics lecturer Geoff Gowan a disservice with my distant recall, diluted by the passage of time.

The reality was that his quiet well-informed advice led us willingly into productive sessions of lactic torture.

Training with top athletes like Brightwell and Cooper often took on a new highly competitive dimension, which featured, for example, six to eight extremely fast "220s" or four or five differential "quarters"[8]. The former regularly demanded a series of near personal bests from me with totally inadequate three to four minute "recoveries", which forced me into the psychology of overcoming the debilitating pain of lactic acid build-up. When we were doing differential "quarters" I found it almost impossible to inject the required acceleration of the differential component with the pace being somewhere between 50 and 52 seconds. Sprint start sessions were of the highest quality too, regularly carried out in the company of sub ten-second men Berwyn Jones, Brian Anson, Reg Holmes, Jim Railton, Nick Whitehead and, of course, Brightwell and co.

Longer sessions like hill repetitions with a flat sprint at the top were routine. Such Sunday morning fare, and much more besides, served up by our popular Pied Piper, Technical College tutor Ian Boyd, attracted a hard core of middle distance men among whom one Glynne Jenkins stood out as something of a tyrant. He was always demanding that we did more than our prescribed training dose, increasing fatigue and delaying welcome refreshments at the Boyd apartment in Hazelrigg Hall, but again there was no apparent coach-based structure. Glynne proved to be the best trainer with whom I ever ran, Gordon Pirie apart, but he was never a competitive threat to me at anything other than cross country and road running. I owe him a debt of gratitude for helping me to learn what my brain and body could take.

The ever smartly dressed "I. G. Jenkins Esq", as he was affectionately known, clearly liked us to believe that he had friends in high places. Glynne was however a pretty selfless fellow for a pseudo aristocrat and enjoyed helping other athletes to achieve their potential rather than his own. On one occasion a few days after I had been inexplicably out-kicked in an indifferent race, he wisely suggested that I worked on the fault, with him sprinting unpredictably and repeatedly off a good pace. All I had to do was respond promptly. That was fine for the first thirty minutes, but as he eagerly drove on for the hour I was forced to throw in the towel. Such challenging company was one of the many privileges and benefits of being a Loughborough student.

---

[8] Laps of variable pace.

My idea of celebrating my 21st birthday in February 1959 was to run for Croydon Harriers in the Southern Cross-Country Championships at the Aylesford Paper Mills in Kent.

See Figure 39 – 21st birthday, Southern Cross-Country Championship XC Aylesford, cheered on by Frank Turk

After an unsensational, yet satisfying run, I returned with my club mates on the Croydon team coach, and to my surprise the driver dropped Frank Turk off with me at the bottom of my road. Frank came back on some pretext or other such as: "books from his wife Myrtle for my mother". While I luxuriated in a muscle-easing bath, unknown to me the driver had gone round the block before dropping the rest of the team off to attend the surprise party they had plotted. I didn't even smell a rat when my mother, Beryl, incautiously called out:

"Beryl's here," to Beryl Proctor's husband Brian, the Harriers distance coach who had arrived earlier. Overhearing, I thought mother was referring to another Beryl, a nurse friend of hers whom I then jokingly invited to: *"Come up and scrub my back".* The Beryl who had just arrived was, I was told, more than taken aback by my rather forward approach.

Enjoy celebrating my 21st? I certainly did in that eccentric way, having ploughed my "rear race furrow" round the fields of Kent, but those unexpected celebrations afterwards were far more rewarding. The whole day proved to be a winner, even if I was not. I am not so sure how my poor father viewed it as, despite all his persuasive powers, at midnight he was unable to arouse massive "Mighty Mouse" shot putter Nick Morgan whose sonorous slumbers prevailed until breakfast the next morning. Only then did loud wake-up calls, a generous serving of bacon and eggs with copious cups of coffee do the trick; the amiable giant finally ambled off, rested and replete.

What turned out to be a protracted, frustrating pursuit of the Surrey senior "half mile" title began in May that year, with an encouraging third in 1:52.2 behind highly ranked international Brian Hewson. I was really pleased to have finished within three seconds of the reigning European 1500m champion, but I kicked myself for letting club colleague Bob Harvey edge me into the bronze medal position. Little did I know then that my county title pursuit would continue for another seven years.

Late that spring I was enjoying a barefoot run on the Loughborough campus beside James Watt's historic steam engine when I sustained what was possibly my strangest injury. A searing pain under one foot led me to think that I had embedded a shard of glass, but on closer inspection I discovered the crushed remains of a bumble bee wedged between my rapidly swelling toes. The dying creature had clearly expressed its distress at being so entrapped in the way that only bumble bees can. It embedded its sting in my flesh. A twenty-minute, one-mile hobble to Dr Smith's surgery that evening brought me scant solace. Taking one look at the swollen extremity the dour unsympathetic Scot declared:

"If ye miss lectures tomorrow ye'll be malingering laddie, just keep it up tonight."

See Figure 40 – Disputed Loughborough dead heat Mike (L) and Wynne Oliver

A week later, and with my 100% lecture attendance record intact I was able to resume running, but only in the relative comfort of trainers!

My first significant recognition came in early June 1960 with an invitation to run in an 800m at the legendary White City Stadium which had hosted the 1908 Olympic Games and were immortalised by the tragic Dorando Pietri marathon saga. I ran 1:50.8 for a respectable fifth which represented a new personal best, and which I soon improved over yards in the Southern Championships, finishing fourth in 1:50.9. A small consolation then was sweet revenge over club colleague Bob Harvey. Never an international himself, Harvey was a doughty competitor, who in later years often helped make the early running for me when I needed a fast time.

It was during the summer holidays of 1960 that I unwittingly put my athletics career at risk for the second time when I ran for my temporary employers, Barkers, Derry and Toms and Zeetas, in a London Business Houses Championships on their leafy ground at Wimbledon. My winning anchor leg in the medley relay was met with embarrassing delight, and with the bonus of a rare but welcome ten pound note being thrust into my hand.

See Figure 41 – Anchoring Barker's and Derry and Toms to historic victory over Harrods at Wimbledon
See Figure 42 – First Athletics Weekly cover appearance and first AAA vest partnering winner Mike Rawson (3)

After another Invitation International at the White City in May 1961 in which I finished a rather inauspicious and battered sixth, the winner, reigning European champion Mike Rawson, was quoted in the somewhat questionable Sunday Sun, under the headline "Thanks Mike", saying that I had enabled him to win by "unselfishly letting him through to win". That is certainly not how I recall the race! To this day I can feel his grabbing hand on my shoulder, and remain incredulous that he was not disqualified. The rough and tumble of the Rawson fracas was followed the next month by an improvement over 880 yards to 1:50.0, plus a Southern Championship bronze into the bargain, and then three days later came a major stroke of luck...

...I had just finished a strenuous morning swimming session at Loughborough, when Bert Kinnear the lecturer called me to his office:

"Fleet, you've had a telephone call from somebody in London about athletics. He said it was fairly important. You'd better call back and find out what it's about, but be quick; your next lecture is in ten minutes!" I was allowed to use Bert's office telephone and pulse racing, quickly called back.

"Thanks for calling back, Fleet, Herb Elliott, the Australian star, has pulled out of the London v Rhineland Cities match at the White City tonight. Would you like the spare place, the race is at 7.45pm?" said the voice 98 miles away. Would I?!

There was no doubt at all, and soon the athletics-mad college authorities had given me the nod.

Kit was quickly crammed in a bag and I was into a taxi and down to the station on the first part of the blurred dash to what turned out to be one of the most exciting and formative races of my career. Having emerged into the evening sun via the daunting dripping tunnel beneath both canine[9] and human tracks, my attention was drawn to the PA announcement.

"...and taking the place of the great Australian Herb Elliott (boos of disappointment), the British Universities Champion and Southern bronze medallist Mike Fleet of Croydon Harriers." (Do I recall murmurs of discontent?).

---

[9] The White City Stadium sported a greyhound racing track outside the running track.

I didn't care, for I felt that I had arrived, and in the outcome, bearing in mind the energy output of the preceding seven hours, the experience proved well worth it.

The PA told it all for me. *"Result of the match and invitation 880yds. 1st Peter Snell, New Zealand, 1:48.4; 2nd Paul Schmidt, West Germany, 1:49.5; 3rd Mike Fleet, Loughborough Colleges and Croydon Harriers 1:49.9. Did I hear cheers? It was a personal best and a landmark first sub 1:50.0 run. I had finished 1.5sec behind one of the greatest Olympic Champions Snell, who felt, according to The Times report, that he had clocked "a highly satisfying time". Described graphically as "...Fleet, large chest heaving with the effort, finished less than half a second adrift of Schmidt the European Champion".*

Reading that gave me the feel good factor.

"Not bad I thought", as I travelled back on the *"milk train"* to the Midlands very early the next morning, readying myself for the conclusion of another week as a physical education student.

*See Figure 44 – "Not bad after a swim." First sub 1:50.0 800m leading
Peter Snell*

That afternoon, my personal tutor Don Anthony called me into his study to remind me that I must make up for the missed lectures the previous day. *"By the way,"* he smilingly added, *"...good race yesterday."*

Well, he was an international hammer thrower as well as a lecturer!

After one more domestic race, a comfortable win in the Croydon Borough 880 yards Championship, followed by an ignominious elimination in a very rough AAA Championships heat, THE letter landed on the front door mat.

Yes, this was my first full international selection.

My experience as the first full Croydon Harriers track international was not to pass without its moments! I must have been pretty keyed up, for I do not even remember Mary Rand, the gorgeous future Olympic gold medallist, being one of seven girls on the parade of athletes with me! The occasion was most memorable for the fact that, just before the race in which I paired up with the experienced Sid Purkiss, a pacey French-polisher from Romford, I become trapped in my tracksuit trousers.

"We know you're playing for time," snapped the unsympathetic marksman.

At that moment, shot putter Mike Lindsay miraculously appeared out of nowhere, and tore me free of my misery... so much for jammed track suit zips!

BRITISH AMATEUR ATHLETIC BOARD

LANgham 3498

54, Torrington Place,
London, W.C. 1.

July, 1961.

Dear Sir/Madam,

I have pleasure in advising you that you have been selected to represent Great Britain and Northern Ireland in the match with Hungary at the White City Stadium, London, on Saturday August 5th and Monday August 7th, 1961 in the following event(s):-

800 Metres (Saturday)
••••••••••••••••••••••••••••••••

I shall be glad to learn by the immediate return of the form attached whether you are able to accept this invitation, together with the other relevant information requested thereon.

All Members of the Board join in sending you their congratulations upon your international selection.

Yours sincerely,

Jack C.G. Crump,

Honorary Secretary.

According to John Rodda, the eminent Guardian athletics correspondent:
"Fleet and Purkiss played their hand a little better in the 800m than A.J.Harris and J.Wenk did against the United States, but were still defeated".

Had I run 0.7sec faster, it was pretty certain that I would have won my first international instead of finishing third, and the press comments might have been totally different. C'est la vie!

See Figure 45 – International debut GB v Hungary. A disappointed third

I complained to the iconic Harold Abrahams about his comments in the press, which implied that I had "eased up". Courteous as ever, he wrote back, and I still have his cherished explanation and apology.

Orchard Leigh,
Hailey Lane,
Hertford.

September 12th., 1961

My dear Michael,

    Thank you very much for writing. May I say at once that I am most sorry if what I wrote caused any offence. Of course one gets an impression of a race, and then has to telephone a report, with no opportunity for real judgment. What I meant to covey to the reader was that you had eased up thinking that you had the race for third place in hand, and that this conscious slowing up, not of course through any lack of guts, lost you the points. My refernce to them not mattering was again because of the large margin of our victory.
    May I conclude by saying how glad I am that you mentioned the matter to me, and wish you the very best of luck.
    In so far as an apology if necessary I unhesitatingly give it.
    Yours ever,

Harold M. Abrahams

A few days later I received a parcel and the following handwritten note from Mary Tupholme, Clerk to the British Amateur Athletics Board.

BRITISH AMATEUR ATHLETIC BOARD

54 · TORRINGTON PLACE · LONDON · W.C.1

Telephone : LANgham 3498

With the Compliments
of the Honorary Secretary

We have these trousers spare – will they fit you in exchange for the ones you got "trapped" in

I asked myself, was this a hint that I might be in line for some more international selections?

It was at about this time that a photograph in which I featured appeared on the cover of Athletics Weekly magazine. It was to be the first of several which caused a few "disjointed noses" among my contemporaries!

Many years later I was delighted to read that Lord Sebastian Coe considered that he had "made it" when he so appeared. This indirect and retrospective endorsement was well worth having.

My eager anticipation for the long awaited trip to the World Student Games in Sofia, Bulgaria, had been mounting all season and especially since June when my Surrey bronze medal winning time of 1:51.3 had cracked the qualifying time.

A visit to Jackson the Taylor in Oxford Street for a uniform fitting was a new experience for me and for most of the team, as was the kind invitation, from Monsieur Parvan Tchernev (I never found why he was not prefixed as Mr.), to cocktails at the embassy of the People's Republic of Bulgaria on 17th July. He presented a clear insight into the unfamiliar world of diplomacy, and into one of the more obscure nations contained behind the Iron Curtain.

Our departure for Bulgaria proved to be a nail-biting affair, with our chosen carrier getting into financial difficulties. The airline first chartered by the British Universities Sports Federation then folded. After a spell of uncertainty, confirmation finally materialised. Some frantic searching had conjured up a venerable Pegasus Airlines of Luton Viking, formally of the Royal flight, but at a price £400 more than the previous quote! A further sponsor had to be found, or we would be remaining at home. Good old Gillette stepped in and saved us from a very close shave at extremely short notice. Relieved team members were not required to add to their individual £10 contributions! The Board had generously agreed to pay any assembly and dispersal costs of team members in excess of the first 30 shillings each. Those were the days! Soon afterwards on the morning of 23rd August, the welcome sight of our "very own" gleaming airliner awaiting us at Gatwick Airport was a joy to behold.

"Where's the new man from Scotland?" was the question on the tips of many tongues.

A tall fellow in a natty trilby hat strode into view. Menzies Campbell had arrived and the team was complete.

See Figure 46 – World Student Games 1961 Fisu I/D
See Figure 47 – GB Athletics Team, Sofia

The rising crescendo of the two Bristol Hercules engines of the Pegasus Viking was music to our ears as we sat tilted back in the old-timer, awaiting take off. For many of us this would be our first experience of flying. With no direct flights to Sofia in those days, we welcomed a brief stop in Munich before heading off up over the Alps to our destination. A couple of hours or so later, and mainly to the embarrassment of the males in the group we were welcomed at Vrazhdebna Airport by group of gladioli bearing girls …I had certainly never been given a bouquet of flowers before, but hope that behind the blushes, I for one accepted mine with due decorum!

We were soon settled into our rather austere rooms at the University, each corridor end occupied by a miserable looking woman, rather unnervingly monitoring our comings and goings on an abacus. The Bulgarian experience, sport apart, was one of great cultural mix and corporate enthusiasm, physical well being, plus the disturbing noise of military convoys on the move for hours on end, for several nights. In contrast, it was a real pleasure to cross their virtually traffic free equivalent of Trafalgar Square to visit the golden domed Alexander Nevsky Cathedral. On the more mundane but nonetheless very important subject of food, I cannot recall either before or since having seen truck loads of unboxed oranges and peaches being delivered to a refectory and hosed down prior to consumption.

The Universiade athletics was based in the Bulgarian National Vassil Levsky Stadium, with its magnificent backdrop of the snow capped Rhodope Mountains. Some of their distant cool would have been welcome trackside.

Before the athletics began, a heroine emerged in the delightful form of diving gold medallist Liz Ferris. This smiling perfectionist won our hearts and set our minds to the tasks ahead.

See Figures 48/48a – "Cross sport inspiration" Liz Ferris

Since then the diving belle, now Dr Elizabeth Ferris, has become one of the most respected women in the Olympic administration. A Research Fellow of Kings London in the Department of Nutrition, she is currently a champion of a different kind, having become a leader of the cause of women in sport and Vice-President of the World Olympians Association.

Another young lady to win a heart was Vera, our Bulgarian interpretress, a striking brunette, who at least emotionally bowled one of our biggest athletes off his feet. One night she responded impressively to his understandable attentions by borrowing her grandmother's beautiful wedding dress to wear for dinner with her admirer. One can only guess whether this gorgeous young lady finished up as a film star or a model, but I thought she was too intelligent for either!

Our male interpreter Janko Stamoff turned no heads, but did his utmost to ensure that we all enjoyed the best he could offer of his country. No effort seemed too much, ranging from a bucket of freshly made curd cheese, coarse bread and grapes, to a luxurious lakeside meal with music and a visit to the awe-inspiring Rila Monastery in the mountains. The visit to Rila Monastery gave us the somewhat dubious privilege of showing devotion to a disgusting looking bible which was greyed by the moisture from the lips of many pilgrims. Despite never having met since, Janko and I remain good friends. He has been a conscientious correspondent throughout the intervening years, his letters becoming more natural with the passage of time, and even more so following the dissolution of the communist regime led by Todor Zhivkov on 10th November 1989.

But I am racing ahead in the literary sense and digress. I was there to represent Great Britain in the 800m, together with John Holt, the future IAAF General Secretary, and to run in the 4x400 team with, among others, Menzies Campbell, who 46 years later as Sir Menzies, served in Parliament as Leader of the Liberal Party. In the large 800m field requiring three rounds, one noticed Irishman Ronnie Delany, the eternal Villanova University student and 1956 Melbourne Olympic 1500m Champion, and Zoltan Vamos, Rumanian Universiade 800m title and record holder and fifth finisher in the previous year's Olympic 1500m. A pre race day "warm-up" with Ronnie turned out to be an insight into the make-up of the great man. The activity involved a brisk pace, and my attentive ear for the generous non-stop delivery of advice, regularly interspersed with anecdotes. After 25 testing minutes he thanked me for joining him, and set about the rest of his workout, party to which thankfully I was not. I made off for the nearest shade and an opportunity to recover!

In an undemanding 800m heat I found that a comfortable second place in 1:56.8 was good enough to reach the semi final the next morning. Then I would I vie with Vamos for a place in the final later on the same day. He just prevailed in 1:49.3 and I also qualified 0.2 sec back. We both beat the existing Student Games 800m record.

All seemed set for a tough final, and so it transpired with that wily, experienced campaigner Delany controlling the race to win comfortably in 1:50.7. Far less experienced and possibly weary after my necessarily quick semi, I finished a disappointed 5th in 1:52.1. The unlucky favourite Vamos was a faller and jogged forlornly home last, covered in black ash. It was one thing to be able to say that I had run faster than the Olympic 1956 1500m Champion and the University Games Champion, but semi final performances do not win gold medals, and certainly another thing to have to say is that individually I came home empty handed when Delany and two others had medals to show for their efforts.

It was a salutary lesson and one which I still preach to athletes whom I coach and hope will benefit from my experiences no matter how far back in time.

See Figure 49 – Ronnie Delany wins World Student Games, 800m. MF 5th second from R

From the British perspective, despite having released our top two 400m men, Robbie Brightwell and Adrian Metcalfe to the senior Great Britain team competing against the USSR, the 4x400 proved to be a much more rewarding affair. Charged with the responsibility of anchor leg and blissfully unaware of the opposition, I took over in third place and held on as best I could to a rather fast fellow who resisted my every challenge.

"Well run Englishman" said a large chap with a stopwatch *"He, Josef Trousil, Czechoslovakia, Europmeister, you 46.9seconds. I Korobkov, Russki."*

That name rang a bell. Five years before it was he, Gavriel Korobkov with whom Jack Crump the BAAB Secretary had shaken hands after the Ponomareva hat stealing scandal and the diplomatic furore surrounding it... the Russian official with the human touch!

The Soviet team leader had noticed me as his team finished well beaten. The bronze medals were ours and I was thrilled, but historically with one disappointment. I had failed to feature in my only major championship podium photograph. For years I viewed the grainy record of our success believing that I had been selfishly blocked out by my team mates. Not so! With hindsight, I realised I was the culprit: I had smuggled my Voigtlander Vito B camera into the centre, but in the excitement I completely forgot the personal need for a pictorial record. I had stepped down from the podium and captured my three colleagues on film for posterity; my presence is confirmed by an unmistakeable shadow in the foreground!

My outstanding athletic memory from that Universiade is of Russian high jumper Valery Brumel's world record at 2.28m, achieved with the now superseded straddle technique under floodlights, in uncanny silence... followed by a euphoric eruption of acclaim and then the emotional playing of the majestic Soviet national anthem for his medal presentation. The closing ceremony was unforgettable too, stunningly spectacular, brilliantly colourful, deafeningly loud. It featured a dynamic display of traditional Balkan dancing by hundreds, maybe thousands, of brightly dressed

Bulgarians, was loudly interjected by huge ear-blasting and subsequently sky lighting fireworks, which my fertile imagination suggested were fired from nearby Russian tanks and was emotionally concluded with a powerful rendition of the Brahms' Academic Festival Overture. I was left with an indelible and inspiring memory. What must it be like at the Olympic Games I wondered?

The next day we were relieved to find that the captain of our trusty Viking had remembered where we were waiting to be picked up, but had us all worried for a while, taxiing up quite some time after we had run out of "life-sustaining" Levs[10] at the airport. An uneventful flight back to the UK via Munich got us back to Gatwick shortly after dawn. Soon after we landed at 6am and with farewells made, I was preparing to enter my teaching career, in very much at the "deep end". The new South Croydon Secondary School year was scheduled to start at 8.30am that morning. Slightly dishevelled and distinctly weary, their recently recruited assistant Physical Education master marched nervously through the school gates. This was indeed new territory and there was no time for a warm-up...

See Figure 50 – Leaving our trusty Viking behind at Gatwick. Mike and trilby-hatted Menzies Campbell with others

---

[10] Bulgarian currency

7

The Working Athlete

My work at South Croydon Secondary School as number two in the P.E. Department brought me over the ensuing months into contact with several youngsters keen on athletics, and led me to a modest start of an interest in athletics coaching. Doubtless at the back of my mind, was the curious lingering exhortation of Britain's finest coach Geoff Dyson who had made his indelible impression on me while lecturing at Loughborough.

"You can't have pole-vaulters without poles," he barked, *"now go back to your hinterlands and spread the gospel"*. As a geography student then as well as a PE person, I thought that I understood him better than most.

Little did I realise then that I had begun my ongoing passion for coaching, which has subsequently encompassed some 12,000 hours of unpaid but result-rewarded coaching. Thousands more professional hours have been enjoyably spent preaching "The Dyson Gospel", amended over the years with acknowledgement to John Le Masurier, Dennis Watts, Percy Cerutty, Ron Pickering, Mike Smith and many more during PE lessons, school games afternoons and at specific athletics and cross-cross country sessions, notably at the outstanding Trinity and Whitgift Schools in Croydon.

The names of three keen youngsters persist from those formative days; waif-like sprinter Pam Bradbury, plus middle-distance runners John Player and Colin Yarlett. One hopes that they enjoyed being coached in my early teaching days. With apologies, I recall little of their achievements, but curiously I do remember where all three lived! Pam's family occupied a tiny Victorian terraced house in West Croydon, which has long since fallen to the advance of the bulldozer. Colin's home on the Waddon council estate is now proudly privately owned, while the unique "Player Pad", then boasting frosted glass windows which announced it as the "Cow Keeper's House", has now succumbed to the clinical anonymity of double glazing. It is still easy to find in South Croydon on the Brighton Road, thanks to clearly identifiable carved angelic scenes retained either side of the front door.

I still coach nearby, just a misdirected discus throw from the Cow Keepers

House across the A23 on South Field at Whitgift School. Well, not actually possible, thanks to the powers that be at the school taking my advice and installing a fine safety cage!

That autumn I ran four more "halves", twice in times fast enough to have seen me first in Sofia, but I must concede that they were achieved in non-pressure races. My mother at least finished the season happy, having been given the set of china fruit bowls which I won in the Fulham Borough Open Meeting at Hurlingham Park. They were certainly good value and remain a credit to their owner and to their manufacturers J & G Meakin, still in use and undamaged 50 years later.

No longer a student and faced with a long challenging summer, hopefully culminating in the 1962 Commonwealth Games in Perth, Western Australia, I stepped up my winter preparation. Longer runs, muddier hills and more weight repetitions were fitted in alongside routine track sessions, road and cross-country races, and of course, my annual Old Mid-Whitgiftian team sport hockey fix.

Track training with Croydon arch rival and good friend Bob Harvey proved extremely beneficial, with the semi-competitive rivalry bringing the best out in both of us. I recall with amazement one eccentric session which we devised, which involved power skipping the bends and jogging the straights for ten laps! I do concede that, with the skid afforded by the cinder tracks, such a session must have been easier then, than it would be now on an all weather surface.

The somewhat limited weight training of my National Service and PE student days developed significantly in the far less salubrious environment of the Croydon Tug of War Club HQ, beside the Arena. The big bonus for me in more ways than one, apart from the "central heating" of a coke burning and fume belching stove reminiscent of RAF billet heating, was the partnership which I developed with Croydon Harrier colleague and international shot putter Nick Morgan. Over the ensuing months "The Mighty Mouse" patiently moulded me into a technically sound and much stronger athlete.

An attractive welcome addition to this predominantly macho environment came with the arrival in our midst of Ann Packer, one of Britain's most talented and personable women athletes, who was then teaching at the nearby Lady Edridge School. Her good looks and high quality perfume gave the squalid place an immediate lift, not least with the stifling of previously routine expletives which had been considered an essential accompaniment to success. Suddenly this fetid world pulled itself out of the Dark Ages, with well-muscled males starting to appear washed, in clean kit and smelling of after-shave rather than sweat. It was astonishing how quickly Ann eased her way into acceptance from the strutting broad-belted body-builders now smelling sweet rather than of sweat, and using unfamiliar expressions of anger like… "B***** hell, oops sorry!" in preference to the previously very common "F***ing hell" or regular reference to certain parts of the male anatomy. The less sexist "A*** holes" came into more common usage, but even that caused any involuntary deliverer to blush and mumble apologies.

The projected productive winter of hockey and training followed, geared towards the 1962 Empire and Commonwealth Games, as they were then parochially known. Due to be held on the other side of the world in Perth, Western Australia, they were a hugely exciting prospect. The highlight of my winter with the Old Mid-Whitgiftian Hockey Club was a goal which I scored against Cheam. Following a seemingly vain ball chase and an air hit by a brain-dead goalkeeper I was left with the chance of a lifetime. My success was reported in the Croydon Advertiser as "…the silliest goal yet seen at Sanderstead!"

My only regret that winter was to have caught a heavy cold which stopped me tackling the nine mile National Cross-country Championship in Blackburn!

The summer season opened early at the Milton Road track, Cambridge, where I ran an unspectacular second for the Amateur Athletic Association versus the University. The occasion proved to be notable, not only for the unique start effected by a youthful groundsman wielding what appeared to be a sawn-off shotgun, but much more poignantly it saw the very low key end to the illustrious career of none other than Australian Herb Elliott, one of the greatest middle distance runners of all time, for whom I had been the late replacement, the year before.

The legendary antipodean athlete, who reluctantly went through the motions on the Light Blues behalf, trailed home last in 1:59.5. He presented a mere and disinterested shadow of the man who had set several world records and who had spectacularly won the 1960 Rome Olympic 1500m with yet another world record in 3:35.6 only two years earlier. My last sight of the great man was of him strolling languidly through a gap in the hedge with never a glance back at the scene of his final "race".

See Figure 51 – White City Whitsun Games. Cover Boy Mike in the lead!

Fourth in the AAA 880yds final in 1:51.3 might not seem to have augured well for my pending Australian adventure, but viewed in the context of a 1:50.4 heat run less than three hours earlier was OK by me, since I was third British finisher and second Englishman. I knew that I would have to run faster but with all my "quarters" under 50 seconds, including an inter-county bronze and that preceded by a 49.0sec semi final personal best, I felt confident enough.

See Figure 53 – 1962 AAA Championships 4th, 3rd English. Mike behind 10 and 17

As the season reached a key stage, a different challenge caught my interest and promised to take the pressure off a little. My attention had been drawn to the one off "Ferdi Koch Mile", a completely domestic challenge at Croydon which, thanks to the generosity of Ferdi, the Club's very good Swiss friend, had a handsome winner's medal up for grabs. Had not some alert Bromley policemen found the forlorn and bedraggled little Swiss runner five miles off course from Hayes Common in thick fog the previous winter, such expansive motivation might never have been on offer! Well...

Believing complacency among the key opponents to be worthy of cultivation, I kept my modest ambition to myself. I really wanted that medal and without declaring my interest for fear of stimulating serious preparation among key candidates, I set about honing myself in isolation for the longer test ahead. After a few private uphill ¾ mile repetitions on the Purley Way Playing Fields beside the A23, with the wind from the east to avoid fumes, plus a solo track session of 8x440yards in 64sec, and there I was, Bannister-like, ready for the race.

No flag fluttered in a breeze on a nearby church tower, needing us to delay until the flag fell; no press corps eagerly awaiting an athletic landmark; no crowd; just eight competitors, Tom Miles the timekeeper, Doug Webb the starter and the lure of the Ferdi Koch Medal glinting on a card table centre-stage facing the empty grandstand.

The gun cracked and eight medal seekers were off. Four laps and a non earth-shattering 4:17.2 later, plus reasonable recovery time, and while

I was still feeling more sick than usual, with my rivals seeming sick with envy, the smiling Ferdi presented me with the medal which I still prize to this day.

The effort had been very different for me, but well worthwhile. It was extended and excruciating. The great Roger Bannister, already high in my regard, immediately went right to the top. He would have finished more than the length of the home straight ahead of me!

After a series of "near misses", an inter club match on a balmy August evening at the Withdean Stadium, Brighton provided the ideal conditions for an assault on the elusive Commonwealth qualifying standard. I was certainly up for it, as was club colleague and friend Bob Harvey who had agreed to set the early pace. Again not quite the Iffley Road epic; no waiting for a church tower flag to drop etc, but it certainly proved to be more than a milestone for me. Close behind Bob at the bell in just over 53 seconds, I took off with 300yds to go, and urged on by knots of cheering Croydon folk strategically positioned every 20yds or so around the track, I didn't dare to let up. On breaking the tape, I looked up enquiringly at chief timekeeper Tom Miles from my characteristic hands-on-knees recovery position. How had I done?

He smilingly confirmed my time; it was 1:48.9. The exciting personal best had the bonus of it being a new stadium and Croydon Harriers record, the best time by a British athlete for the year, equal 7th in the UK All Time rankings and, most significantly, it was a Commonwealth and Empire Games qualifying time. It is difficult to describe the relief and excitement created by that successful effort, and I could only imagine the supreme joy evoked by any athlete turning such a key to the ultimate Olympic door.

To his great credit, club colleague Bob Harvey, no token pacemaker, finished a worthy second in 1:54.8. In third place, and as far as I can confirm the only other finisher, was a delighted John Cobley of Brighton who clocked a personal best of 2 minutes.

See Figure 54 – 1962 happy Quartet, White City Harriers, Bob Harvey, Michael Soubry, Mike Fleet, Doug Webb

I had two more scheduled domestic events in which to run. One was the Glasgow Floodlit meeting at Ibrox Park, where I won both the quarter and half mile races. I successfully "negotiated" two very suitable prizes with the extremely inebriated steward. I also availed myself of the opportunity to wash where George Young, one of the all time great Scottish footballers had scrubbed down. Such was the claim of the plaque beside the Rangers' galvanised plunge bath!

One month and one day after I achieved the qualifying standard, the postman delivered my eagerly anticipated, blandly-typed selection-confirming missive from the AAA Headquarters at Torrington Place W.C.1.

"Dear Mike,

We are pleased to advise..."

There was no need to read on,...... I was Australia-bound!

AMATEUR ATHLETIC ASSOCIATION

LANgham 3498

54 Torrington Place,
LONDON. W.C.1.

1st October, 1962.

Dear Mike,

We are pleased to advise that you have been selected to represent England at Perth, for the British Empire and Commonwealth Games (November 24th – December 1st). The duration of the trip will be almost four weeks, leaving England on Saturday evening, the 10th November and returning on Tuesday, the 4th December.

Will you please advise BY RETURN that you are available.

As the Party is not sufficiently large enough to cover all events with a competitor, a certain amount of doubling-up will be necessary. Your main event will be taken into consideration, but it is possible that you may be asked to double up in other events. Details of these will be sent to you immediately all acceptances are received. Details will also be sent re Kitting-out, Inoculations, Vaccinations, etc., etc.

Yours sincerely,

LES GOLDING
Honorary Team Manager
England

In the intervening weeks came an intriguing athletics adventure in Kampala, which was part of the Ugandan Independence Celebrations. This provided me with my first experience of jet flight aboard a sleek Comet 4B of East African Airways, flying together with mile World Record holder Derek Ibbotson, big discus thrower and shot putter Mike Lindsay, earthy team manager Phil Gale, plus the Archbishop of York and his retinue. It all proved to be something of an eye-opener both for me, and for the Archbishop too, who was particularly discomfited by the big man's unceremonious in-flight can-crushing antics.

See Figure 55 – 1962 Welcome info from fellow NUT. Updated UK All-Time Rankings

Of course today, such a trip would be seen as potential "athletics suicide", involving long flights and racing at altitude without acclimatisation.

See Figure 56 – East African Airways Comet 4B

Our graceful aircraft banked smoothly over the vast shimmering expanse of water that is Lake Victoria and straightened its approach to Entebbe. As we continued to descend, smoke rose from hundreds of fires in the wooded land below, suggestive of the preparation of many an early post-dawn breakfast, and a spider's web of red African dirt roads beckoned the enthralled British athletes.

Housed in the barely disguised "Nakasero Press Hotel", clearly the temporarily vacated maternity hospital, we found ourselves in curtainless rooms with the bonus of "interesting" multi-tapped sinks. Phil Gale insisted on more privacy, and reluctantly accepted accommodation in the bedding store, some of the contents of which became our curtains. The experience put me on a fast learning curve to un acclimatised competition at altitude, on grass and in a race featuring a dozen unsophisticated Ugandans, plus a couple of other Europeans. The barefoot locals clearly revelled in running higgledy-piggledy at fiendishly fluctuating speeds, leaving a confused Englishman and his token white "brothers" from France and Germany all taken aback by the disarray.

My modest performance of 1:56.0, achieving 5th place in the field of thirteen, remains the best time I ran in Africa, and apart from a staff/school run eighteen years later, it was my last serious half-mile run on grass and, of little consolation, my fastest run on that surface. Derek Ibbotson struggled too, only managing to complete his four laps in about 4:11, for neither altitude nor temperature had entered the equation of our late arrival in Uganda. However several javelin throwers unaffected by the aerobic imposition of the venue were witnessed "improving" their performances when they surreptitiously advanced the pegs used to mark their throws!

Kenyan President Jomo Kenyatta was in regal attendance, complete with trademark fly switch and not surprisingly attracted considerably more attention than the athletes. Fortunately, his personal guards were far too pre-occupied at ground level to notice the juvenile antics of a rotund fly-switching Englishman on the balcony. We cringed at the naïve imitative charade enacted by our team manager and tried to convey by body language that for the moment, he was certainly not one of us. We put his behaviour down to relief at being free for a while from the confines of his blanket cupboard bedroom!

Ibbotson was in his element as a prankster too, and later he managed to get himself pictured in the Speaker's chair in the Ugandan Parliament, but when his "infallible test" of genuine cut glass failed and he broke one of the British Ambassador's best EIIR champagne glasses, he finished up with proverbial egg on his face! The ambassador's wife eased his embarrassment.

"Don't worry about it, dear, there are plenty more where that came from!" she simpered.

The Ugandan Independence Ceremony in the Kololo Stadium was, if anything, more chaotic than my race. My official invitation to the Milton Obote Investiture only offered an occupied space on the ground in front of a Pathe News cameraman's tripod. All VIP seats had long before been opportunistically commandeered by excited locals. Despite having to remain crouched below the camera, I was captivated by the unfamiliar pageantry and by the mayhem which unravelled before my incredulous gaze. It ranged from formal pomp to spontaneous dancing and ululation from the gathered masses, to a dramatic simulated Lake Victoria helicopter rescue which caused panic among the previously captivated crowd, many of whom prostrated themselves at the arrival of the roaring monster from the sky. Finally the old British flag was lowered, giving way to its Union Jack-free successor complete with its proud emblem of a crested crane, raised to an accompanying roar of approval from the thousands of newly independent Ugandans.

On 1st October, my name nestled unobtrusively to the rest of the world, but in "ten foot" letters to me in two column inches of the Daily Express,

"M
Fleet," with my initial on one line and the rest on the next, I was the last of six athletes listed for the 440yds, the 880yds and the 4x440yds relay.

My selection for the Empire and Commonwealth Games in Australia was confirmed.

No words can represent the elation I felt then and for several days afterwards. Doubtless along with many of the other observant hot-blooded young men selected, I secretly hoped that Janice Catt, a stunning Welsh qualified Chelsea College PE student long jumper would be selected to compete for the Principality. Sadly, despite clearing a very respectable 18' 8¾", she was overlooked by the short sighted Welsh selectors, and her many admirers faced the prospect of having to concentrate on their events without distraction!

See Figures 52 and 52a – 1962 "Welsh distraction" Janice Catt in action

With the Perth trip of a lifetime looming large six weeks away, I set about recharging my batteries. Several searchingly hot mid-day hill sessions of 3 x ¾mile on the Purley Way Playing Fields were soon under the belt followed by some fierce 660 yard repetitions on the Southern Railway Sports Ground at the end of my parents' garden. Then it was off to the sand dunes at Merthyr Mawr in South Wales with my former Loughborough room mate, discus thrower John Sheldrick, for a few days character-building.

We arrived at Candleston Farm intact after a minor crash while distracted trying to identify some hairy creatures grazing beside the road, and hardly had time to pitch our tent before an important looking little man turned up and started to give us the third degree in a high-pitched Welsh accent.

"What do you think you are doing here boys, this is private property?" he quizzed.
"Oh yes we know sir, we've got permission," said John, confidently towering above him.
"So who has given you permission?" queried the little man.
"The Welsh Athletics Association," I replied.
"Do you have a letter from the Welsh Office?"

...and so it went on, until I explained that our visit was part of our build-up for the Games in Perth.
"So who are you then boys?"
"Well sir I am Mike Fleet and this is John Sheldrick," I informed our inquisitor.
"And what are your events boys?" asked the little man seemingly not yet

convinced.

"I'm doing the discus and Mike is a half miler," John replied.

"Didn't you run in the Welsh Games at Maindy in July, Mike?" asked the little man.

I had run a reasonable second there in 1:51.0 and confirmed the fact.

"You're welcome boys, I am Arthur Williams, President of the Welsh A.A., you must come round for tea. My wife and I live not far away in Port Talbot."

Recognition and status had won the day, but then the pound of flesh was negotiated!

"You will come up the valley with me and I'll introduce you to the folk up there," said Arthur grabbing a megaphone. *"Come up in my car".*

We clearly had little choice and complied. Soon we were being driven up and down the hills and along the tightly knit roads parallel to the main valley thoroughfare in a nearby mining community.

"This is Arthur Williams here," our host repeatedly and embarrassingly announced through his loud hailer.

"Come on up to the miners' hall and meet some English Commonwealth and Empire Games athletics stars."

Such immediate and somewhat premature hike in status soon had the desired effect and twenty or so inquisitive folk arrived to shake the invaders by the hand, and to ask us unintelligible questions in richly accented English. I was persuaded to jog up a hill and back with an energetic group of lads, while John demonstrated discus spins and picked up an array of the heaviest items to hand to inspire his admirers. Then to a round of hardly deserved applause we left our new found friends en route to chez Williams for some welcome tea and biscuits before being driven back to our two man Perth preparation camp.

After the public introduction to the principality we then found ourselves left virtually in peace with plenty of time to attack the famous dunes. With much gritting of teeth and with an accumulation of grit in our shoes we strove onwards and upwards! The image of Australian Herb Elliott being harangued into action by the cavorting Percy Cerutty on dunes the other side of the world at Portsea was my inspiration for the expedition. With hindsight and half a century of coaching experience I wonder at the wisdom of our programme, but we certainly felt fitter and more focused.

Five weeks later on 10th November, two tougher and rejuvenated athletes assembled with a diverse plane load of sports men and women at Heathrow Airport for Qantas flight 738. Our flight to Perth via Rome, Teheran, Delhi and Singapore aboard a shining kangaroo emblazoned Boeing 707 took about 23 hours, making the Western Australian coast somewhere north of the grimly named Shark Bay, before heading south to arrive considerably ahead of schedule, prompting the captain to take us on an impromptu sightseeing trip up above the shimmering Swan River!

I arrived fresher than most, having followed the advice of more experienced travellers and included a towel and soap to enable a cooling shower at the final steamy Singapore stop-over. We were all sprayed by Australian Health Department officials before being allowed to leave the aircraft and be presented with bouquets of fascinating Kangaroo Paw blooms. We then had to walk over disinfectant soaked straw, before finally stepping onto hot Perth airport tarmac.

Luxury accommodation in a new bungalow development at City Beach set us up nicely, and after almost twelve hours of soothing sleep I found that as well as lodging with great athletes Derek Ibbotson and hammer thrower Howard Payne, kindly team manager Les Golding was on hand to provide early morning tea and unobtrusive discipline.

"Time to get up boys."

My first conscious day acclimatising in the Antipodes drew to an end by way of a clearly unsuccessful disco where I saw a large group of athletes ,several of whom I knew. The centre of attention was an attractive English superstar exponent of another sport whom I and the others surrounding her, hugely admired. I joined the group and her eye met mine. Wow...!

"Would you like to come to the beach?" she invited.

"Was I imagining things... would I?!"

The ten minute walk took us over the dunes to City Beach. A full moon illuminated a millpond Indian Ocean as it gently lapped on the sands. There was a surprise, an unbelievable kiss and we talked and talked until my flight-induced fatigue returned and in any case the village curfew called. We wished each other good luck for our respective competitions and returned to our quarters in the nick of time. We never met again. Hopefully inspired by the encounter, she went on to a silver medal winning success; sadly it had no such effect on my result.

Our resident kookaburra provided an unwelcome early morning call every day, eased slightly by the tray of soothing cups of tea served up by "Uncle" Les Golding, our kindly co-habiting team manager.

Three rounds of the 880 yds in Western Australia's "Mediterranean" summer at the Perry Lakes Stadium were made tougher with the heats and semis being programmed on the same day, but it worked out well, with safe seconds and thirds earning a place for me in the final. I "warmed up" gently, seeking shade where the temperature was still over 100 degrees and occasionally jogging through the water sprays refreshing the grass outside the stadium.

In the final, according to my records, "I simply wasn't strong enough. Snell and Kerr were in a class of their own" and, having clearly tried to beat them taking on the pace early, I also played into the hands of two other less ambitious, perhaps more sensible athletes who edged me back to 5th in a relatively modest 1:50.0, which even so was still my equal second best of the season, but oh for my Brighton time – which would have been good enough for bronze medal on that scorching summer day "down under" in November! My enduring memory of that race, was of Peter Snell coming alongside down the back straight, eyeing me up and down and quickly assessing the "threat" before changing gear and leaving me "for dead". He went on to win in 1:47.6 with Jamaican George Kerr taking the silver medal in 1:47.8.

See Figure 57 – 1962 Commonwealth final. Unusually then chasing Kenyan with Peter Snell waiting to strike
See Figure 58 – Peter Snell holds off Geoge Kerr for Perth gold – MF 5th

I still believe that it was the right thing to have tried to take on the Olympic gold and bronze medallists and guess that it was no disgrace to have run respectably against them, rather than to have tamely tried for a more accessible bronze.

What was foolish, I now realise, was to deviate from my pre-race training routine a few days earlier, by trying to replicate Snell's reported 3x440yds in sub 49.0sec. I managed three sub 50sec runs in half an hour, albeit with rolling starts, which only went to prove that the New Zealander was faster and stronger than me. It clearly left me more tired for the tests ahead and used up a valuable day of recovery. The moral is not to get sucked into something different and demanding so close to an important event. I ought to have placed faith in my well-established routine.

Despite some astonishing sprinting by the gazelle-like Rhodesian Seraphino Antao, 100 yds in 9.5 sec and 220 yds in 21.1 sec, rumour had it that the fastest performance of the Games was by an intrusive bush fly, which almost got into the lungs of middle distance colleague Bob Setti, before being violently expelled as he sprinted home in his semi final.

See Figure 59 – Personal best page from the record book

Many years later a lovely Welsh lady, a former long jumper who had hoped to be selected for those Games, gently chided me for sending her a post card from Perth which thoughtlessly told her what a great time I was having there. Clearly I had not chosen my words considerately
The following winter featured much tough preparation including the nine mile National Cross-Country Championship on Coldhams Common, Cambridge, unique for its cloying mud, which at times converted light racing shoes into something akin to deep-sea divers' boots. I classed my struggling 632nd finish in the field of 1,300 as a valuable investment in the fitness bank for the summer ahead.

In March I made my sole and somewhat undistinguished indoor debut at the Empire Pool and Sports Arena Wembley, competing in the Amateur Athletic Association inter club medley relay championship. Our 2:59.2 clocking must still be a Croydon record. The cigarette smoke-filled environment was not one which I would wish to experience again. Far tighter than usual post-race lungs and sore eyes were the short-term legacy of that occasion.

A full winter hockey programme too, playing for the Old Mid-Whitgiftians helped to restrict boredom and retain speed and fitness.

A 1:51.8 clocking against Cambridge University in May despite defeat indicated that I was on track for a good season in 1963. Wins for London in Munich and in the Southern Championships were encouraging too, but a dismal 9th in the Amateur Athletic Association Championships was cause for concern. Fortunately I managed to bounce back with a 1:50.8 win in the Brockman Trophy at Wimbledon Park, thanks possibly to the adrenaline rush of a car crash en route to the track. There were no injuries and the driver, international shot-putter Nick Morgan, managed to knock the car back into shape with one his 16lb implements. Soon after, I was selected to run for England against Italy and foolishly, I ran with a heavily strapped injured ankle. It was only the anger at my unco-operative "team mate" Alan Dean, who dogmatically refused to contemplate tactics, which motivated me to overcome the pain plus all my rivals into the bargain.

See Figure 60 – Southern 880 yds title winner at Welwyn

Full Great Britain status then finally materialised in mid September when, first partnered by Ilford French polisher Sid Purkiss and later, Brighton's pacey policeman Chris Carter, I had runs against Hungary and Sweden in London and again against Hungary in Budapest, followed by an unforgettable first ever team victory over the Russian Federal Republics on their own soil in Volgograd.

See Figure 61 – Win in controversial shorts v Sweden at White City

It was at one of the home internationals that I discovered that I had forgotten my shorts. With no speculative kit supplier at the White City and appalled at the prospect of borrowing some, the only recourse was to telephone my mother. To her lasting credit the brave lady overcame her innate fear of travelling on the London Underground to deliver a pair of my favourite home made shorts and maintain my decency.

She had already seen the awful issued kit, and ever the patriot, risen to the challenge, quickly making me comfortable alternatives in red, white and blue nylon. The rather rakish white ones made a reasonably successful and unnoticed outing in the Hungarian match, then I foolishly won in the even more obvious non-uniform blue pair and mother's handiwork received a high degree of notoriety. My non-conformity was spotted by the national press and led to a paragraph at the foot of a Daily Express column headed...

WHY DO OUR GIRLS HAVE TO LOOK SO SHABBY? ...MEN, TOO
Even the British men didn't look like a team.
David Jones in all-black:
Mike Fleet in blue shorts;
Robbie Brightwell in scarlet.
No one could have been disappointed by the superb performance.
But must they look so tatty?
In a fortnight's time the British team goes to the Soviet Union. Couldn't someone do them proud and supply them with British Uniforms?

Patricia Welbourn

Had the writer been male I would willingly have offered the issued shorts for a personal trial... without the essential Vaseline[11] of course!

---

[11] Much of the issued kit seemed similar to sackcloth or other rough material.

What I claim, tongue-in-cheek, as my sole "World Record" was achieved when I won the 800m for Great Britain on the occasion of our unique victory over the Russian Federal Republics in Volgograd in late September 1963. Thanks to the foibles of Central Russian weather we were welcomed with a dust storm, followed by a torrential downpour which inundated the track. Undaunted, the Russian authorities evacuated the stadium, and called in the army who duly soaked the sodden cinders with diesel and seemingly in no time at all, lanes 4 to 8 were dry enough to use.

The race unravelled in my favour, and I won with a decisive kick over the final 150m in 1:49.1 and achieved the "World Record" for the 800m[12] run in lane 4! I was surprised to learn from one of my Russian rivals that he had been in the army for five years and that his work was athletics! His specialisation had clearly not helped him against a fully employed Surrey schoolmaster and a Sussex policeman. To this day I still harbour doubts about the benefits of total specialisation in sport.

My home-made shorts, much smarter and far more comfortable than the issued counterparts, went unnoticed in the excitement of the occasion.

A word or two about mother's skill would not have gone amiss in Pravda and would have earned a hallowed place in my scrap book. I was however promised copies of action shots by a Russian photographer who laboriously insisted on writing down my name and address. Was this part of the KGB design I wondered as I foresaw my details being recorded for their great big Black Book. Three months later my fears were partially allayed when I received two excellent photos of the 800m.

See Figure 62 – Volgograd "World Record" in lane three
See Figure 63 – Volgograd letter re Photos

Another interesting feature of that encounter was the escalating lack of co-operation from the Russian officials, and a blackout on the match situation once the points swung in our favour. The scoreboard "broke down", but at the conclusion of competition, news of the British win emerged, and to their credit the sporting home crowd rewarded us with a standing ovation.

Intent on obtaining a match poster before we left the scene of our triumph, I endeavoured to charm the dour woman in charge of our changing room with my bar of Cadbury's Dairy Milk chocolate, and it

---

[12] We started off the stagger in lane 4 and Russian officials ensured that the distance was accurate by the judicious use of cones.

did the trick, as planned. The eye-catching poster which featured a fine drawing of Russian long jump legend Igor Ter-Ovanesyan, was gently removed from the wall, rather too efficiently folded and exchanged for the coveted chocolate bar. While I could hardly conceal my delight there was nary a smile from the facilitator. Her face, became more relaxed, possibly in anticipation of the treat in store. Later, the whole team, except for long distance runner Don Taylor, signed it. I had forgotten that duty-bound to his tough training regime, he had disappeared into another dust storm, face masked with a red scarf, to notch up a few more precious miles. Many years passed before I was able to catch up with him again at Tooting Bec for the omission to be remedied.

A translation of this poster is reproduced here:

The Russian Committee of the Union
of Sporting Associations and Organisations
Track and Field Federation of the Russian Federation
of Soviet Socialist Republics

CENTRAL STADIUM
INTERNATIONAL MATCH
OF
TRACK AND FIELD

ENGLAND - RUSSIA

(United Team) **(United Team)**

In the English Team will be the following champions: D Hyman, R Brightwell, B Tullough, Metcalf and also the winners of the 1963 match who were competing for Great Britain: including: M Herriot, F Allsop, M Lindsey, M Bignal-Rand, J Grievson, P Radford and others

The sporting honour of the Russian Federation is being defended by sportsmen of Moscow, Leningrad and other cities of Russia the world famous track and field athletes: V Brumel, I Ter-ovanesan, G Popova, T Press, T Shelkanova, G Zbina, A Michaelov, E Ozolin, V Bulyshev, N Sokolov, T Chenchin, V Kreer, A Zolotarev, G Kondrashov, Y Turin and others

PROGRAMME OF MATCH

28 September 29 September
at 16-30 at 16-30

28 Ceremonial opening of the competition 110m hurdles etc. 20km Walk etc. **29**

September September
1963 **1963**

The chief track and judge of overall categories is **A Abdullaev**
Competition begins at 16-30
Tickets can be bought at the kiosk of the central stadium,
also at the office of the collectives of physical cultural
undertakings, institutes, technical colleges and schools
Cost of tickets 30 Kopecks
VENERATED CITIZENS OF VOLGOGRAD
We invite you to watch this most interesting match

Translation by Chris Garrett.

See Figure 64 – Russian poster for a bar of Cadbury's Dairy Milk chocolate!

The second leg of that European tour to Budapest was prefaced by a seemingly interminable technical delay, the boredom of which was broken by impromptu cabaret performances by fellow athletes. Was it my imagination or did Adrian Metcalfe, one of my flamboyant friends, penetrate the inner cabin ceiling fabric of the non responsive Tupolev 124 with the point of his umbrella? Just in case the KGB are still active and seeking the British vandal, I find it convenient to forget his name!

A Russian flight engineer, clearly a professional, buttocks aloft from a trap in the floor, was unimpressed by the athletic talent around him and totally unmoved by unravelling pandemonium. He finally emerged, apparently satisfied that he had returned the aircraft to working order; the trapdoor was replaced and we were taxiing towards take off and the flight to Budapest to the accompaniment of unnerving creaks and cracks from the protesting airframe. What a relief it was to disembark in Hungary even if near midnight, and with no customs officers ready to check our bags, but with grim looking passport controllers grilling us and applying lengthy and pedantic scrutiny of our prized documents. Even more concern ensued when our passports were taken away and locked up at our hotel. Our understanding then was that Britons NEVER handed their passports over when abroad!

Budapest, a beautiful city in two parts, with old Buda on the hill and Pest on the plain, bisected by the far-from-blue Danube, still bore the scars of the 1956 uprising against Soviet oppression. Numerous bullet marks were clear to see on buildings, especially at street corners.

On match day we waited fruitlessly more than half an hour for the promised transport, before making our way on foot to the vast Nep Stadium. Was the non-appearance of our coach transport part of a more sinister Hungarian plan to wear us down?... Memories of a visit to a Dutch paper mill!... With time running out we set out for the stadium on foot. The vaulters proceeding, at opposite ends of their poles, like anorexic pantomime horses, clearly attracted more attention than the other blue track-suited Brits marching purposefully through the capital. We must all have appeared a somewhat bizarre group amid so many far more fashionable pedestrians.

Chris Carter turned the tables on me in our 800m one/two while I at least had the satisfaction of heading Peter Parsch who had beaten me in a previous encounter. The match resulted in another fine win for our team.

Post-match stadium exploration, courtesy of the hospitable head groundsman, revealed a vast, finely furnished VIP lounge and bar, and gave us a first class overview of the arena and the surroundings. Our guide proudly told us he had been among 50,000 boys who visited Britain in 1929 for a scout jamboree at Arrowe Park, Birkenhead. In common with all the other boys there, he recalled having been generously given pocket money (1/6, eighteen old pence, I later discovered) to spend in the city.

The only redeeming feature of the return flight on a chintz curtained Ilyushin 18 of Malev Airlines, was that it got us home. The Hungarian pilot had clearly not come to terms with the need to fine tune his turboprops to eliminate the de-synchronous wobbling sound, which tormented our ears throughout the journey. After an experience like that it was amazing how soothing the routine buzz of an airport like Heathrow appeared.

Two days later the season came to a low key close for me with an "Also ran" at the Birchfield Floodlit Meeting, and with inexplicably untapped energy, I disco-danced into the early hours to such wonderful numbers as Sweet Georgia Brown.

Throughout the frustrating early 1960s, my senior international career was born, peaked and declined disappointingly early, in no small measure due to among other things, the dreaded, debilitating almost unmentionable haemorrhoids. I've never understood why that notorious condition generates so many jokes, although my game of awarding "Ministry of Silly Walks" marks on the hospital ward all those years ago later made all of us suffering have a laugh at each other.

A significant season of athletics was over. An autumn of routine school-mastering followed, with some welcome hockey, and mandatory cross-country running training in preparation for the Tokyo Olympics.

8

My Unscaled Mount Olympus and Beyond

1964 was Tokyo Olympic Year, the "Big One" for me.

By then well-established as assistant PE Master at Selhurst Grammar School in Croydon, under the experienced eye of the Head of Department, the seemingly neckless J.B Thomas, the ex London Welsh hooker, I had become accustomed to the exciting but much less privileged post-Loughborough life of the serious athlete.

See Figure 65 – Selhurst Grammar School Team

"Time off to represent the Amateur Athletic Association against Cambridge University during term time; can't they get someone else?" queried C.F.R. Ackland, the unsympathetic Headmaster.

"...I am certainly not giving you leave of absence for that – it's not as though it is an international fixture. If you still want to go, you will have to apply formally to the Education Office in Katherine Street!"

I wondered maliciously how many days he had been off at "conferences" during the fly fishing season! He must have been a fly fisherman, for he was often to be seen wearing a somewhat bedraggled deerstalker hat! Dismayed but determined I went ahead and to my delight and surely to his disgust, I was allowed one day of unpaid leave to take up the selection.

I finished an angry second in the 880yds for the AAA against the "Light Blues" at Milton Road in 1:51.9, but the time did however seem to augur well for Olympic year since it was my best ever opener.

See Figure 66 – Brightwell's Inter Counties "Bombshell" colour

Two weeks later, and a winning Inter Counties heat in 1:51.0, set me up, so I thought, for a good chance in the final, but I had not reckoned with quarter miler Robbie Brightwell stepping up a distance, steaming through at the bell and taking John Boulter with him en route to a winning debut by a tenth in 1:48.1. I improved to 1:50.0. But third was not good enough and frustration continued into June when a gun to tape effort in the Surrey final came unstuck, and the relatively unknown nineteen year old David Cocks came through in the last few strides to win by a tenth of a second in 1:49.6, on the now historic and grassed-over Motspur Park track.

Despite my best efforts and the help of several sporting friends throughout the season, I only managed to shave a tenth off that time a week later in Madrid at the Kanguro Meeting. I was again found lacking in the final stages, but I only had myself to blame for an over zealous first lap of 50.9sec. It left the challenge of the second like a mountain to climb, and played right into the hands of Barros, the Spanish champion and record holder. I clocked 1:49.6 as a fading runner-up. That time remained unbeaten for the rest of the season. The Valle Hermoso Stadium (Happy Valley Stadium) did not quite live up to its name so far as I was concerned.

Second places don't win toy kangaroos, and later that evening I found that even the fountains and lights in the Plaza del Sol seemed to be in sympathy, fading like I had earlier in the day, just before I could photographically record their midnight splendour for posterity.

Ten days later I was lucky enough to run a winning, but not earth-shattering anchor leg 880 yards for London against New York, in the inaugural match at the exciting Crystal Palace National Recreation Centre athletics stadium. The post-match buffet notably featured Ribs of Aberdeen Angus.

Beef, Spring Lamb Cutlets in Aspic, and Sherry Trifle were much more worthy of recall than my run, but I must say that I remain privileged to have been an active participant in the first competition on the now historic track.

See Figure 67 – London v New York Crystal Palace match Menu

With Olympic hopes slightly dampened but still alive, I was given a boost when I received an invitation from Robbie Brightwell, GB team captain for Tokyo, to join his Senior Advisory Cmmittee aslongside such stars as Ann Packer, Peter Radford, Mary Rand and Bruce Tulloh. I was clearly still seen to be in the Olympic frame.

Not so, for the rest of the season dimmed into obscurity. I took an indifferent fourth in the Southern Championships, failed to reach the A.A.A final, and followed up disappointingly too with a fourth place in the Welsh Games.

Things really fell apart when it mattered most at Crystal Palace in an England v Ireland and Invitation International. My undistinguished sixth sadly sent any lingering Tokyo hopes almost beyond the Olympic horizon. One more tiny glimmer of half mile hope came with a 1:50.8 run in an Inter Club event at Carshalton, a frustrating fourth equalling my quarter mile best of 48.7 sec, after which I found myself subconsciously going through the motions as races slowed one by one. Any lingering lights of Olympic optimism finally went out after a dismal, disinterested 1:58.0 apology in the Birchfield Floodlit Meeting in September.

See Figure 68 – John Le Masurier's dreaded "Kiss of non-selection" list

My UK number one ranking achieved some seven hundred days earlier, had paled into irrelevant insignificance, so that when it really mattered I found myself a second and a half slower, jaded and unnoticed in ninth place.

I had clearly succumbed to the pressures of trying too hard when I wasn't physically up to the task. With hindsight I should have taken a mid season break and given myself the chance to recharge the batteries. It really might have been better than battering my muddled head against the hypothetical brick wall. I should also have heeded tell-tale signs and sought medical advice sooner, for my undisclosed concerns were later confirmed as being caused by much dreaded and debilitating haemorrhoids.

How fortunes can change! Watching the 1964 Olympic Games recorded from afar, on a TV set in a Wimbledon electrical shop window, I was hardly surprised, and indeed delighted that New Zealander Peter Snell won the 800m in Tokyo. It was much more difficult to take on board the fact that the silver medallist, Bill Crothers of Canada, was among the athletes whom I had eliminated in the Perth Commonwealth Games two years earlier.

Chris Carter, former 800m colleague and friend to this day, the eloquent John Boulter who wrote "See you in Tokyo" on my Russian poster in 1963, were the British athletes who deservedly carried our two-lap flag in the

Kasumigaoka Stadium.

The third competitor was Alan Dean, a Midlander whom I had no difficulty beating the previous year in the England v Italy match despite having a sprained and heavily strapped ankle. He won his selection thanks to a timely third in the AAA Championships. He failed in the Olympics and was hardly heard of afterwards. Chris ran a respectable 1:49.1 fourth in his heat and was eliminated, but clearly gained from the experience, for two years later he set a British record of 1:46.6. John made the semi final.

Two postcards thoughtfully sent to me from friends competing in Tokyo went a little way to ameliorate my distress at not making the grade. That Menzies Campbell and Robbie Brightwell could take out time from the greatest sporting test of their lives to put pen to paper in my direction remains a greatly appreciated gesture.

Welcoming many of my friends and former team-mates back early one autumn morning at Heathrow Airport from their Tokyo triumph, was certainly an occasion of mixed emotions for me. A splendid if somewhat incongruous champagne breakfast probably eased my sadness at not having been part of such a great success. I was none the less extremely proud to have been associated with one of Britain's finest Olympic teams. How many other athletic teams have come back with four gold medals?

I had previously been privileged to compete alongside the golden track and field trio: long jumpers Mary Bignal, Lynn Davies and 800m runner Ann Packer, when Great Britain beat Russia in Volgograd. I had also been tested to the limit, as lead cyclist during a national 50k walk championship at Loughborough by fourth gold medallist, Ken Matthews.

Other more tenuous links with them included being very willingly dragged back to a Russian supermarket by Mary to show her where I had purchased an unusual set of pottery animals, and helping to arrange "digs" for Ann with our Downsview Church friends, the Stockdale family when she was Physical Education teacher at the Lady Edridge Girl's School in Thornton Heath. The school, affectionately known as "LEGS", among whose students my sister Judy then featured, is now no more, thanks to Sainsbury's urban advance. In those days, she recalls residents in the roads around Selhurst Park, home to Crystal Palace FC, were often treated to the sight of an attractive Olympic Champion in the making, sprinting by as fast as many a car.

One cherished outcome of that occasion over 40 years ago is the fine gallery of four giant photographs of the British Olympic Champions on show at the Croydon Harriers Headquarters. They had been a feature in the display at Heathrow Airport which welcomed the athletes back from Tokyo in 1964.

See Figure 69 – 1964 Olympic Gold Medallist, Lynn Davies

"Where did those come from?" I wondered aloud to a fellow supporter, admiring the five feet high action shots. My enquiry as to their source led me almost immediately to Stan Levenson, athletics correspondent to the Daily Worker, a now defunct communist newspaper.

"Could you use them?" he asked, pre-empting any request of mine.
...Could I?!

A couple of weeks later a Daily Worker delivery van drove into the Croydon Arena and the photographs of the British quartet of Tokyo gold medallists were unloaded. They have been admired by visitors over since; the more so recently, thanks to the featured stars themselves who have kindly sent the signed messages which now embellish their pictures.

One bonus of being left at home, had been my availability to link up with Harold Abrahams and Dr J.M.Tanner author of the book "What Makes an Olympic Champion?" for the most significant broadcast of my three-programme radio career on "What makes an athlete?".

The Croydon Harriers AGM the next month witnessed the watershed election of a green-horn General Secretary. Subconsciously I must have known that there would be more satisfaction in trying to run athletics than to solely run in its events! Had I however looked into a crystal ball and seen the 35 years which ensued, I would probably never have accepted the nomination! By the time of the next Olympics at altitude in Mexico City, I would be 30!

Not getting any younger, I still clung on to the elusive dream but clearly with diminishing single-mindedness. At that time too I started to develop my interest in coaching which diluted my personal application to training and competition.

John Le Masurier, the much respected Chief National Coach, had for some time been encouraging me to extend my Loughborough qualifications, and when I finally agreed, he kindly explained what had to be done to achieve the status of AAA coach. A few months later, the same genial gentleman gave me what I felt was "third degree" in the context of my unique chosen selection of events, 400m, 800m and hammer. I passed, but I guess it was thanks more to the entertainment value of my hammer demonstration which exuded enjoyment rather than skill, and to impeccably compliant performances by my specially selected "guinea-pig" athletes. I do however believe that John was well aware of how seriously I took my chosen events, and the depths to which I had delved in pursuit of perfection.

My coaching status, ie hitherto unqualified, now became much more meaningful, and I began to look for personal development and greater recognition. Ten years or so further on, and three failed interviews for positions as National Coach, suggested to me that it was not to be and that I should remain satisfied with my lot, and so it has remained.

39, Teddington Park,

CONFIDENTIAL

Teddington,

Middlesex.

Dear

    As you have read overleaf it is my intention to form a Senior Advisory Committee within the British Team, and it is with this in mind that I am writing to you.

    I feel it is imperative that I ask you to assist me in making the Olympic Team a success. Your experience, status, and integrity make you a natural choice for the Committee mentioned above and your acceptance would be a source of considerable assurance and satisfaction. Would you be willing to sit on this Committee?

    I am determined to make a success of this job, but am aware that without your co-operation the task will be immeasurably weakened. Therefore I would ask you to consider this matter most carefully and let me have your decision as soon as possible.

Yours sincerely,

Copies to:

Peter Radford.	Mary Rand
Adrian Metcalfe,	Dorothy Hyman
Mike Fleet	Ann Packer
Bruce Tulloh	Mary Peters
Brian Kilby	Sue Allday
Mike Lindsey	
FAIRBROTHER	
~~Gordon Millo~~	Alsop?
John Cooper	
Ken Matthews	

9

The Downhill Run

With the Tokyo Melody of Helmut Zacharias still nagging in my subconscious, post-Olympic 1965 proved a pretty flat year. I only ran nine "halves", winning just three with a season's best of 1:50.8, achieved for want of a better word in 7th place in the Welsh Games. Alan Simpson fourth in the Tokyo 1500m, finished a frustrating 1.5sec ahead of me, but how much more frustrated must he have been to have missed the silver medal by 0.2sec in a race of nearly twice the distance!

Downhill running is never the easiest of techniques and in the context of a declining athletics career, it is especially difficult to accept that improvement is less likely to feature on the agenda!

Eight blue nylon surgical stitches sealed in my scrapbook for that year are a grisly reminder to me that it was far from a good move to cut in front of a tall hyper-extending long jumper in a medley relay. John Howell of Herne Hill Harriers, the other athlete involved, was very concerned and apologetic, but it was really my poor judgement which led to both my legs remaining scarred to prove it.

Advancing age is an effective leveller, and with the passage of time I became all too aware of others who "also ran", not previously considered as threats, were more and more confidently ahead of me from the gun, or producing unfamiliar and unchallengeable final sprints. Clearly their less-abused legs were also a key factor. Mine were protesting and didn't I know it!

In 1966 I unwittingly gave my waning middle-distance career a fitness boost by starting school ski trips. My body responded really well to the benefits of dynamic action at altitude on the slopes above Sauze D'Oulx in Italy. On the third of these highly action-packed sorties I stopped off at the Kappanna Kind Restaurant near the top of the main lift and was about to ask two rather scruffy individuals whether I might sit at their table for lunch when my ski instructor friend Alberto Zarini kindly invited me to join him. As the lunch progressed he expressed his surprise at seeing the head of Turin Police dining nearby. The scruffy fellows finished their "Tripa casserole", the speciality of the house, got up and left. Soon too did the head of police. At the end of the afternoon, on completing the chairlift descent into town, I couldn't miss seeing an animated throng of caribineri there, or sensing an excited buzz pervading the streets of the busy little alpine resort.

I later discovered that my scruffy potential lunch companions had been arrested in a burst of automatic fire as they stepped off their chair at the bottom lift station. They were members of the notorious Marxist Leninist "Red Brigades Gang" which had been responsible for the kidnap, murder and subsequent beheading of Aldo Moro, a former Italian Prime Minister. Who knows what might have happened had an ill-shaven English schoolmaster ridden down at the same time?

That year too, I made a brief sortie into the periphery of technical running and set a short-lived Croydon Harriers 440 yards hurdles record of 57.3sec. All was fine until a well-meaning enthusiast showed me the film of my eleven short sprints, interrupted by ten rather ragged high jumps. My Loughborough pedigree would not permit further humiliation and I immediately retired from the discipline.

Before eventually winning the Surrey title, I had won the Southern Counties title, finished as third Briton in the AAA Championships, albeit 4th overall and made several international appearances while the county title continued to elude me.

It was not until 1967 that I was able to write in my record book: "Ambition was achieved in the pouring rain, with that oh so elusive Surrey win in a modest 1:53.6. Successfully nursed a pulled thigh muscle the final furlong". Sometimes it seems experience does really pay off! In 1967 the frustrating issue had finally been settled. The curious affair of the elusive senior half-mile title, although sounding somewhat Conan Doyle-ish, had been a problem that only I alone could solve, not Sherlock Holmes and Dr Watson. When it came to the event and in the knowledge that there would be few more chances for me, I concentrated superhumanly, relaxed when a tender thigh muscle tweaked at the bell and, nursing myself along behind a premature and overly energetic burst from rash, race-favourite John Greatrex, I awaited my moment. As he faded in the home straight, my confidence grew and I splashed home first, mud spattered but overjoyed in 1:53.6. It was indisputably a case of nirvana at the ninth attempt.

See Figure 70 – In the bag!...The oh-so-elusive Surrey title

"The Mike Fleet Surrey Half Mile Title Saga"

Year	MAF Position	Time	Result of Final
1959	Heat 1	1:57.1	
	Final 3	1:52.2	1st Brian Hewson, Mitcham A.C.
			2nd Bob Harvey, Croydon H.
1960	Heat 2	1:58.6	
	Final 3	1:53.4	1st Brian Hewson, Mitcham A.C.
			2nd Tony Milner, Walton A.C.
1961	Heat 1	1:53.8	
	Final 3	1:51.3	1st Peter Milner, Walton A.C.
			2nd Tony Harris, Mitcham A.C.
1962	Heat 1	1:55.1	
	Final 2	1:53.7	1st Bob Harvey, Croydon H
1963	Heat 1	1:55.2	
	Final 2	1:55.2	1st Terry Keen, Hercules A.C.
1964	Heat 1	1:51.2	
	Final 2	1:49.7	1st David Cocks, Belgrave H.
1965	Heat 1	1:56.0	
	Final 4	1:54 7	1st Kelvin Bromley, Walton A.C.
1966	Heat 1	1:55.0	Withdrew from final, Injured
1967	Heat 1	1:54.1	
	Final	1:53.6	1st Mike Fleet, Croydon Harriers
1968	Heat 1		
	Final 2		1st Nick Lovatt, Mitcham A.C.
1969	Heat 3		
	Final 2		1st Tony Harris, Mitcham A.C
1970		1:54.6	
	Final 2		1st Martin Winbolt-Lewis

To put that specific struggle into some kind of perspective, my research has revealed that my sole modest winning time is better than that run by eleven of the last twenty Surrey County 800m Champions!

Significantly, a young Woking sprinter named Nicola Murray, several times Surrey and South of England sprint winner and English Schools' finalist, won gold that day too. I noted her achievement out of the corner of my eye. In later years, as Mr and Mrs Fleet, we were delighted to discover our possibly unique status as concurrent Surrey Champions who subsequently married.

See Figure 71 – Nicola in ESAA 200m Championship MF photo Nicola timekeeping at Olympic Trials with "Stan the Man"

In the intervening years I had been county half-mile runner-up four times, had finished third twice and withdrew from the final once due to injury, having qualified with an unconvincing try-out run in the heats. Discretion was the better part of valour. The camphorated "White Horse Oils" and then state of the art electric massaging device wielded by club physiotherapist Stan Holness both failed to do the trick on that occasion.

Despite losing so many Surrey finals, I have happy memories of them and really enjoyed their cut and thrust. I was indeed extremely fortunate to have been in action during such a highly competitive period. My fastest Surrey time, in 1964, a 2nd placed 1:49.7 (after a 1:51.2 heat), was in stark contrast with the pitiful two-man race 43 years later which was won in outside 2 minutes. Had I left the timekeepers' stand where I was on duty that day and strolled two laps, I could have added a county bronze to my tally at the age of 69! Only one athlete has bettered 1:50.0 in the championships since 1989.

There were however glimmers of hope in the county in 2007 when Aldershot protégé Rikki Letch took the U15 title in 2:06.4 and 13 year-old, fourth-placed Jordan Maurice, whom I have had the pleasure of coaching at Croydon, ran an equally eye catching 2:09.54. Letch is just one of the constant stream of outstanding athletes who "teethed" at Aldershot Farnham and District, and who has now changed allegiance to Windsor Slough Eton and Hounslow. I have enjoyed being being Team Manager for Rikki at Surrey Schools and South of England Schools level, when I experienced at first hand his indomitable fighting spirit, which, added to his natural talent, make him a force to be fully respected. With 50.27sec 400m, 1:51.06 800m, 4:01.2 1500m and 9:20.3 3000m marks to his name, he is ruffling more than a few feathers among senior runners. His fantastic 800m time achieved at 16 knocked mine achieved at 18, which so surprised the athletics world over fifty years before, well into the shade.

Further afield and less well known to me, another aspiring Brit, eighteen year old Niall Brooks of Sale Harriers gives great hope for optimism having already run 1:47.99. Who knows, Liverpool's young senior Michael Rimmer, already a sub 1:44.00 man, may yet have it in him to break Seb Coe's 1:41.73 and become the first man to set a UK record wearing a personalised T-shirt[13].

With such challenges to motivate them, the contenders for future United Kingdom middle-distance running stardom promise much, but their potential must be very carefully nurtured for it to bear fruit. One dreams of a crop of future Coes, Crams and Ovetts, and with the bright sun of London 2012 rising quickly above the horizon, some dreams will surely come true.

The technological advances in athletics were really brought home to me at an insignificant inter-club match at Crystal Palace in May 1968. It provided me with my first experience of track running on a surface other than grass, wood, tarmac, crushed stone or industrial ash. The spring derived from, and the silence of running on, the new all-weather Tartan track gave my ageing limbs a new found boost, but unhelpfully provided little clue as to what was happening behind me. No informative crunch of spikes striking cinders, just the barely audible patter of feet on rubber, and the sound of heavy breathing! I never heard the much younger Messrs Morton and Roseman strike, not that I was able to do much about it when they did. Clearly assisted by the new surface to the 1:53.6 clocking which saw me finish third, I wished I could start it all again, but at 30 years of age that was an unrealistic hope. I wondered what the thousands of aspiring athletes waiting in the wings around the world would achieve on the amazing new surface.

The days of dear old cinder were clearly "burning out" in tandem with the days of Archie McTaggart, Britain's doyen Head Groundsman and David Morgan his successor at Motspur Park.

See Figure 72 – The great Sydney Wooderson setting a new mile record of 4:06.4 at Motspur Park in 1937

There was an exciting flourish for me that August when, as the invited hare in a British Games International 800m, I duly reeled out the requested 54 second opening lap and then decided to see how well I could

---

[13] Michael Rimmer always races in a customised T-shirt or a T-shirt under his team vest.

hang on to younger bloods who had benefited from my earlier pace. My 1:48.9 clocking in 6th place raised a few eyebrows and gave my White City chapter a happy ending. It turned out to be a UK age 30 best.

Statistician Andrew Huxtable gave my morale a further boost two months later, when his "Top UK Brother and Sister Ranking List" was published in a short-lived magazine, "Women's Athletics". Together with sister Judy's[14] 440yds time of 61.3 sec, my 1:48.9 880 yds run earned us 1,684 points according to the Portuguese Scoring Tables, to place us fourth behind Michael and Mary Tagg, 1,906.5, Robert and Rosemary Stirling, 1,774 and Godfrey and Audrey Brown, 1,732[15].

See Figure 73 – Mike with sister Judy

The launch of the National League the next year provided me with the incentive to continue competing. It was nice to win an 800m in an eminently forgettable time for Croydon Harriers in their August match at Southampton.

I concentrated on 400m running in 1971, and curiously won my first and only Surrey title in 50.1sec, my slowest time of the year. My other 400m races, including the county heat, were all sub 50sec efforts.

Near the end of that season, an example occurred of an athlete, somewhat past his sell-by date, being sucked into irrational competitive stupidity by an irrepressible brain.

With ten years of water having flowed under the proverbial bridge since my eye catching, very fast but unsuccessful chase unwittingly behind the then European 400m champion, I found myself trying to relive former glory in the wake of Alan Pascoe, an Olympian and 48.59 sec 400m hurdler to be, and nine years my junior.

Limpet-like I hung on until in a virtual state of collapse, I staggered over the line an uncomprehending, but respectable second, so I was told...

Such was my state of exhaustion that I was incapable of driving home, and another kind athlete shouldered the dubious responsibility of retuning

---

[14] Judy married Peter Stanyard, a Croydon Harrier and keen rugby player. Peter was later best man at my wedding.

[15] Godfrey won Olympic silver in the 400m and gold as anchor man in the 4x400m and Audrey won silver in the 4x100 in Berlin in 1936.

the rag doll shadow of an athlete to my shocked parent's house, from which I had moved many years before.

Summoned the next day to a wan shadow of physicality, the doctor stated that my temperature confirmed more than fatigue. I must remain in bed! Several days passed before I was well enough to retrieve my trusty "Minor 1000" from the National Recreation Centre.

I resolved never again to try to replicate my one off, successful "Trousil Chase", and have ever after advised all athletes in my care to closely evaluate their condition before any demanding competition.

The 1972 Munich Games saw the exorcism of my personal "Olympic ghost".

One early summer morning the telephone rang. Stan Biggs a fellow club coach breezily urged me to buy a week's athletics tickets for £25.

"You know what I feel about the Olympics," I blustered *"and £25 for the tickets too!"*
"Well how about it then?" he urged.
"Er, I am not sure, I need time to think it over."
"OK then, I'll call back tonight by 9pm if I haven't heard from you" and the phone went dead. Well before the witching hour I decided to take up the offer, and the rest is both personal and international history.

In seemingly no time at all, following a demanding solo drive to the Bavarian capital, I availed myself of a reciprocal gesture to my parents' kindness many years before, from Herr Dill, the father of my "German sister" Gine. He gave me the use of his business flat not far from the stadium, stressing that it must be for my sole use. I simply could not believe how many close and homeless friends I had suddenly acquired! At times the chain on the door proved to be essential in barring determined squatters. Soon I was witnessing many fabulous athletics performances which have become lifelong sporting memories, but all too soon were overshadowed in a much more poignant way.

After becoming reconciled with my dashed Olympic dream, I was then surprisingly told by German friends that I was lucky to be leaving. A major terrorist incident was unravelling and it appeared that there was the distinct possibility of the Games being curtailed. News crackled through on the car radio of the mayhem at Furstenfeldbruch Military

Airfield from which the terrorists were trying to effect their getaway. Even with my limited German, the eyewitness commentary conveyed an horrendous scene, with the added frightening background of shouting, the crackle of gunfire and roar of helicopters overhead.

And so it proved, as I later learned, that the attack tragically took the life of athletics coach Amitzur Shapira, the only member of the targeted Israeli contingent whom I knew.

At 34, and with my own international career and representative travel well and truly over, I resolved to give as many of my coaching charges the opportunity to experience "international competition" at acceptable level and set about maximising my contacts abroad to that end. Two years later I managed to run a 1:54.2 800m behind one of them, Alan Carr-Locke at Papendal, the Dutch National Centre near Arnhem, and felt satisfied that the job was being done. Alan, who had trained with David Hemery and me in Richmond in 1968, never reached his full athletics potential, but his vocational skills moved him on to another kind of gold in the United States, where he is credited with the design of a computerised medical records system for Boston Massachusetts.

That year too witnessed my last sub 50sec 400m run in the club National League cause at Cwmbran. Four more individual 400s followed in 1973 and a token final 800m race in outside two minutes rounded off a career of some 300 "halves". To my great delight in 1974, I rallied sufficient strength in my over-used legs to win my only Amateur Athletic Association medal, a much to be cherished silver in the 4x400m relay Championship at Crystal Palace. My magic lap was clocked at 49.7sec.

In a new "international" development, I was recruited by Mark "The Rabbit" Winzenreid[16] to act as fortunate courier for his all female Big Eight Conference Tour[17] of five European countries including competitions in Belgium and Switzerland.

Meanwhile, Holland, France, Germany and Sweden were about to feature on a developing Club itinerary, which would cement old friendships and form new ones, many of which are ongoing to this day.

Freed from the demands of selection-seeking athletics, I joined the first

---

[16] The more often than not self-appointed hare in American-based half-miles.

[17] A former NCAA-affiliated Division I-A college athletic association based in central USA.

Croydon Harriers European tour to Freising in Bavaria in 1969. We were extremely well looked after by our host Helmut Weinzierl, whose brother Franz had been the exchange catalyst while studying in Croydon and joining in with our club activities. Helmut's team of helpers couldn't do enough for us. Three girls for instance cycled several miles every day to bring fresh bread and fruit for breakfast at our beautifully situated hostel perched on a river cliff. Volunteers were always on hand to act as couriers for our coach driver and they also readily acted as invaluable interpreters.

It was German efficiency at its beneficial best and was the precursor of an enduring friendship and a great "augmented Club" international team visit for the opening of the Savoyer Au Stadium in 1978.

With the scent of a successful new activity fresh in my nostrils, "I sniffed out" a Swedish contact, former international and coach Bose Aggebon, and with his essential help, organised my first overseas club tour the following year. Thanks to the hospitality provided, this proved to be my motivation to capitalise on an ever-growing list of continental contacts, which have developed into exchange with clubs across north-western Europe. Sporting, social and cultural horizons have accordingly developed to everyone's benefit both home and away, with new doors opening for many more club tours and the forging of many friendships, including with Monika Lundblad, an outstanding 800m runner coached by Bose.

On that 1970 tour, first class accommodation was provided free for us in a community house not far from Stockholm where we were initiated in the delights of sauna, especially when beer was poured on the coals.

Perfectly structured competition was organised for us and we were also given a privileged insight into the delightfully formal home hospitality of the country with the ladies, surprisingly for us, ensuring that the gentlemen were comfortably seated first and well "fed and watered" throughout. The size of the T-bone steaks and the flavour and effect of rather too many peaches marinated in brandy, is a memory which will never fade.

Another lesson learned somewhat nervously was that Swedish folk have no inhibitions about skinny dipping and were clearly surprised when we asked where to change before a programmed lake swim.

We cast aside our doubts and clothes to follow rapidly-disappearing Scandinavian derrieres into the inviting depths, and afterwards, the mandatory post-swim picture (sorry, not for publication here!) took far longer than the swim to set up.

The Swedish contact evolved through an introduction by Monika Lundblad to two athletics enthusiasts, Erling Hansson and Roland Soderlund, who subsequently accommodated Croydon groups at Sodertalje in their beautifully situated lakeside hostel.

The scene another year, on a warm summer night in an unlit lay-by beyond an autobahn service station, somewhere in Central Germany, was reminiscent in my mind of the Cold War Gleinike Bridge between Berlin and Potsdam where spy exchanges took place and other more clandestine business was enacted. I was in charge of a touring group of club athletes and almost two hours late for my rendezvous with none other than local official Herr Schmidt. He was the recommendation of the eminent non-related Herr Schmidt of the Deutsche Leichtathleteik Verband at the 1976 Montreal Olympics.

I had only corresponded with the local Herr Schmidt, whom I hoped I would soon be meeting. I nervously approached glowing red rear lights of the only vehicle to be seen in the gloom. Once alongside, the door opened and a smartly be-suited man got out.
"Fleet?" he demanded.
"Ja ich bin Mike Fleet!" I responded timorously.
"Fleet, you are late!"... did I hear his heels click, I wondered?
"I am sorry," I replied.
"You are welcome," he replied and to my great relief, extended his hand and warmly shook mine.

We were soon installed in a smart little hotel on the edge of a small industrial estate, appropriately adjacent to a healthy looking asparagus field for which crop the area was famous. Herr (local) Schmidt had lived up to his word.

I still relished another "international challenge" which offered itself over two laps in Leverkusen on that trip, and I managed to win the "B" race in 1:56.9, which at the age of 39 left me pretty pleased. The German lad who chased me home, sportingly shook my hand, and with some measure of incredulity at the outcome, queried
"Wie alt sind sie?"
"Ich bin neununddreissig," I gasped.
"Mein gott!" he exclaimed admiringly...

This series of fascinating and rewarding club tours continued with me as leader of "Croydon the European Harriers"!

Little did I realise five years later, as the Skinners coach carrying a tired but excited group of Croydon Harriers pulled up in an interesting little German town that I would soon be looking back on a finished competitive career... well almost!

This was Schwetzingen, noted for asparagus, its rococo castle and our contact, the soon to be encountered "Special one" – no not Mr Mourinho but the somewhat frightening red-haired local official Tosca with whom I was to be billeted! I hopped off the coach beside a call box and dialled her number.

"Frau Oberst?" I queried at the sound of a very masculine voice! Not the wrong number please, I hoped, with twenty-four athletes relying on my organisational skills.
"Ja, ist das Mr Mike?"
"Ich bin Mike, in der nahe von schloss," I replied hoping that I had correctly confirmed who and where I was!
"No problem," ...how many more frustrating times was I to hear that expression in the days ahead!... *"I come!"*

A forbidding looking, but I have to say smiling, woman soon appeared atop an impressive upright bicycle, and we were in business. The red-haired widow was keen to tell me of the time when she must have been a blonde youngster, as one of Herr Hitler's chosen and protected maidens, she spent her youth safe and keeping fit in the mountains! One wondered what other pleasures had been on hand for the privileged young of Nazi Germany protected far away from the conflict?

The end of my possibly over-long competitive career resulted from a 400m race while in Tosca's "custody" a few days later in Ludwigshaven. The anticipated adrenalin buzz carried me rather too enthusiastically past the 150m mark, after which my achilles tendon complained of overuse in the only way any self-respecting achilles tendon can. It sharply tweaked its warning! The latter stages of my foolishly completed run were lost in a blur of extreme discomfort. With the misplaced pride at stake of never having dropped out I stupidly ran on, only to sustain a tear with 50m left. Even more ridiculously I hopped home in a time of 55.2sec in 3rd place.

Uncannily that was almost identical to my first timed one lap, 26 years earlier, when I had been thrilled to beat the Whitgift Middle School 440yds standard with a 55.6sec clocking. I looked back down the finishing straight and believed that it is was the scene of my final competitive strides. My racing career appeared to have gone full circle.

A sympathetic Tosca produced a vinegar compress which I could only presume was meant to preserve me rather than to cure me! I guessed that I was not worthy of any of the wartime wonder cures which might have been used on injured "special ones" and hidden in her memory. Despite her kindness, the redoubtable Tosca, clearly unaware of my painful sleepless night, was vacuuming her apartment at 5am the following morning! This was an unwelcome awakening I had to experience again when on the reciprocal visit to England and in the absence of anyone else willing to put her up or should I say put up with her, I felt obliged to reciprocate her hospitality and crack-of-dawn flat cleaning habit. Thankfully she at least didn't dare to venture beyond my firmly closed bedroom door!

As so often happily evolves, good things follow bad, and so it transpired during our next competition in Bruhl, home town of world tennis star Steffi Graf, where, naturally she is feted for her exploits with a tennis racquet and also, not surprisingly, remembered as a one-time near 2-minute 800m runner.

There, my luck changed while I was being harangued by the demanding Tosca over my inability to deal with unfamiliar German race entry slips. When the sixth slip was rejected and screwed up, the frustrated lady stormed off. I then heard a deep soothing English voice behind me.

"I think I can help you in a minute," said a friendly looking athlete. *"I'll be back."*

True to his word the "Englishman" soon returned with a little girl in tow. *"I'm Fritz Emmert, I'll sort your entries out and as I see you are injured perhaps you would be kind enough to look after my little girl, Kim, when my wife competes, while I keep your entries up to date?"* So the deal was struck in return for helping to keep his daughter entertained by trapping

Grashüpfer[18] under a beaker, from which an enduring friendship was born. It transpired that Fritz, teacher of English and dedicated anglophile, had lived and worked in England, and was proud to have competed in the green and white of Woodford Green AC. I can forgive him that!

"We live in a lovely little country town called Rimbach, you would like it better than this. How about making your next trip to us?" Fritz invited *"Sounds great to me,"* I accepted, shaking his hand.

Fritz and his wife Gudrun, a fine sounding name for an athlete although inappropriate for a hammer thrower, have since hosted several club trips plus many personal ones to the Odenwald, as well as returning to England from time to time.

See Figure 75 – 1974 AAA silver in 4x400 Mike to Roy Fox
See Figure 76 – Mike with Fritz and Gudrun Emmert

While my coaching commitments increased, so my competitive activities decreased and were mainly in support of the Club, in particular its effort in the British League. My penultimate appearance in that competition saw me run in the same race as an astonishingly talented young fellow of nineteen called Steve Ovett, already a champion. I wittingly didn't say race or compete against but also ran does come to mind as being appropriate.

At the bell reached in 56seconds, I was almost as close to Ovett as I was at later Croydon Harriers 1980 discos, when he was dancing with whichever of his delightful young ladies he had in tow. Was it the lavishly beribboned blonde Lesley Kiernan or the rivetingly classical Rachel Waller? No matter, the star man clearly had impeccable taste for females!

But I digress. At the finish of that league encounter in Liverpool, thanks only I guess to the young Steve's compassion, he won easing down in 1:52.3 over 4 seconds outside his best, while I struggled home 5th in 1:54.2.

See Figure 77 – A youthful Steve Ovett shows the way

In the following year, 1983, while on holiday in Canada, I rather rashly raced one last 400m lap on the Richmond BC tarmac track. With the Gods on my side I got round without mishap in 53.0 to set a Croydon club

---

[18] Grasshoppers

Veteran 45 record which stands to this day. Not bad in trainers, though I say it myself!

After that, an occasional 60% track sortie, especially on club tours and for the even rarer ceremonial duty jog, hardly put me at risk of further injury or of becoming a laughing stock. Running, and in particular racing had become much more the prerogative of youth. That is to say with one more exception towards the end of the 1980s, when I was persuaded to partner David "Awesome" Lawson, as second string for the Trinity staff in the 1500m against the junior boys.

"Awesome", fifteen years my junior and famous for falling backwards into the school swimming pool on more than one occasion, and a proficient modern pentathlete into the bargain, headed off into the distance. Way behind, I managed to salvage some of my age 50+ reputation by out-jogging the foolhardy, exhausted youngster, who had precociously tried to stay with my victorious colleague. So, fittingly, my racing career had finally run full circle on the new field of my Alma Mater at Shirley Park. This somewhat insignificant event had been poignantly completed within a few yards of where almost thirty years earlier, my parents had celebrated their silver wedding anniversary at the Shirley Park Hotel which previously occupied the site.

With the personal competitive bug finally laid to rest, I seriously set about coaching and developing the careers and experience of others at various stages on, as I like to call it, their "Ladder of Athletics Success".

Our routine training sessions, club competitions and championships were supplemented by further tours. Next in line came the eagerly anticipated first visit to Rimbach in the Oldenwald region of Germany, courtesy of the Emmerts and their delightful friends, one of whom was the 1972 Olympic long jump silver medallist Hans Baumgartner. That tour turned out to be a triumph of organisation and enjoyment, the latter especially as the result of a seemingly endless flow of jokes from Hans.

Who said the Germans do not have a sense of humour? Reinforcing this evidence in later years, Fritz became an avid "Dad's Army fan" and introduced Captain Mainwaring and his raggle-taggle platoon to many a class at the Martin Luther Gymnasium, the school where he taught. John Cleese of Fawlty Towers fame and noted in this context for his classic, "Don't mention the War", became popular too.

Each tour had its own personalities and rare moments. Not least among them in entertainment value was a trip to the little walled Stadt Hersbruck in Franconian Schweitz featured our least popular host Karl Heinz Dottl. I hasten to add not with us, the visiting Brits, but with his fellow Germans. Our coach drew up in the attractive town centre, amazingly for once, bang on time. I clambered down from the coach in front of a relaxed looking group of drinkers, confidently expecting our contact Dottl, a highly efficient correspondent, to be downing lager with them in the mid-day sun. Hadn't he done well too, I thought, to have hosts ready and waiting! Alas, my idealistic illusion was soon to be shattered.

"Herr Dottl?" I queried, approaching the group with a smile.
The group of locals looked uncomfortable and I heard a muttered response which being translated was roughly:
"Not bloody likely, he is a bad man!"

Not a good start I thought, with images of paedophiles and worse rushing through my mind. But thankfully not so, and following a successful telephone call when contact was made with the elusive Karl Heinz, I later discovered that it was because of his role as the town bailiff that he was almost universally despised. Hence the earlier gruff response in the town centre.

Thankfully he was friendly enough with the custodian of the Hersbruck youth hostel, a cheery moustachioed fellow who much resembled a butcher's pavement manikin complete with blue apron, for the bulk of our group to be safely, if somewhat spartanly, accommodated in two large dormitories.

The hospitable Dottls, for that is certainly what they proved to be, generously opened their home to three of us "elder brethren", and it was during our time with them that Karl Heinz, fairly well oiled at the time, I have to say, got us into one of the most entertaining of scenarios I have ever experienced. It was at about two in the morning, a time when all self-respecting athletic folk would expect to be in bed, that Karl Heinz decided that we men needed an ice cream. The only place where our requirement could be satisfied was an outlet in the town square. Despite our protests we were bundled into his car for the five-minute drive. Thank heavens it was that short and at that time of night, for no other vehicle was encountered as our drunken driver hugged the centre of the road albeit, to our relief, at about 20 mph, thereby avoiding the houses and shops dangerously situated on each side! We pulled up rather too sharply for comfort outside the clearly and not surprisingly closed Hersbruch ice cream parlour. Several loud shouts of DOTTL, plus a few bangs on the ice cream parlour door and hey presto, success, it was opened, if a little grudgingly by the bleary-eyed proprietor.

"Wir möchten ein grosses Mandeleis mit Sahne," our leader demanded, disregarding my loudly protested dislike of cream!
The order duly appeared accompanied by four glasses of Schnapps! Despite reservations, duty had to be done and not until everything was consumed did we have any chance of returning home to bed.

On the unnerving drive back with the middle of the road evidently now even more difficult to follow, Karl Heinz started rambling on about a clock which he had:

"bought in Lossiemouse in Engeland,"
Foolishly I tried to correct his geography.
"I think you must mean Lossiemouth in Scotland, Karl Heinz," I suggested.
"Ja, Lossiemous in Engeland," he shouted back unswayed by my correction.
"You vill come und see heem, he ist in der bedroom."
The mind boggled at that unearthly hour at the thought of three Englishmen being ushered into the bedroom where his wife was asleep, to view some horological trophy. Karl Heinz turned on the bedroom light, whereupon his naked wife, understandably shocked, leapt up and dived under the dressing table, leaving her more than significantly impressive rear protruding for all to admire. Discreetly we made to move but our man was determined.

"Ach eet ees nussing," he explained pointing at Frau Dottl's expansive buttocks, *"eet ees only die skin!"*

"Der Lossiemouse clock ist hier!" he continued. We made admiring noises and retreated to bed.

The following morning everything was back to normal as if nothing had happened, with our fully clad hostess smilingly serving us breakfast. Was there, I wondered, the merest suggestion of a blush on her cheeks?

The excellent performance of our team there, enhanced by family friend and Canadian double-Olympian Thelma Wright, an Ellen Tittel look-alike,

Fig. 76f – Mike with Helmut Weinzierl in Freising 1978.

Fig. 76g – Croydon Harriers and guest stars in Germany for Freising Stadium Opening.

Fig. 77 – A youthful Steve Ovett shows the way. Mike (L) in vain chase after youthful Steve Ovett (R) in British League 800m.

Fig. 79 – Grange Hill TV "English Schools sprint final!" MF photo.

Fig. 78 – Generous Dalton Grant's Eberstadt medal. MF photo.

Fig. 80 – Mike taking Selhurst Grammar cross-country boys for a five miler. Croydon Advertiser photo.

Fig. 81 – Bob Benn (L) racing bend at Wimbledon Park. MF photo.

Fig. 82 – Yacin Yusuf Post European U23 1500 ESAA 3000m Victory. Mark Shearman photo.

Fig. 83 – Martyn Rooney and coach Mike after UK Junior 400m win. Chris Carter photo.

Fig. 82a – Mike & Yacin Yusuf in Gothenburg European U23 Championships 1995.

Fig. 84 – Who forgot his vest? Henry Rono "The Croydon Harrier!" Mark Shearman photo.

Fig. 85 – Now I know how mother felt! NF photo.

Fig. 88 – Loud hailing. 2009 Lexus 10k Mike with his personal mike. Ian Gillett photo.

Fig. 86 – Timsbury Manor Group world record hammer thrower Harold Connolly USA (L), Mike at back and Oliver Cutts (R).

Fig. 89 – Announcing at 2010 Inter Services Championships "Mike with the Mike" and Squadron Leader Jason Davenhill at RAF Cosford.

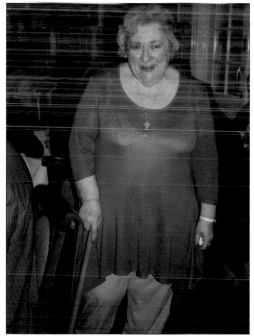

Fig. 87 – "Galleann" Organ, CPFA. Sporting Salt of the Earth. MF photo.

Fig. 90 – Mike and Gerry Cranham "Maestro" photographer of the 1960s. Mark Cranham photo.

Fig. 91 – Mike (L) Official Shepherd accompanying Glen Cohen, David Jenkins and Bill Hartley to the Europa Cup 400m Start at Crystal Palace.

Fig. 94 – Amitzur Shapira. Photo Israeli Embassy.

Fig. 92 – Mike with Shirley High School Big Match Kit Stewards Crystal Palace.

Fig. 95 – International Athletes Club Charity Football team and All Star XI. Bobby Robson back row centre, Mike back row second from end Right.

Fig. 93 – Mike, Nicola and Beijing Volunteer with "Bird's Nest" Stadium behind.

Fig. 96 – Mike with Lord Weatherill, Mary Berkeley and Don Faircloth at "The Speakers House".

Fig. 97 – MFG re-union photo at Croydon Harriers 75th Anniversary Dinner 1995.

Fig. 100 – The awesome Niagara Falls, one of the Wonders of the World. MF photo.

Fig. 98 – MFG 2010. Graeme Fanner Photo.

Fig. 101 – UK 800m Number Ones 48 years and 4 seconds plus apart. Mike with Michael Rimmer 2010. Nicola Fleet photo.

Fig. 99 – The poignant Hiroshima Atom Bomb Memorial. MF photo.

Fig. 102 – Sir Roger Bannister congratulates Kip. Keino after Pentland Anniversary mile at Iffley Road, Oxford 1994. MF photo.

3:59.4, Thursday 6th May 1954

Fig. 103 – Roger Bannister completes the first ever sub 4 minute mile. Iffley Road Track Oxford. PA photo.

Fig. 104 – Prolific record breaker Alf Shrubb.

Fig. 106 – Judy Oakes Commonwealth joy 1994 Victoria BC. MF photo.

Fig. 105 – Donna Fraser supreme Croydon Harriers female sprinter in full stride. MF photo.

Fig. 107 – Ann Packer wins at White City. Gerry Cranham photo.

Fig. 108 – Mary Peters. Gerry Cranham photo.

Fig. 110 – Dorothy Odam-Tyler practising post war Western Roll. Inset Dorothy age 91, 2011.

Fig. 109 – Mary Rand. White City action. Gerry Cranham photo.

Fig. 111 – Martyn Rooney in very tight 400m Beijing Olympic final chase, second from left. MF photo.

Fig. 111a – Martyn Rooney's (3rd L) home straight dash in Beijing Olympic 4x400m final. MF photo.

Fig. 113 – George Chuter javelin potential (inset MF photo) now England rugby star. Getty image courtesy RFU.

Fig. 112 – Stephanie Twell Young Olympian. MF photo.

Fig. 115 – Oliver Bradfield. MF photo.

Fig. 114 – Danny Cipriani, huge athletics potential is rugby union gain. Getty image courtesy RFU.

Fig. 116 – Beth Carter. MF photo.

Fig. 118 – Emilia Gorecka/Ruth Haynes. MF photo.

Fig. 117 – Peter Chambers Lexus Croydon 10k
Runner-up age 15 2010. Peter. MF photo.

Fig. 119 – Croydon's quadruple Olympian Donna
Fraser welcomes emerging star Twinelle Hopeson
to "Wall of Fame!" mural by Jeanne-Marie Eyers
and Susan Beresford. MF photo.

Inset, Twinelle Hopeson the club athlete.
MF photo.

Fig. 120 – Jessica Judd win SEAA title by a "straight" Ashford. Inset Victor characteristically waits for vanquished to finish. MF photos.

Fig. 122 – Kelly Holmes with Loulou Rowlands. MF photo.

Fig. 121 – Record breaking Lawrence Okoye, Croydon Harriers at Bedford 2010. Keith Mayhew photo.

Fig. 123 – Katerina Thompson. MF photo.

Fig. 124 – Ned Quiney breaks the 5m barrier at Crystal Palace 2010. MF photo.

Fig. 127 – The Magnificent Arthur Wint. 440yds start at Motspur Park 1946. Getty Image.

Fig. 125 – David Barrington beats computer results! MF photo.

Fig. 128 – Carolyn Franks discussing finer points of javelin throwing with Wilf Paish. MF photo.

Fig. 129 – Linda Harrison enjoying her athletics! MF photo.

Fig. 126 – The fair and knowledgeable Jeanne Coker. MF photo.

Fig. 130 – Dedicated Derek Hayward on ESAA duty. MF photo.

Fig. 131 – Valiant team manager Matthew Kiernan prepares plunge in pursuit of points. Martin Rowe photo.

Fig. 133 – "Grass Roots" multi-tasker Peter Radford. Trinity photographer.

Fig. 132 – The "Chippy and the Pedagogue" Terry Lapins and Paul Weston with their England Athletics Officiating and coaching Awards. MF photo.

Fig 134 – Achilles Relays "Anchor Man" Mark Steed centre at Iffley Road with John De'ath, and fellow blue Alan Sexton. MF photo.

Fig. 135 – Bannister First Sub 4 minute mile Anniversary Achilles Relays Programme. MF photo.

Fig. 136 – Tommy Thomas long time South London Harriers secretary photographer Ed Lacey Centre. Alan Black Photo.

Fig. 138 – The devoted Don on duty while awaiting a hip Replacement. MF photo.

Fig. 137 – Don Turner presents Surrey gold to Shirin Irving, one of Britain's brightest multi event hopes. MF photo.

Fig. 139 – Jessica Ennis at full stretch in Long Jump. MF photo.

Fig. 140 – Jenny Meadows and Mike after Barcelona medal ceremony 2010. Nicola Fleet photo.

Fig. 140a – Jenny Meadows en route to European Indoor silver medal, Paris 2011. Mark Shearman photo.

Fig. 141 – The London Olympic Stadium nearing completion, spring 2011. Nicola Fleet photo.

Fig. 143 – Happy CRY Moment after Lexus Croydon 10k. Philippa Stanyard and Scottish cricketer Neil McCallum, now Mr and Mrs Neil McCallum with Martyn Rooney 2007. MF photo.

Fig. 142 – Heart washed and modelled by mother, Beryl Fleet at age 96. MF photo.

Fig. 144 – Cecilia Barriga in Surrey Schools action. MF photo.

Fig. 145 – CRY Logo.

and an unfortunate incident in which Scottish international triple jumper John Brierley had his wrist broken by a flying dustbin angrily thrown at his, until then, proudly worn Bayern Munich shirt by an inebriated local football fan, would have been the "routine" highs and lows of the trip, but they paled into insignificance in contrast to the "Eet ees only skin" incident. In recent time Thelma has become a highly-respected globetrotting IAAF cross-country representative and John Brierley, a senior lecturer at Oxford Brookes University and Commonwealth Games Team Manager.

On one of Croydon Harriers several visits to Fritz Emmert and his athletics-loving community in Rimbach, a very tall sixteen year old Martyn Rooney was sidelined as his body took on a further growth spurt and "complained" at any effort in the only way that any self-respecting body can, with pain. The young man had no option but to rest. His calmly controlled frustration was a credit to him. Already a fine performer, he was clearly displaying the attributes of an athlete who had his eye firmly on the future.

See Figure 78 – Generous Dalton Grant's Eberstadt medal

Ever the efficient German host, good friend Fritz Emmert embellished one memorable tour by booking our group into the world famous Eberstadt Hochsprung Meeting. Would it be a success across the disciplines we represented I wondered? My fears were quickly allayed as Dalton Grant, the top British jumper of the day, quickly got our lively youngsters on side.

He proved to be a big bonus among the likes of Cuban star Javier Sotomayor and winner on the day, Artur Partyka of Poland, who cleared 2.34m. Dalton rapidly built up a rapport with our raucous youngsters, who were certainly no respecters of silence when concentration was called for! Dalton revelled in it, and after the event, much to the delight of his new-found Croydon admirers, willingly signed autographs, patiently posed for photos and donated specially-labelled wine he had won to the admiring adults waiting in the wings.

Then came the jewel in the crown! Young shot putter Jemal Ezel asked if he could hold Dalton's medal.

"You can do more than that; you can have it," replied the patient star, generously, removing the gong and placing it around the wide-eyed young

fellow's neck.

One would have to go a very long way to find a better ambassador for our sport. Dalton is a champion in that context. The medal, thanks too to Jemal's generosity, now hangs proudly beneath a photo which our hero high jumper suitably signed in gold. He was certainly a winner in our eyes.

On another tour, the additional sport of mediaeval moat fishing in Holland caused a furrowed brow for me as group leader, when a whistle blower drew my attention to some surprisingly quiet plastic bag anglers, who had probably never before seen "tame" carp almost within reach. Luckily for me, the "anglers" were inept, and the fish too cute and elusive to capture, so a possible international incident was avoided!

The hunger caused by the boys' sacrifice of their packed lunches, floating clearly visible, and being enthusiastically consumed just out of reach by the canny carp, went unsatisfied for long enough to make the miscreants suffer. All was forgiven after apology followed admonishment and our role as athletic, ambassadors reinstated.

Over the years, though not now competing, I continued track running, albeit in trainers, and inevitably getting nearer the back of my developing squad. More and more I was enjoying the therapy of steady training runs with good friends. There were the reminiscing runs with my former schoolboy rival Phil Collins and there were conditioning and scientific sorties with good club friend Chris Scott.

The runs with Phil were more often than not in part on Kenley aerodrome, a former World War II fighter base, happily to the accompaniment of hissing gliders gently circling in the thermals overhead rather than the imagined angry roar of Spitfires setting off in pursuit of marauding Messerschmitts. It was surprising how much the memory of our youthful encounters came back as we trotted therapeutically around the perimeter track, and were later recalled with characteristic embellishment over our post-shower mugs of tea at Iver House. On one amusing occasion while showering there I sensed a presence, and on swilling the shampoo from my eyes, looked down to see Phil's then diminutive daughter studying a certain part of my anatomy from embarrassingly close range.

"*Hello N…*" I said, simultaneously re-establishing my dignity behind a towel.
"*Daddy's is a different colour!*" chirped the inquisitive child.

Being confident that my friend's "parts" would not be significantly different in hue from mine, I recounted the incident but did not seek proof or otherwise of his daughter's claim!

Runs with Chris, considerably younger than me, but thankfully a long and triple jumper way back in his Rhodesian schoolboy days, were less demanding and more educational. Chris, then a British Airways captain, whom I disparagingly dubbed "Bus Driver in the Sky", would more often than not come up with some fascinating information which had previously eluded me. Among many other previously un-encountered gems I would enthusiastically lend ear to his wealth of knowledge on the weather, the explanation of condensation on chemistry beakers and the theory of airflow over wing surfaces according to Enrico Bernouilli. Secretly I always hoped that these often detailed deliveries would lead to a slowing of pace. At least while listening to them, I could concentrate on breathing!

Running these days does not feature in my fitness regime, that is apart from the odd surreptitious but necessarily gentle surge to prove that I can move faster than walking pace when umpiring lower eleven Old Mid Whigiftian (changed to Trinity Mid-Whitgiftian 2010) hockey matches.

The wind was briefly taken out of my sails not so long ago by athletics friend and journalist Peter Mulholland, who told me that my 1962 UK All Time ranking of equal 7th with a time of 1:48.9 for 880yds is equivalent to 1:48.27 for 800m. This would put me in 163rd place in the 2010 UK All Time rankings, now topped by the 1:41.73 of Lord Sebastian Coe, driving force of the 2012 London Olympics. Happily I have now been assured that my long-accepted 1:48.2 still stands as the most accurate conversion, with me restored to 161st place!

Coe's world record time has now been superseded and the current world record holder is Kenyan David Rudisha who ran the distance in an astonishing 1:41.01... but watch out for Martyn Rooney.

10

Pastures New

Still incurably competitive, I felt that the time was ripe to transfer my attention from track to field. The attraction of coming to terms with the intricacies of tackling technical events was I felt a move in the right direction for they neither demanded VO2 uptake nor created debilitating lactic build up. Brains making up for brawn, I would kid myself! Such involvement gave me an extended competitive role allowing me to emphasise athletics as a team sport as well as an individual one. The much maligned filling of vacancies with limited ability but serious intent in the pursuit of points acquisition is something which I will always encourage as long as it is safe, sensible and not forced. Surely such participation generates healthy understanding between the disciplines.

The technical challenge for me of the throws, coupled with the sociability of the athletes involved, especially at veteran level, led when the need arose, to many an enjoyable competition with cheery and helpful rivals. It also provided the coach in me with invaluable hands-on insight into the events which I was teaching students.

I guess that when it came to offering coaching advice, the generally larger and clearly more experienced throwers knew that whatever I gleaned from them would never lead to me becoming a threat. My thinking as a team man was that a humble odd point gained from my "explosive" efforts might further the Croydon club cause. When "competing" against far superior rivals, I evolved a system of relative percentile performance. So when confronted by the genial "Big" Eric Barker, former British veteran record holder in the shot, I would galvanise my limited resources and aim for 50% of his distance to count as a success. On rare occasions, the friendly giant would sportingly concede defeat with a well intended but crushing handshake!

The competitive flame continued to burn brighter than the athletic body which belonged more appropriately to the cinder tracks of days gone by. This, I found to my cost, as recently as 7th May 1990 at the official opening of the re-laid Croydon Arena. I had been given the honour of leading the biggest field ever assembled there to run the inaugural "First Bright Red Lap" on the new all-weather running track. Everything went smoothly to plan, until with 30m to go, a sharp little lad struck decisively for home. My brain wanted to respond. My body would not! Hands aloft, he gleefully stole my thunder and disappeared into the anonymity of the crowd. A golden glory-seeking ringer, indeed! A clear picture of him remains in front of my out-of-joint nose to this day. Just let me get MY hands on that unidentified little so and so!

The following month my career in film took off with a vengeance when I was recruited as coach, starter and technical adviser for that classic of athletics films, sadly not "Chariots of Fire", but the much more down to earth school kids TV series "Grange Hill" To be more specific, just one episode of the school-centred saga. This starred Rene Zagger, more recently of "The Bill" and "Silent Witness" fame, playing the role of Mick Bentley, a burgeoning student athlete running for glory in the English Schools Championship 100m final.

Thanks to good friend and athlete Martin Rowe, I discovered fairly recently that I had, many years earlier, featured[19] unwittingly as a mermaid on a Pathe News clip from the shores of the Indian Ocean at Perth, work in this medium posed few problems for me in familiar athletics terms. However the task of coaching the seven Croydon Harriers and Trinity School athletes was a daunting task. I had to make them look genuinely fast while running slowly enough to lose to the predestined and relatively slow Zagger. It proved a fascinating challenge, made more difficult by an ingrained desire of serious athletes to win! One also had the brief to ensure that he looked impressive in his moment of glory. Somehow the project was a success but not before numerous retakes and many a laugh as I screamed at my athletes to slow down and let the star through. To have been on a par, if only for a few days, with my local locksmith Lee McDonald who regularly played Zammo in the series, must surely have worked wonders for my street cred in and around Wallington.

See Figure 79 – Grange Hill TV "English Schools sprint final!"

In my active days, the Korean War was rumbling on and we athletes acknowledged the heroics of those involved by naming some of our toughest training challenges in Lloyd Park, Croydon after their daring allied exploits in the Far East. Multiple "attacks" on "Imjin Ridge" and "Pork Chop Hill" were regularly tackled as an integral part of winter

---

[19] This came to light a few years ago, to much hilarity, when it was unearthed by an enterprising and brilliant young IT specialist, staunch Croydon Harrier, Martin Rowe. I was blissfully unaware in 1962 that folk back home were watching our foolish revels in the comfort of their local cinemas.

training. We imagined ourselves repeatedly delivering counter attacks to relieve mega-hero and subsequent VC, Sgt Bill Speakman. Those wonderful challenges remain, while their historic relevance is lost to contemporary athletes, especially cross-country runners toiling up them on many a winter Saturday. Another favourite was the "Ovett Hill", named in honour of Steve, the Olympian who joined us many a time on this tough 600m Shirley Hills incline, and made it look so easy. He regularly totted up ten repetitions compared with an outstanding club effort of eight on the hill, which now only provides a minor challenge to the powerful Croydon trams which have been routed on it.

Coaching which had already brought "rewards" of varying types, ranging from being pursued by an irate pitchfork-carrying Battersea Park keeper, to the delight of assisting six Selhurst Grammar boys into the first eight of the Surrey Schools Cross Country Championships now became much more of a priority.

See Figure 80 – Taking Selhurst Grammar cross-country for a five miler

The lesson from not reconnoitring a Battersea Park knoll before sending twenty young athletes over it, was well learned. They dutifully followed my instructions, only to cleave an unwanted path through the beautiful bed of daffodils and round a large beech tree on the unseen side, before racing back to the track totally oblivious of the ire about to be provoked. Never again did athletes in my care disappear, lemming-like over an unknown horizon!

Over the years, individual and team successes have been many and varied, ranging from County and County Schools to Area, National and English Schools title winners, and an European Junior and World Junior Championship medal winner, Martyn Rooney, who also ran outstandingly well in the World Championships and who set a UK U20 record, to erase none other than Roger Black's performance from the books.

400m and middle distances apart, I have also been fortunate to help coach many Surrey Schools relay teams to their English Schools triumphs, on one occasion marginally missing out on gold when the threat of rebellion loomed, with the "star" refusing to use the correct baton hand for his delegated position. I succumbed to the pressure of his team mates, much against my better judgment and changed the order rather than including a reserve. After we came a very respectable second to an outstanding West Midlands team, the young man came up smilingly to receive my praise. I quietly pointed out to him that the team had been two metres ahead before his change, three metres behind after it and that his subsequent brilliant run had recovered four of the five lost. The calculation was beyond him!

Many seemingly keen young club athletes often fail to last beyond their first few appearances, and I certainly was not confident for the future of a disgruntled lad who arrived one beautiful spring evening supported on crutches.

"I'm Bob Benn and I'm fed up with football, and I want to be a serious athlete," he confidently declared, "this broken leg is the limit."

I could not fail to be impressed, but certainly had doubts.

Having discussed the accident and the injury in detail I gave him some exercises and we agreed to meet again after his plaster had been removed. The phone was there should he have any problems.

On the due day, five weeks later he was there free of plaster cast and crutches.

"I want to jog a lap," he declared.
"No way," I decreed, "but you can walk two, one in each direction slightly faster than you have been doing."

He set off far too enthusiastically and came back more than chastened.

I could see he had the right spirit but needed reining in.

"I like your attitude, but I will not help you unless you do what I say and exercise patience," I advised. "I'll set you a schedule for the next three weeks after which you ought to be able to train normally."

After three more weeks of remedial walking, slow running rather than jogging plus plenty of local muscular work he was ready and raring to go. The problem was to hold him back, but it was well worth it.

One Saturday lunchtime in 1978, I answered a telephone call from the very same Bob Benn who had run well in the 4x400m relay for Great Britain in the European Junior Championships in Dortmund the previous year.

It went something like this.

"Hi Mike it's Bob."
"Hi Bob, how are you?"
"I'm fine, thanks but I've got a problem."
"Oh, tell me about it and I'll try to help," I replied, imagination racing.
"Well I've just been invited to run for Britain against the USSR later today at Crystal Palace.
"Hey that's great, congratulations."
"But I haven't accepted yet."
"Why the hell not?"
"It's my mother's birthday," he muttered
"So?"
"Well, I've just eaten a big birthday lunch and had a few drinks!"
"Are you afraid of throwing up? This could be your only chance of a full international, and what better present for your mother? Go for it."
"Yep, see what you mean," he mumbled, *"I'll accept."*
"See you there", I shouted, *"the alcohol will relax you, and good luck."*

A few hours later he beat the Soviet second string in the individual 400m, and a little later hauled the GB team back into contention with a good run in the 4x400m, before David Jenkins anchored the team to victory. The crowd just loved the red-headed reserve who, when it really mattered, came up with the goods, but thankfully not his celebratory lunch. That proved to be his only senior international selection although he had a notable career on the international Grand Prix circuit as Steve Ovett's most reliable hare.

See Figure 81 – Bob Benn racing bend

Just how much of this book you have to take with a "pinch of salt" I will leave up to you, having read the following more recent account of a telephone conversation I had with Bob. After the social niceties I got down to the serious business of verifying my copy.

"Now, Bob can you confirm this?" I asked, *"Was it Kip Kieno's teeth or Henry Rono's which were embedded in your elbow in a last bend melee at Crystal Palace, causing an injury, needing stitches which you refused so that a famous scar could develop?"*
"I don't remember anything like that," he replied unhelpfully. *"The only odd incident I recall, was when I was forced to leap over Mike Boit as he crashed just after a mêlée following the first bend break at the beginning*

of a race in Kingston, Jamaica!"

"And what was the injury you sustained?" I asked optimistically.

"I don't remember any injury," he responded again equally unhelpfully, *"...but I must have beaten the club high jump record as the unfortunate Boit crashed sickeningly to the ground,"* he added.

I knew that was not true either, for that record stands at 2.24m to John Beers set in Oslo in 1973! Bob did kindly investigate his elbows for tell-tale scars just in case his memory was playing tricks with him too. No luck there!

So Mike Boit, when you read this book, it's up to you! Please confirm the authenticity of the Kingston incident by writing to me and kindly sending a signed, smiling photo of yourself to:

"Figment of My Imagination",
Memory Lane,
Dream On,
Cloud Cuckoo Land UR1 2NO

Some years later, I was more than impressed by a young Somali lad, complete with shorts way down below his knees, who won the Croydon Primary schools 800m by a street. The young Yusuf Yacin, as I had erroneously called him from then on for several years, responded well before fading back into the Roundshaw Estate for a while, now well known for another of its sporting sons, the wheelchair sprint to marathon phenomenon Paralympian David Weir. When he reappeared on the athletics scene the very polite Somali teenager politely informed me that his name was actually Yacin Yusuf and that he wished to resume his athletics career. He achieved distinction as a schoolboy athlete, winning an English Schools 3000m title and having registered the rare distinction of winning the prestigious six-mile Knole Run in Trinity School colours at Sevenoaks not just once, but twice. It was a great thrill to accompany him to Gothenburg for the European U23 Championships.

See Figure 82 – Yacin Yusuf (78) on his way to ESAA 3000m victory
See Figure 82a – Mike & Yacin Yusuf in Gothenburg U23 European
Championships 1995

Dubbed "Mary Poppins" by the benevolent Sir Eddie Kulukundis because of my ever present blue and white brolly, I almost danced and sang as my diminutive charge, having been battered and bruised, finished faster than everyone in the 1500m final. Faster even than winner Rui Silva who later went on to win Olympic bronze, but my man had sadly run out of track to make up ground beyond eighth place of twelve.

Most recently, Croydon Harrier star, Martyn Rooney, who joined the MFG[20] at thirteen and who moved on to Loughborough at nineteen and the direct care of my friend Nick Dakin, the Director of Athletics, has brought great pleasure and satisfaction through a continuing string of fine achievements. Rooney's first International Championships, the European Under 20s in Grosseto, Italy, turned out to be an adventure and a challenge for both of us. He had gone on with the team and I followed privately a few days later, having learned he would not be racing due to the revelation that, despite UK Athletics scrutiny, his possession of an Irish Passport had gone unnoticed until he checked at the Championship Headquarters. The first time I became aware of the problem was when my phone rang a few days before I was due to depart.

"Hello is that Mike Fleet?"
"Yes it is, who is calling?"
"Zara Hyde-Peters, UK Athletics in Grosseto. Are you sitting down, I have some bad news about Martyn?"
"No I'm standing up, what's the problem?"
My mind was racing, was he injured ill or worse. I certainly knew that it couldn't be a drugs problem...
"It's his passport, it's Irish."
I heaved a sigh of relief.
"Is that all, that's a relief?" I responded.
"Are you serious Mike, you must be joking. He will not be allowed to run," Zara almost shouted.
I quickly told her two emotive names.
"Yes, but thank God he hasn't joined Sam Haughian and Ed Prickett!"
Both were outstanding young athletes who had had their lives tragically cut short in the preceding months.
Zara immediately understood my earlier seemingly blasé response.
"You're right, Mike," she replied," *but what are you going to do?"*
"If he's not being sent home, then I'll be coming over," I assured her.

As my Gatwick-bound train was about to pull out of Purley a couple of days later, Nicola, my wife, shouted out urgently into the crowded carriage that she had just been called on her mobile by trusty Centresport Tours maestro Graham Botley. He had given her the name of my transit hotel

---

20   Mike Fleet's Group.

in Pisa. It was Hotel Leonardo. By the time she reached home, there was another message from an apologetic Botley to say that he had inadvertently supplied an incorrect hotel name. Multiple unsuccessful efforts were made at contacting the blissfully ignorant mis-directed traveller, including an attempt at ground-to-flight contact by pilot friend Chris Scott. Several hours later, just short of midnight, a bemused Pisa taxi driver insisted, correctly, that no such hotel existed in the city! He deposited me in a dubious looking establishment, where the manageress was a striking Romanian lady with dazzling carrot-coloured hair, and where I spent a nervous but uneventful night. In the morning I made my way back to the station and headed post-haste for Grosseto.

The abashed Botley met me on arrival and transported me smoothly to my hotel, the very basic Quattro Stradi nestling strategically beside a service station on a traffic island site fed by four roads, and with the railway line 20 metres behind as a bonus!

The unravelling Rooney saga apart, it was evident that I was in for a testing time.

Martyn, the epitome of calm, was over the shock of his ongoing Irish nationality by the time I arrived, and after a really good chat we decided to proceed as closely as we could to what we would have done in the normal course of events.

He was to carry on as if nothing had happened and would warm up with his team mates at the given times and would run a time trial 300m soon after the relay final. All went to plan and it was all put down to experience.

See Fig 83 – Martyn Rooney and coach Mike after UK Junior 400m win

On his return, Martyn was met at Heathrow by his expeditious mother Marie, who promptly handed him the necessary UK passport application form.

The critical document soon arrived and the Croydon-born athlete the Irish would have welcomed strode purposefully into the British fold.

Since then he has produced a string of outstanding performances. These include his UK U20 record of 45.35sec which removed the previous time by Roger Black from the books, a European U20 400m silver, two World

Junior bronze medals and several stunning sub 45sec 4x400m legs in senior World Championships.

He followed these fine achievements with a brilliant 44.60sec run, the 8th best British 400m of all time in the fabulous Beijing "Bird's Nest" Stadium which earned him a coveted place in the 2008 Olympic final. His immediate disappointment at placing 5th in a slower time was indicative of an athlete with a fiery ambition.

I am certain that he would be quite stunning over 800m. It is my opinion that he possesses the astonishing ability to run sub 1:40.0. In one of only three "serious two lappers" at 18, he gave a clear hint of his potential by clocking 1:50.5 in third place and complaining, hardly breathless, that he had "run out of track".

Nowadays, regular sorties of other Olympic aspirants to run Lloyd Park "Rooney Lung Busters" are made more attractive to ambitious youngsters, by the clearly beneficial effect they have had on Martyn in his formative pre-Loughborough days. I must add that coaches who confine their involvement to the upper echelons of athletics are missing out on some of the most rewarding aspects of the sport. There's nothing to match sharing the uninhibited joy of a boy or girl setting a personal best Not far behind comes the satisfaction of a senior club athlete acquiring the difficult technique of a new discipline. So often the ability to show that you know exactly what you are doing regardless of standard is hugely satisfying.

I often ask myself, "What is success?" and "At what point is it achieved?" I regularly come up with different conclusions. Of course the measurement of success is dependent on the subject, plus his or her potential and ambition. I believe that by being successful, eg achieving realistic progressive targets throughout a career, any athlete should feel fulfilled even if family, career or illness cut it short before full potential is reached. The better an athlete becomes, the narrower is the margin between success and failure.

So many of the young athletes who have passed through the MFG, my training squad, having run faster than I ever did between thirteen and eighteen, that I often wonder what they might have achieved had not something more important diverted their action elsewhere. The 2:05.00 800m boy at 15, and the 4:16.17 14-year-old 1500m runner are just two of many I could give as examples. There have been numerous teenagers who have been two or three years ahead of what I achieved some fifty years ago, and one 16-year-old girl has been regularly running 800m races faster than I did at the same age.

Of course one could not expect the progress of a young woman to move in parallel to that of a young man, but I believe the athlete in question has the potential not only to surprise the athletics world a few years hence, but also to surprise herself. Inhibitions have to be cast aside and new challenges tackled with confidence and no small element of bravery.

I have had the huge privilege of helping hundreds of athletes to achieve successes ranging from the first Martyn Rooney sub 45sec 400m to the completion of the London Marathon in just over 5 hours, from throwing the javelin 60m to having the confidence to drop one in at a metre or so to score vital points and from converting fitness-seeking housewives and mothers into competent club athletes.

11

Coaching Not Poaching

With the passage of time and with less to go for personally, I found the opportunity to channel my frustration into more serious coaching. This proved to be both challenging and very rewarding at all levels.

Currently my coaching activity centres on a thirty-strong mixed, all age, multi-ethnic group of very committed athletes affectionately known as the "MFG". We are in action twice weekly at the Croydon Sports Arena, with the addition of regular hill and fartlek sessions in Croydon's magnificent, undulating Lloyd Park. The arena and the park have now been rendered even more user-friendly by the introduction of the excellent Tramlink service which serves East Croydon main rail station, Beckenham, New Addington and Wimbledon.

The present regime has evolved smoothly over more than fifty years, with a prolonged overlap during which it went alongside my personal training and competition. Gradually the balance changed and with more coaching quality, the numbers increased to current levels. Right from the start of my coaching involvement, having benefited from circuit training at Loughborough, I led midweek winter training sessions, first in the gym at Shirley High School with its sadly missed ropes and beams and not so sadly missed coir mats, to the far more spacious Trinity School sports hall with its sprint turning boards, plentiful non-slip rubber gym mats and fine basketball facilities.

The days of packed Wednesday night sessions during the half terms either side of Christmas seem to have become a thing of the past. Perhaps the ropes were the yester-year magnet, or maybe it was the challenge of taking on the then active coach at beam circling that was the attraction. It is interesting to note that veteran athletes form the majority of the group these days and that the high levels of their application and measure of their achievement in competition are relatively superior to that of most of their contemporaries.

As a coach I may appear an eccentric dresser, having graduated from my dogmatic, strictly track-suited post-Loughborough days, to the present, now favouring a broad brimmed cricket hat throughout the year. In practical terms it does keep the rain off my spectacles and the sun out of my eyes. Furthermore, in the interests of being easily found, I favour bright orange, yellow or red tops, and in summer long golden socks and, I am told, overly long shorts, but I defy any athlete, inquisitive parent or newcomer not to find me! My aim is not to be mocked but to be easily identified during coaching sessions and at competitions and it seems to work, sometimes rather too well. I call the policy my "Lighthouse Syndrome", standing out brightly like the traditional coastal warning, but that is as far as it goes, much more on a friendly foundation than a frightening rock, for I want to advertise my presence rather than warn people away.

The passage of time has, I believe allowed my coaching to progress in parallel with my reduced competitive activity. The former is now sporadically limited to attacking Club veteran throws records. While acknowledging the seriousness of many veteran athletes, I try to make a point that in many cases officiating allows one to return something tangible to the sport rather than putting more pressure on a declining force of judges, starters, timekeepers etc. In many cases too there is the added advantage of avoiding the embarrassment of novice-like efforts!

In addition to my rewarding club involvement, I enjoy delivering regular summer and winter sessions for the Trinity and Whitgift Schools in Croydon and acting as coaching starter at various schools' sports days. On such occasions I instruct my marksmen not to be afraid to hold up a hand and talk to the invariably nervous and minimally instructed Usain Bolt-aspiring young sprinters, especially on how to acquit themselves during what is the tensest point of any competition. Such a policy has helped many a shaking child to smile and be relaxed, and saved many an otherwise prematurely fired 40p worth from being wasted.

I also enjoy working on County Schools' courses, benefiting from the interface with younger coaches as well as that of stalwarts like former cross-country international Mick Firth with his wealth of distance running and coaching experience, and helping to hone Surrey Schools sprint relay teams to national championships performance level.

Without ever aspiring to equal such eminent and dedicated a coach as the late lamented Wilf Paish MBE, I have always respected his work and have endeavoured to follow his example as best I could. Doubtless he could double my estimated 12,000 coaching hours over the past 50 years.

Similarly I still aspire to the great knowledge, patience and charm of National Coach John Le Masurier, my mentor in 1964.

From my earliest days as a qualified coach when I started with a group of a dozen or so athletes at Crystal Palace, I now endeavour to regularly give personal attention to more than thirty. I now rely on the crucial help of two junior coaches and, of course, senior athletes and parents.

Timsbury Manor was one unfortunately transient training opportunity which appeared in the 1960s, from which my group coaching and personal expertise greatly benefited from what it had to offer.

The Manor, a delightful red brick building standing in several acres of grounds near Romsey in Hampshire and critically boasting salmon rights on the famous River Test, had been acquired by millionaire Oliver Cutts. He had developed it as a centre for training for the benefit of all athletes ranging from club enthusiasts to members of the International Athletes Club and specialist coaching groups.

See Figure 86 – Timsbury Manor Group world record hammer thrower Harold Connolly USA(L), Mike at back and Oliver Cutts

It was a staffed Athletics Youth Hostel by the genial Des Pond and his family and featured specific facilities which included a sprint straight in the kitchen garden, a throwing circle on the front lawn and a half-mile running circuit, plus all the impedimenta and weights any serious athlete could wish for.

There was even a large dog kennel which once served well as a short term detention centre for an over "zealous" young man in unfamiliar mixed company. Suitably humbled he soon returned to sporting society a reformed character!

A rare encounter there with the then US hammer throwing great Harold Connolly during a Hammer Circle reunion was indeed inspirational to everyone there, more so when one saw, close up, the disparity between the world record holder's arms. His every word on technique and training was analysed by the active disciples and coaches alike and, when it came to texture of the Manor's new hammer circle, again the great man's decrees were attentively absorbed. Hard though Doug Birch, our Croydon thrower, and I tried after that, we never managed to persuade the Croydon Parks Department to replicate such smooth perfection!

128

Surreptitious attempts during Timsbury weekends to lure naïve trout or even stupid salmon with worms, safety pins and finishing tape, all ended in abject failure, as ultimately did Cutts' project.

It was later to transpire that his manorial magnanimity was not all that it was made out to be. Cutts, allegedly a rags to riches man, held misguided aspirations to grandeur, and word had it that he tried to pave the way towards an unlikely knighthood with floral gifts to Princess Margaret too.

Some years later I learned the law caught up with Cutts on several counts, and that he was obliged to spend a considerable length of time courtesy of Her Majesty's Pleasure for, among other things, extortion!

My pre-Commonwealth Games training at Merthyr Mawr had sown the seeds for several successful club visits to Candleston Farm near Ogmore by Sea and the magnetic challenges of the huge sand dunes nearby which drew many from further afield than Croydon.

The long journey to South Wales for a weekend was soon forgotten as athletes and coaches alike revelled and sweated in the tough environment, where the work of wind and sea had conjured up terrain unequalled anywhere else except in Hungary. The value of tough training on the spectacular sand hills and its contribution to conditioning could initially be judged each night by the voracious appetites of the runners, and their profound slumbers which followed soon after supper.

Having always considered myself in the coaching context as a creator rather than a collector, I believe that the sport has accordingly been much more rewarding for me than the other coaches who seem to delight in claiming that they alone can move an already talented and progressing athlete further forward.

In my view, it's possible to assist an athlete without applying acquisitive pressure. For example, during the 1977 English Schools Championships, as a well-established coach with some hopefuls in action, I found myself consoling another athlete, a sobbing, waif-like Surrey girl who had just failed in the junior 800m. Little could I have imagined then that the dejected Wendy Smith would emerge ten years on at the 1984 Los Angeles Games as Wendy Sly, a world star, to win something which had been beyond my reach, an Olympic silver medal. The erstwhile failing young half-miler had progressed to become a woman of steel, striding strongly into the record books in the first women's Olympic 3000m, the race sadly made notorious for the athletics world by the controversy surrounding the clash between American favourite Mary Slaney and Zola Budd, the Briton adopted from South Africa. I would like to think that my empathy at the time of her schoolgirl failure played a part in her very special future. I sometimes wonder too how my career might have unravelled had I experience a similar "disaster" at such a tender age?

I find it an interesting exercise to try to compare the success of an athlete brought through to world class level, with that of, dare I say, the delightful, and, dare I also say, overweight young mother who arrived on my coaching doorstep, seeking entry into the demanding world of those fit enough to finish the London Marathon. Having satisfied myself that her ambition was serious, I made the customary request for such a candidate to get a GP's appointment and hopefully obtain from it a clean bill of health.

That was surprisingly forthcoming, accompanied by additional sage advice which I was relieved to know that the doctor had kindly saved me from having to deliver... "and you will have to cut down on chocolate, white bread, butter, jam, pastry...!!!!"

I am delighted to record, that in the ensuing ten months the lady in question did enough to survive five hours on foot, and complete the 26 miles 385 yards around the streets of London and over Tower Bridge. As a direct result I became the delighted owner of an official souvenir Mars Mug as my "reward", which remains second only to satisfaction at the measure of her achievement.

I have yet to have the good fortune to help an athlete to a national standard marathon, but have been pleased to help two women who, I believe, fulfilled their potential with runs of 3 hours 9 minutes and 3 hours 15 minutes, one of them only eighteen at the time.

While of course it is fulfilling to coach a national champion or an international, I genuinely believe that many an "ordinary" athlete, if there really is such a person, is in reality some kind of champion in his or her own right when having achieved the very utmost of God-given talent.

Never expecting any reward from coaching, other than a share in the achievements of athletes, I cannot deny the delight that the valued Mars Marathon mug gave me, nor can I forget the wonderful gesture of a then young Ian Grant's mother, who spent goodness knows how many hours knitting a magnificent heavy-duty, cable-stitch sweater, which continues to keep me comfortable on cold winters' days some thirty or more years later.

Very satisfying too was an email received just before my 72nd birthday, recalling the day during National Service when football miscreant Jim Ewing appeared at the RAF Jever track...

"Mike,

I'm fairly sure that I have long faded from your memory. But you appeared in my life at a most opportune moment and helped to change its direction, so this is a belated thank you. I had never run on a track before and was stationed in Jever as a reconnaissance photographer, but having disgraced myself one day in a soccer game I went to the track to exorcise/exercise my demons. You were there, and after watching me run offered such encouragement and advice that from that point on, nothing mattered as much as running.

To cut a long story short, in 1962 shortly before I was demobbed, I was placed second in the RAF and combined services one mile run in 4:11[21], received an athletic scholarship the following year to a small college in Texas, eventually finished a PhD in English Literature, and have taught English in Texas, Mississippi and California for the past 40 years.

Needless to say I have followed your career as closely as I could from the US and you remained an inspiration, even later when I was a successful Masters runner. At 70 I am training again with hopes of competing as a senior so maybe contacting you at this late stage will add fire to these slowly burning embers. At any rate, my deeply felt thanks for helping change the direction of an eighteen year old Scotsman's life.

Jim Ewing"

I was truly touched by Jim's message. He had certainly remained firmly in the memory bank, but is there far more clearly now. With my aching knees and my legs limited to walking these days, I feel more relaxed in the knowledge that someone else's are carrying on the good work, for Jim must be an inspiration to many others on his side of "The Pond".

---

[21] Jim's memory served him very well to within 0.2sec of total accuracy. He ran 4.11.2 at Uxbridge on 11th July 1962, to rank 55th in the United Kingdom. He went on to record a very respectable mile best of 4:06.0.

Thanks too, to broadly smiling ten year old Gideon who once gave me a hug after training. Sadly, with current child protection regulations as they are I would be foolish to risk such uninhibited tactile gesture, even when a child is injured or disappointed. Could it be misguided reverse ageism, for there are no such restrictions between adults? At times one has had no choice but to be alone and at risk, dealing sensibly and expeditiously with injury, sickness and distress. Almost without exception, I have had thanks from both sufferer and parents alike.

And so it can be seen, coaching and spreading the athletics gospel is a truly fulfilling activity. As a coach I have to share both success and failure and, on fortunately rare occasions, tragedy too. The premature death of Cecilia Barriga of an undiagnosed heart condition is regularly recalled in what I believe is a happy and charitable way when I ask for donations to Cardiac Risk in the Young in return for any of my photographs requested by athletes or parents.

I hope to be able to continue coaching for many years to come. My aim is not to be too set in my ways but to be alert and receptive to developments which complement my existing routines.

My policy has always been, and remains, to be relevant, challenging and adaptable.

12

On the Other Side of the Track

The complexity of athletics has, as I have discovered to my benefit, the great advantage of offering a wonderful choice of less physically demanding roles for those wanting to remain involved in the sport once competition ceases to be a realistic option. The windows of opportunity are such that anyone with interest can find a useful and rewarding niche.

They range from starting, timekeeping and judging to the hidden, in photo finish and results rooms or under grandstands checking implement weights and ensuring their return. One wonders how many hidden Austin Foxes[22] there are in the world of athletics. Only the vigilance of one of these unseen heroes prevented the theft of several very valuable international standard disci (discuses) by a very large track-suited felon at one of my club's major promotions. Similar alertness also prevented the acceptance of a UK discus "record" achieved with an underweight implement.

Hard though I found it to accept that the passage of time was taking its toll, I gradually conceded that the more sedentary aspects of the sport could still be satisfying, with all the ingredients to challenge, stimulate and produce fulfilment. Officiating does not provide individual victories or records, but does produce the feeling of satisfaction from knowing that a job has been well done, and is capable of providing other kinds of achievement within the sporting context.

When all these roles are happily filled, the promotion of athletics speeds along as smoothly as Usain Bolt in one of his sprints! Who knows, at the end of his exciting career the great man may, one hopes, become an inspirational coach or, if he prefers, a daunting behind-the-scenes custodian of discuses.

Committee man

Life after competition, for me, took its roots subconsciously I believe, way back in the 1950s when, as Trinity School athletics captain, I had to learn the social graces of welcoming visiting teams and thanking host schools

---

[22] Austin Fox, long-time staunch Croydon Harrier athlete and dedicated official.

for their hospitality. Also to a degree some team organisation and athlete motivation had to be learned as part of the responsibility. Once involved in any ancillary activity, as I have discovered, the enthusiast can be gripped by its magnetism.

Over the years I have thoroughly enjoyed the exploration of many of these new avenues, accepting on more than one occasion that ambition elsewhere had to be curtailed. A big bonus too has been learning about the fascinating athletics careers of colleagues, who of course may also have tales to tell of life outside sport. Many a wizened and seemingly insignificant colleague has turned out to have been an Olympian to whose superiority I have readily conceded.

Things evolved during the distant dynamic days at Loughborough when one juggled with the balance between study, athletics training and student life, as well as fitting in committee work. My experience on committees was enhanced by working on a team with such significant luminaries as Derek Hayward, later of Kangaroo Club and English Schools fame, cross-country Secretary David Saul, who later deserted athletics for a millionaire life-style captain of a luxury yacht and the Premiership of Bermuda, and the almost imitable "Stand with your feet closer apart" Anglo/Greek technical lecturer coach, Basil Stamatakis.

We were the initiators of the Loughborough versus the Amateur Athletics Association match, wearing the trademark African violet track suit, and also, at the time we thought, the creators of an innovative athletics team vest design which incorporated diagonal violet and maroon stripes. Not so the latter, as I discovered from the photographic display at the Loughborough Centennial Graduation in 2010. There on display was the team of 1948, splendidly attired in vests just like those we believed we had pioneered in 1960.

My duties then as press secretary held the added attraction of a handsome weekly 10/- (ten shillings in old money, 50p today) payment from the Loughborough Echo, as bait for reliability. How times have changed! Nowadays one is lucky to get credit for contributions or photographs, which are generally viewed by copy-hungry journalists as free publicity for our clubs and for athletics in general.

Next came National Service sport which seemed not to need committees, everything emanating from the station gym, where the PFO and his corporal issued instructions, team selections, travel details and issued kit.

My job as captain of the Royal Air Force Jever team seemed to be that of formal trophy recipient on behalf of the team, and to learn that the commissioned ranks did not find it easy to be told what to do by an "other rank" colleague. In fairness they generally co-operated fully, although on occasions the glory leg in the sprint relay was in dispute when a mere middle-distance runner claimed that he was the fastest man available!

Things seemingly developed from modest beginnings during those heady days way back in the 1960s, when co-editing my club magazine "The Harrian" with my mentor Frank Turk, complete with eye shade and blue pencil behind the ear, we excitedly stapled cover to copy on an ancient German stitch stapler in the Croydon Youth Office. The Youth Office is no more, now transformed to the far more popular, but less philanthropic Tiger Tiger Bar, while the venerable stitch stapler languishes in relaxed retirement in my porch, acting as an excellent stand for trailing plants.

The need for young blood on the Croydon Harriers committee in 1964 prompted a "peaceful revolution" within which a naïvely willing Fleet armed with all his new found Loughborough expertise but blissfully unaware of his administrative inexperience was persuaded to take on the role of club secretary. Little did I know what I had let myself in for. One of our earliest and not universally popular "modernisations" was the removal of the formal tea break with its eagerly consumed bread and butter pudding. From then on business became the priority with tea on the hoof and a rich tea biscuit if you were lucky!

Apart from a gap to enable me to acquire a hard-earned belated, and I guess much-needed, Diploma in Management Studies, I "outlived" all the original "Gang of Twelve[23]" and only finally stood down in 2002 due to wear and tear. Not quite the continuous 41 years of pioneer Harriers secretary Jack Lisney, but he was the captain of a virtually crewless ship during World War II, and to his great credit he kept the flame of athletics glimmering in Croydon despite the blackout and other privations of those austere times. The small but enthusiastic club which he nurtured in the 1940s has now grown into a four hundred strong family-based organisation, participating in leagues catering for virtually everyone's interests. From the modest beginning, when the club contested a dozen summer fixtures, it now encompasses over sixty while the winter programme reflects a similar expansion.

During my tenure as secretary, I quickly learned that to be a successful

---

[23] Members of the 1964 Croydon Harriers take-over committee.

fighter for the cause, one had to rely on a willing and competent ground crew to pick up the loose components.

In the very early days, my parents, with whom I was still living at the time, fulfilled that role uncomplainingly and extremely well. Later wonderful "assistant secretaries" made up for the skills of which the RAF deprived me. All parents of athletes, Valerie Allen, Vivienne Sterry and Pauline Waters somehow overcame the conundrums presented by my generally rushed longhand and shorthand thoughts to produce concise correspondence, meaningful minutes and non rambling reports. Time and time again, the faux pas, the split infinitive, innuendo and even litigation challenging items were discreetly removed.

See Figure 85 – Now I know how mother felt!

Only now can I fully appreciate and acknowledge the great job they did, and I just wonder how many other club secretaries have, over history, been sustained by similarly public-spirited, unpaid professionals.

Other committees took up my time in parallel too and I learned of the importance of links with the local authority and with higher athletics bodies both at County and County schools level and above. These were far less attractive with smoke-filled rooms, pontificating but doubtless wonderfully dedicated officers and post-meeting bar refreshments. They provided little attraction for me.

In recent years, I have been privileged to serve in a truly philanthropic organisation, which can I recommend as the ideal committee, that of the Croydon Playing Fields Association which is inclusive, genteel and effective, although seemingly in a time-warp. Thanks to the expansiveness of Chairman Edward Handley MBE, it sends its servants home after issuing grants and protecting sports grounds, with a warming glass of high quality white wine. I defy anyone to find me a committee which not only does that, but which also permits the resident cat to attend, albeit ex officio, complete with his own chair.

Dedicated long-time secretary Anne Organ, a charming Victorian-natured woman of wonderfully distinctive character, is in her own words "mother to all men, never a threat to wives; a veritable galleon in full sail, a woman who always asks her male mini-cab drivers if they are properly dressed – they can't drive safely if they are uncomfortable," she asserts! Ann delivers the minutes in tantalisingly hushed tones to an attentive committee waiting on her every word as has been the case for over 50 years. "Item 5 Eleanor Shorter Fund, nothing to report". I have no recall of anyone having had the courage to enquire just what the Eleanor Shorter Fund is, let alone just who Eleanor Shorter was!

See Figure 87 – "Galleann" Organ, sporting salt of the earth

However, in common with most of the representatives of local sport on the CPFA Committee, I am pleased to publicly acknowledge my gratitude to them for their generosity with grant aid to individuals and clubs, and for their vigilance and foresight with regard to playing fields and ancillary facilities.

Official

Happily my experiences within the athletics officials' community have revealed that those involved work very much with the athletes' interests at heart. There is in general a good rapport between the performers and the measurers. It is, however, not always sweetness and light, and from time to time unforeseen problems, rivalries and personality clashes lead to disagreements. Overall, officials, who some athletes clearly think are paid, thoroughly enjoy making a significant contribution to the sport.

See Figure 91 – Official shepherd accompanying Glen Cohen, David Jenkins and Bill Hartley to the Europa Cup 400m start at Crystal Palace

Starter

As a youthful post-competitive starter I found the "brotherhood" generally welcoming and informative...
..."*Always make sure you have sufficient blanks with you,*" was advice which avoided any embarrassment, although I must confess to having been a shade quick with the trigger at some local schools meetings in order to protect dwindling stocks of my .38 Smith and Wesson shells.
..."*Protect your ears*" was undoubtedly extremely important as was...
..."*Make sure the chief timekeeper has acknowledged you before getting the race under way*". Thanks to this advice, I have made many friends in the timekeeping fraternity, and have retained most of my hearing which thankfully allows me to join in the more than occasional banter.

One of my earliest, and certainly most memorable duties with the guns, was as assistant to the legendary Ron Jewkes at a London University v

Royal Navy match at Motspur Park on a distant May evening. It must have been May, for the rich purple of the nearby rhododendron bushes is still etched in my memory.

"Right young man, you're doing the 100," directed the well-organised expert.

Little did I anticipate the test soon to unfold. Ron kindly advised on procedure and told me that he would act as recall from the path outside the track by the bushes.

"On your marks...set,"....bang!... and bang again!
"Warning to number 8 in lane 3," I announced.
"Not me," announced the guilty naval runner.
"You're quite right Mr Starter," came a raspy response from my red-clad mentor surrounded by purple blossom.
"On your marks...set,"...bang!... and bang again!
It was the Navy man once more.
"Number 8, Lane 3, disqualified," I announced rather too timorously.
"You must be joking," shouted the athlete in question, the colour of his face closely matching that of the rhododendron flowers. *"You can't disqualify me. I'm Surgeon Lieutenant *******, and I am the Navy Team Captain!"*
"You're quite right Mr Starter," came the characteristically raspy, response from the bushes again.
"Leave the track at once," he further instructed, *"you will have more time now to attend to your duties as captain."*

There was no problem with the start of the 4x110yds relay at the end of the meeting, when I had the distinct impression that number 8 got away significantly behind the others!

I would like to think that over the years, having covered numerous meetings, often at the last minute, for a colleague who regularly succumbed to better offers, plus numerous local schools championships, that my skills became honed to an acceptable level. At one point I somewhat rashly set about obtaining the prerequisite reports for upgrading. Duties at distant Oxford and Woodford elicited heartening comments and assurances that the necessary documents would be forthcoming. Despite reminders, they never did, so I can only presume that I was seen to be something of a threat or that the gentlemen in question had passed on. Happily I was not deterred by any missing acclaim and have thoroughly enjoyed setting hundreds, possibly thousands of athletes about their business in the nicest possible way.

On a club trip to Sweden I learned the local starting instructions as usual and was nearing the end of a session to familiarise the athletes with the routine...

"Pa edra plaster," I instructed and runners duly complied.
After giving the time to settle I called them confidently into the set position.
"Fardiga"... And once still, the internationally understood executive of my clapper sent a 400m bend start into action.
"How long are you staying in Sodertalje?" a Swede enquired in embarrassingly impeccable English.
"You must do this at home. Would you like to be a starter at the Swedish championships at the weekend?"
"That's a very flattering and tempting invitation," I replied, *"but I have to return to England with my group on Friday."*
"Oh, I am sorry," said my new found friend, *"it would have been really nice to have you work with us."*

The matter was closed, but what a feather that opportunity would have been in this Level 3 starter's cap had I been able to accept! I have yet to meet a low grade British starter who has officiated at a national championship abroad!

Many years have passed since then, featuring a host of starting duties predominantly at modest but extremely rewarding club and school level from which possibly, with hindsight, the most entertaining episode evolved. I call it:

"The Salutary Tale of the Grumpy Gnome, the Colourful Clown and the Stroppy Starter."

Not so long ago, my long-since dead competitive fire was briefly rekindled by an ever increasing list of very indifferent veteran records taking up space in the Croydon Harriers handbook. These had all been set by one incurably acquisitive elderly athlete of seventy plus. So soft were some of his marks that I decided to challenge them in areas where my knowledge of the technique would compensate for the damage caused by the passage of time to my throwing persona.

The scene of this drama was set for a Croydon Arena based Southern Counties Veterans' League fixture at which I had been asked to act as starter, but at which I was also determined to put on one final act as a competing athlete, alternating between the role of starter and that of competitor.

This would be a veritable doddle, I foolishly thought, not accounting for the dogmatism of the league secretary, competing colourfully in the guise of a red and yellow clad "Clown", nor for that matter the tenacity of the "Grumpy Grey Gnome", holder of the records about to come under attack. I happily set the first race on its way and went over to take my first discus throw oblivious of what was about to evolve.

"You've missed the first round – you can't compete now," proclaimed the Clown as I dutifully removed my red blazer to reveal the requisite club vest, complete with number, ready for the fray.
The Clown, smiling contemptuously, turned away and threw his tiny spinning saucer into the near distance, encouraging the reluctant implement with an overly loud shout.
"Don't be so stupid," I exclaimed, *"I only agreed to be starter on the understanding that I could compete."*
"It's against the rules," came the riposte.
Digging deep to recall a teenage strop, I picked up my bag and stomped away, declaring in thinly disguised rage:
"You're now the starter; I am going home!"

The exchange had clearly been louder and more obvious than I thought, for my wife, Nicola, had left the timekeeping team 80m away and, firmly taking me by the elbow, told me in no uncertain terms not to be so childish!

Grudgingly I agreed to resume my briefly abandoned duties, only to discover that the "diplomatic corps" had been at work and was told that I could after all compete in the discus as a non-scorer!

Rapidly reinstated and with no time to get the specific weight discus for the M70 category, I grabbed a larger implement, a 1.5k "monster" and despatched it all of 16.53m.

"Did you beat the record?" enquired Kim Thornton, an enthusiastic Croydon veteran standing nearby.
"I think so, but I am not sure," I replied. *"Must go to start the next track*

event."

A few minutes later, Kim returned smiling.
"Mike, you beat it by more than a metre, congratulations."
"Thanks, but no big deal. I'll have a go at the javelin later."

At that moment the dethroned discus record holder emerged like a *"Grumpy Gnome"* from the announcer's box to declare:
"That can't stand as a record, you were non-scoring!"
"I assume that you still want a starter for the rest of the match," I queried throwing in my bargaining chip.

After two disappointing javelin throws, the better of which was 15.45m, I felt that, with various aches and pains dominated by a threatening cramp in the groin, discretion was the better part of valour, and when Kim confirmed that the old record had been erased I heaved a sigh of relief, smiled smugly, retiring from the event. Thanking the officials and confirming that all had been recorded for posterity, I left with a spring and a vaguely disguised limp in my step, to complete the remaining starter's duties of the evening.

With those "achievements confirmed in print by two intrusive lines on page 20 in the 2010 Croydon Handbook, I hereby declare my definitive retirement from competitive athletics... until the next time".

Timekeeper

Being, as I presumptuously thought, pretty good with the stopwatch as a PE teacher and seeing how quickly Nicola my wife had become an accomplished timekeeper, I deemed the time right in my mid-sixties to sit the Surrey timekeeper's test at Walton. It would be, so it seemed, a doddle. Two sets of starts, one from 100m, and the other from 200m with groups of volunteers, after a suitable time lapse, simulating an eccentric variety of finishes following a 20m run. I encountered no real problems except from watering eyes in a searching headwind. When it was over the candidates retired to the clubroom for welcome tea and biscuits to await results and find out how well we'd done. Did I say WELL!

"Sorry Mike, you've failed" was the verdict from the scrutineer, who was thoughtfully breaking the news out of everyone else's earshot. I couldn't believe what I had heard and wondered if my years as a starter, even with ears shielded had after all caused damage. Even worse was to come!

"What was my mark," I spluttered questioningly.
"Two percent," came like a bolt from the blue!

Even I was lost for words!
I found myself disbelieving in the car park. It was a clear case of *"into the car and away"*. Timekeeping clearly was not for me!
But hold on a minute! I thought that I had done pretty well, and I knew that my concentration had been second to none with the total absence of competition day distractions. I went back in and asked to talk through my abysmal failure.

The chief examiner for the day was Stan Burton, one of Britain's finest exponents of the art.

"Give me time to analyse your results and I am sure we'll sort things out," he kindly offered.

Half an hour later I had been reassured that although my results were wrong, they were the most consistent!

"It's not so bad as you might think," said the understanding Stan. *"You're either wrong at the start or at the finish. Six months working alongside top timekeepers and you'll be fine. Especially whenever you're at the same meetings as I am!"*

Six months later after a miserable rain swept test at Basingstoke I had my doubts, but before we left for home, the same kindly Stan smiled and said,*"I think you will be all right this time."*

Perhaps he knew a thing or two, for when the results were circulated a few weeks later, I had scored 98%.

Never one for competing at any distance much beyond 799m, I have always admired long distance runners for their endurance and tenacity, but wondered at their perceived wisdom. One of them, incidentally the aforementioned compassionate scrutineer, now a valued friend, is Don Turner of London to Brighton, Comrades Marathon (Durban to Pietermaritzberg and vice versa) and 1 hour to 24 hours racing pedigree, enthusiastic leader of the Surrey officials Monday walking group, with whom I now get my regular fitness fix.

My previously ill-informed opinion of these "eccentrics" has been completely revised since Don, and many of his determined kind, have proved to be significantly more normal than I am. Together with international shot-putter Judy Oakes and me, Don shares a birthday, 14th February, and we are annually subjected to public embarrassment as Valentines, before of course having to buy the drinks!

One hears that there will be no timekeepers at the London 2012 Olympic Games, with total faith being placed in highly sophisticated systems which have been successfully tried and tested at all the major meetings for many years now. But lingering doubts remain for there must always the possibility, no matter how remote, of power and back up failure. I recall the Surrey County Championships when I was among the timekeepers after the final event of the meeting, a fiercely fought 400m, we were approached by the winner:

"What were my 100ths?" he asked politely.
"Not happy with your time then, because we are?" responded the chief timekeeper.
"What do you mean?"
"Well young man, 100ths aside, with the electrics down that was the only event all day for which the times taken as back-up by all ten of us contributed to the published result."

Taken aback somewhat, the young man spluttered, *"Thanks very much. I suppose that when it comes down to it times are really secondary and this is really what matters,"* polishing his gold medal proudly. He walked off smiling.

Field Judge

I happily slot in wherever necessary and enjoy learning from my more experienced colleagues. I take a pride in my hooter blowing and avoidance tactics when a discus or javelin slips in the wind. There is invariably a good rapport between field event officials and the competitors. I recall two interesting incidents where international athletes were lined up in the same event as club-standard competitors. On one occasion at Dartford, Fatima Whitbread and her cohorts expected the wet runway to be kept dry for her throws. Happily, a compromise was reached so that each athlete had the chance of having the surface water cleared - an outcome which would not have arisen without the presence of the superstar athlete. This was achieved by officials standing firm for the common good.

Sadly not so on the second occasion, when, having three times called "no throw" to an athlete whose spear landed near the Commonwealth Games standard, I found myself eased out of the duty by the meeting referee and the fourth flat throw 'earned' the athlete in question an unjustified selection (in my opinion!). Lesson learned, I now always seek shared duties on validity.

At the other end of the scale, as field referee for primary school championships, old-fashioned routines persist and I constantly try to introduce proven and safer methods for judges. Once I was asked how I knew it all, by a young man who introduced himself as a headmaster. I complimented him on his elevated status and reached in my pocket for the rule book, to which I assured him I regularly needed to refer. We now exchange cordial greetings and he orchestrates extremely efficient long-jump competitions where the children in question have the runway to themselves for each jump while the others wait quietly and then applaud.

Not so long ago, after a break in officiating in the discus at Tonbridge School, I fell into conversation with a man of about my age who was doing a great job raking the long-jump pit.

"You're Mike Fleet aren't you?"
"Yes, but you've got me at a disadvantage," I replied.
He introduced himself as a Highgate Harrier who had enjoyed watching my swashbuckling but not always successful tactics when I had raced way back in the White City days.
"Oh, you were a hero of mine," he said.
"It's a relief that I didn't disappoint," I proffered, and to reverse the embarrassing spotlight, asked *"What did you do?"*
"Cross-country running was my favourite."
"What do you rate as your best performance then?" I queried.
"Must have been the Southern when Frank Sando won, I made the top 100."
"Ah yes, at Aylesford Paper Mills on the 14th February 1959," I confirmed.
"Good God," he spluttered *"you're right... amazing!"*
"Must get back to my team" I excused myself quickly while the going was good before he asked more, which might have spoilt the effect.
I had celebrated part of my 21st birthday running for Croydon that grey winter's day, finishing way behind my pit-raking colleague!

Announcer

My chance to try out announcing came at the world-famous Motspur Park a few years before its then unannounced and subsequently sad closure. Someone was needed to help the well organised, well-informed Peter O'Brien, who also had the good fortune to be endowed with one of those classical broadcaster's voices and a great understanding of athletics.

Clearly I was seen as the ideal foil with the potential to bring a bit of hands-on experience as former athlete and practising coach to the scene. With no apologies I was known to be spontaneous, eccentric, well-informed and the possessor of a somewhat more earthy delivery.

Peter was very helpful and constructive, and I am indebted to him for making me aware of the athletics meeting as a whole. My present-day attention to the starter's needs, the high jumpers concentration and the inclusivity of athletes, officials and spectators has grown from those beginnings.

Pre-event preparation is essential to enable one to inform all concerned of qualifying conditions, athletes to watch out for, and records at risk. It is always my aim to provide regular, non intrusive delivery of results and points positions in order to engage everyone in the event.

The Surrey Schools Championships remain high on the Fleet announcing itinerary, as do the Achilles Relays at another historic venue, Iffley Road Oxford. There I annually make it my business not only to promote team spirit in athletics, but also to remind following generations of the unique moment on the old cinder track there on 6th May 1954 when Sir Roger Bannister, then just Roger, ran himself into the realms of legend to become the first man to run the mile in under four minutes. The magnificent trophies for that meeting convey a great deal of British athletics history too, bearing the names of athletes of yesteryear, all worthy of a place in a hall of fame.

Nowadays I have fun contributing I hope, to the atmosphere at the annual Lexus Croydon 10k Road Race and the Surrey County and Surrey Schools Cross Country Championships, plus numerous inter-schools events into the bargain too. Most recently, thanks to, kind invitation from Squadron Leader Jason Davenhill the RAF Championships secretary, none other than the upstart Davenhill who successfully wiped my Trinity School half-mile record from the books, I have had the pleasure of being "ex-SAC[24] Mike on the mike" at the RAF Championships at Cosford.

---

[24] Senior Aircraftman, my final rank during National Service days.

In 2010, Squadron Leader Jason Davenhill, holder of the Boys 400m hurdles record having been given the tip off that his Surrey Schools Senior 54.2sec of record, set in 1988, was at serious risk, came to Kingsmeadow for the Championships clearly to see fair play. Relieved that the key challenger did not materialise and the record remained unscathed, he then reverted to his role as the Royal Air Force Championships secretary, inviting me to announce at their Championships. I readily accepted, reluctantly agreeing with his proviso that I would not do simulated flypast imitations or even think about humming the Dam Busters March during the steeplechase!

The ensuing commissions at RAF Cosford, for announcing I must add, not officer status, since I happily remain SAC (National Service Rtd.), turned out to be extremely enjoyable. Helped by efficient station staff, my stumblings over in-house abbreviations were thankfully kept to a minimum, and the supply of results, event draws and other information were promptly and unobtrusively provided. An additional delight on my debut was the opportunity to announce a very rare event in another sport, namely a winning goal for England in the soccer World Cup in South Africa.

On the second occasion, the hosts got one up on their army and naval guests for the Inter Services Match by staging a loud low strafing of the stadium by a pair of resident German made Tutor aircraft. Clearly the intervention merited an announcement. "Army and Navy guests eat your hearts out" I crowed with a measure of bias, naturally having checked, as the rapidly departing pilots must have done, that no unsuspecting pole-vaulters were soaring skywards!

Not to be outdone, a Naval athlete appeared behind me, making loud ship's siren noises, to declare the impending arrival of HMS Ark Royal, soon to be followed by an important looking Army representative clearly not to be dealt with lightly who declared that, but for a significant diversion in Afghanistan, the place would have been surrounded.

I deemed it prudent to restore normality.
...RESULT, 1500m...1st...

It was also my great good fortune to be co-announcer at the last six of the famous London Athletic Club Schools' meetings, latterly held at the Copthall Stadium, Hendon. The venue was moved following the demolition of London's White City Stadium where, as an excited schoolboy in the 1950s, I had first experienced the thrill of competing in a major arena.

I enjoyed working as joint announcer during those years with former international high jumper Alan Dainton at the less impressive Copthall Stadium, but sadly the meeting has now disappeared from the athletics calendar.

I took pleasure in announcing the success of Jeffrey Archer's son, a promising middle-distance runner (before the "Flaming Ferraris" of City fame absorbed his attention) and of noting the rise of Southend High School as a force to be reckoned with in schools' athletics alongside the likes of Harrow and Millfield.

The long-time organiser Geoff Williams of Highgate School declared his intention to retire two years in advance but naïvely, head in the sand, no one believed him on the Independent Schools' Sports Committee and when he went, there was no heir-apparent to take on the mantle.

I still hold the lingering hope of resurrecting this historic meeting, which way back in 1956 gave my then embryonic athletics career such an important kick start.

As an announcer I have made it my mission to inform, entertain and sell athletics. I aim for inclusivity, acknowledging all aspects of the sport on show, and hope that as a result of my involvement there is a better understanding and fuller enjoyment of the occasion. The National Cross Country leaders may well be lapping the tail-enders 4K adrift with hardly a glance, but without the tortoises, clubs would frequently be unable to close in a team. Equally in track and field competition, without the big thrower drafted into the sprint relay at the last minute, a critical match-winning point can be lost. These people deserve credit, as do rain-soaked or frozen officials, as do those all too often "entombed" equipment officers under the stand, and the first-aiders who stand by to staunch blood from spike wounds, deal with anaphylactic shock caused by virulent flies from neighbouring lakes and ponds. Maybe the most important reason for this is to help meet the requirements of vexatious modern health and safety regulations, which if not fulfilled, prohibit competition from taking place.

Sometimes a flat meeting needs an injection of humour, so the unfortunate veteran faller rising like a python's head from a yellow coil of stadium hose, or the vaulters arriving like elongated cartoon dachshunds, can be highlighted to raise a timely laugh.

Opportunistically, too, I annually draw attention to the timekeepers' and judges' transhumance for the steeplechase during the Surrey Schools Championships at Kingston – which draws attention to their good works.

I was quite flattered when told of top field official Peter Crawshaw's comment about my contributions on air:

"Mike's announcing is like Marmite, you either love it or hate it, and I like it!"

Team Management

This is probably the most challenging of the roles I have had the pleasure of tackling. One is not only dealing with known athletes but also with unfamiliar individuals across all disciplines, who are deserving of equal care and attention.

I have always made it my mission to do my utmost for the athletes and to make them all feel important as part of a team. Awareness of each other is paramount.

The ability to empathise with both success and failure is not easy, for athletes in general are highly strung and can very quickly be affected by outside influences.
For the big English Schools' hope, who registered three no throws having shown winning form in the warm up, I was able to find a large enough statue behind which to allow the distressed athlete to let the tears flow and discover that the world really had not ended. His career in athletics, possibly having gained from the unfortunate experience, moved on to a really impressive level.

A more unusual case was the young athlete who stopped during 3K races, only to explain that he "wished to thank the man who cheered," or that he "wished to vomit". Both reasons doubtless seemed valid to him, but to me as team manager the points forfeited raised my blood pressure. I chose my moment carefully and each time emphasised the need to maintain pace during races and also advised against the consumption of Bath buns on the way to the start!

Different situations call for different solutions and concealing my feelings of frustration can present quite a challenge!

Today, persuading people, especially youngsters, to fill gaps for points at club level is surprisingly hard. In my day, I was willing to do anything within the bounds of safety in the cause of my team, but not so many contemporary athletes see it that way. It appears that they think a low-grade performance is demeaning rather than seeing it in the broader perspective of helping the team.

Keeping an eye open for the unexpected has also proved a challenge on more than one occasion, with the "Gateshead shorts incident" being truly memorable: Having advised all the Surrey Schools' athletes of the strict rules pertaining to the wearing of regulation shorts, I was appalled to see the potential senior boys 200m winner sporting eye-catching lycras which had clearly also attracted the attention of two blazer clad dowagers who were homing in on their unwitting target. Grabbing a traditional pair of ghastly golden shorts, I cast caution to the wind, cleared the barrier and made an ill prepared comeback to sprinting. I managed to beat the much younger dowagers by a short head and stunned them into surrounding the similarly non-plussed teenager while he donned the essential kit. Decency prevailed, honour was done and he went on to win the English Schools' title.

On another occasion, this time during a National Young Athletes Cup Final, I was concerned to see my nominated third-leg runner in the under 17 boy's 4x100m relay team standing beside the track, whilst an undeclared athlete was on the track in his position. Again with speed I thought I had lost, I risked my reputation grabbing the illegal boy off the track and pushing the other back in his rightful place. The selected team won and the right lad got his medal. The star of the team, who had recruited his friend into the squad, resigned from Croydon Harriers the following season and later left athletics under a cloud during the Barcelona Olympics.

Very recently I discovered two talented and clearly distressed girl athletes whom I knew from a rival team, spike-less in the mud of the National Schools Cross Country Championships at Manchester, with a few minutes remaining before their race. Rivals or not, I could not ignore such need, and advised them to run as they were should their missing team manager looking after their spikes not be found. Fortunately I got word to the announcer, whose urgent tones summoned the absentee official to hasten red-faced and breathing heavily to the start. One of the youngsters then stormed to a fine fourteenth in the field of three hundred plus, well ahead of any athlete in the Surrey team!

I am proud of my roles as assistant team manager for the AAA in one of their traditional representative matches; for the Surrey AA at Inter-Counties Championships; for the Surrey Schools' AA at many English Schools' AA Championships (I am also sprint relay coach for the Surrey team); and more recently with the South of England Team at the UK School Games. These have all been rewarding and enthralling, and compensate to some degree for my not having achieved National or Olympic management roles.

Meeting Promotion

The Croydon Harriers Open Field and Hurdles Meeting, predominantly my "baby", had its seeds sown thanks to the very popular Bracknell Open Relays meeting, which to my mind was at the time the best of its kind, but which clearly offered an end-of-season competitive opportunity for technical athletes. A quick courtesy call to Bracknell meeting boss, genial Canadian Dave McJannett, resulted in him giving our project his blessing, and the new event was born in September 1967 with the Crystal Palace National Recreation Centre Stadium as the magnetic venue.

From a modest beginning it grew in popularity and quality, attracting many top athletes during its 23 year existence. Highlights included Canadian John Beers' 1974 Commonwealth 2.22m high jump record and Bill Tancred's British All Comers Discus record 62.10m set in 1973.
On one notable occasion, at my request, the 1968 Olympic 400m hurdles champion and world record holder David Hemery sportingly acted as prize steward and celebrity presenter. The event was further enhanced when a distinctly impressive looking group of individuals appeared in the main stand, their spokesman querying:

"Say fellah, what gives with this meet?"
It having been clarified as an Open meeting, entry to which required a fee, the American Olympian, none other than Willie Davenport, responded with bemusement.

"Gee, back in the States you guys would be paying us! How many of your sterling pounds will it cost for us to compete?"
"How many of you are there?" I asked, playing for time.
"Seven or eight man" he offered.

Naïvely I suggested a then seemingly exorbitant sum of £50. Out came a wad of notes and too late I realised that I could have sought and received significantly more.

Davenport himself did not compete, but sportingly agreed to stay around as VIP prize steward alongside fellow hurdler Hemery, while more immediate worthies like another Olympian hurdler Mamie Rallins graced the occasion with very welcome competitive panache and dash.

The Croydon Harriers Open Field and Hurdles Meeting would have returned in 2010 in conjunction with the South London Athletics Network; not at the inspirational but neglected Crystal Palace where a prohibitive pricing policy more often than not leaves the stadium of memories like a concrete Marie Celeste; nor at Croydon where the "sacred" soccer pitch must not be sullied by sector markings after July. The hospitable Sutton Arena's gain would have been the other venues' loss, but unfortunately the track certification was not in place and cancellation was our only option – my first ever such experience.

It is my hope that the new event, featuring mixed age-group jumps and throws, will generate more interest and that presenting performers in order of achievement will prove more straightforward to handle for a worryingly ageing band of officials. The aim is for the event to establish new and secure roots for its future in the athletics calendar. The technical athletes deserve their annual field day!

Several other "one offs" have proved enjoyable challenges, more often than not being generated by short visits to our area by teams from abroad.

Australians, Dutch, Germans, Kenyans, New Zealanders and Swedes have provided the catalysts for many different and interesting competitions to be created around their talents at the Croydon Arena or at Crystal Palace. Certainly for across-the-board ability the Rift Valley Kenyans took some beating, but our European friends have always come with strong athletes, and I recall somehow managing to obtain a late AAA Championship entry for German sprinter Peter Weidl, from Rimbach. That kind of "magic" would only work nowadays, I imagine, for athletes like Usain Bolt!

...Oh and I must take this opportunity to remind wealthy New Zealander "Sugar Daddy" of North Shore Bays Club that he still owes me the deposit for a booking option which I took out on his behalf at Tooting Bec track many moons ago.

I had a much happier experience with a visiting team from the University of Petroleum and Minerals from Dahran in Saudi Arabia. Due doubtless to the integrity of their coach, former international triple jumper Derek Boosey, not only did they pay fully upfront for a match at Crystal Palace, but they also gave my club a generous donation and entertained me to dinner at an exclusive restaurant.

One still has fun thinking up different and interesting challenges to attract schoolchildren into athletics. Using recall from way down memory lane in the 1960s, I have also re-introduced Paarlauf as a training activity, and it has proved sufficiently popular for it to feature in my plans as a competitive option too.

I have successfully introduced inter-school concentric "All Run Together for Fun Challenge" cross-country races. In these, all ages start at the same time using the same start and finish, running round similarly configured loops, Russian Doll style, one inside another. There are three loops, one small, one medium and one large, so that all ages cover suitably commensurate distances.

The popular Croydon Harriers inter-schools "Catch as Catch Can Races" also see all ages running at the same time. The distances are adjusted for age by the addition of early added loop handicaps, while the youngest athletes go straight on to the main course. These variations on the yacht handicap[25] prove successful because they allow younger athletes to show their potential alongside their seniors. Another attraction for athletes, parents, supporters and officials alike is the compact nature of the event. Our aim is to come up with a team result of a "first come first served" nature, with all ages having a fair chance of finishing at the same time, so that it's quite possible for juniors to beat seniors.

"Boring athletics" needs refreshing injections of variety to enable it to compete with the attractions of the "major sports", and I hope that in my own small way I help to keep its head above the rising waters of other sports vying for talent by promoting meaningful and enjoyable events. Be on your guard, parents and supporters, as in the future you may find yourselves a participating prerequisite to validate your club team.

...we were left to further contemplate our relevance! We consoled

---

[25] Yacht handicaps allow runners to go off early according to age or ability.

ourselves with the thought that at least for the foreseeable future, athletes at lesser meetings all over the world would continue to rely on the manual timekeeper to provide their qualitative benchmarks.

However, times are changing rapidly. Not even manual sand-raking is sacrosanct as evidenced at the Beijing Olympics, with wonderful machines doing a better job, dare I say, even than the creator of the finest long-jump landing area I've ever seen. Being complimented on his precision, the perfectionist confided that, as custodian of the croquet lawns at Hurlingham Park, such work came as second nature.

With progress, if that is the right word, the promotion and presentation of athletics may yet become fully automated, but thankfully that will be way beyond the days of my useful involvement. To the huge and largely unsung band of officials I can only doff my dirty cricket hat and wonder at their commitment with thanks.

The well established Lexus Croydon 10k which continues to keep one busy as now spawned the Streets Ahead Croydon Half Marathon which is the comfortably shared promotion of the Croydon Harriers and the Striders of Croydon and will doubtless keep the author out of mischief each spring from now on.

See Figure 88 – Loud hailing. 2009 Lexus 10k Mike with his personal mike

Further aheld, in Somaliland the proposed Hargeisa 10k mooted by Yacin Yusuf, promises to provide not pastures new, but a warm and rewarding challenge.

Photographer

Little did I realise, all that time ago back in the sixties, as a delighted Athletics Weekly "Cover Boy" courtesy of ace athletics photographer Gerry Cranham, that some fifty years later, I would be an occasional photographic contributor to the bigger and better colour version of the legendary sheet-anchor for all serious enthusiasts in the sport. My action shots regularly feature in the local press and on school and club web-sites and notice-boards, generating interest in those featured, their teams and our sport.

*See Figure 90 – Mike and Gerry Cranham, "Maestro" photographer of the
1960s*

The mists of time leave no sharp image of the first action shot I captured on film, but I guess that it was of Otto, the family dachshund, who despite the limitation of his short legs could certainly out-run me when we were both young!

Graduating from my father's pre-World War II "Ensign Box" and often accidentally taking snaps of unsuspecting subjects when my trigger finger was hungrily tapping the shutter, I moved on to a smart Ensign Ful-Vue which recorded the 1953 Coronation procession for me as I held it, otherwise unseeing, above my head. It was with that trusty friend that I believe I took my first action shot of athletics. The historic action took place at the Paris University Club match in 1956 against the London Schools and is of an unknown, oblivious shot putter who remained in picture while the sprinting subjects of my interest had long since beaten the shutter action of my ageing camera and exited the frame!

The Ful-Vue camera remained first choice until my RAF days in Germany, when I invested in a superb little Voigtlander Vito B, some of the results from which appear in this book, albeit mostly taken for me by friends. I had inadvertently "smuggled" it back home from Germany forgetting that it was in my case. It was duly confiscated and held at Moorgate by Customs and Excise until I had raised the £5 which facilitated its return.

Ful-View sporting images had been more often than not blur-dominant, but when the Vito B replaced it, sharpness of the moving object became routine. On occasion, with luck, I even achieved the sought-after Cranham-like contrast of sharp speeding subject and blurred foot, hand or background.

In this way, the new camera faithfully recorded images of legendary runners Stan Eldon, George Knight and Frank Sando heading the 1959 Southern Cross Country Championships and Jim Railton, later to become National Rowing Coach, winning the UAU 100 yards in 9.9sec later the same year, and of course Gordon Pirie. It was still in worthy action in Sofia for the 1961 Universiade.

I developed my interest in photography with the Vito B until malfunction persuaded me to "go Russian" with a beefy, loud but trustworthy Zenit. A far smoother second-hand Yashika beckoned next, and with that, I had the very good fortune of an exclusive shot of the controversial "South African Brit.", Zola Budd winning a secretive 1500m in 4:10.0 at Norman Park, Bromley. Unfortunate Croydon Harrier Heather Fenton was recorded for posterity right across the Croydon Advertiser Group distribution 500m behind the South African. Sadly, business vision has never been one of my strengths and I did not perceive the potential crock of gold at the end of the rainbow in Fleet Street!

My most recent advances as a cameraman have been courtesy of a first class Canon EOS 350D and on to my "best yet" Canon EOS 450D which has helped me to raise £1,000+ in modest donations to Cardiac Risk in the Young (CRY). When Athletics Weekly uses any of my work, they contribute to this worthwhile cause; however, the best the cash-strapped local press can offer for my regular photographic input is the occasional credit. Whilst this is disappointing on a personal level, I'm pleased that they do print so many of my action shots, since I see this as publicity for Croydon Harriers, Trinity and Whitgift Schools where I am very fortunate to coach their athletes.

I will never cease to be amazed by the wonders of modern technology and how it has leapt forward in the photographic storage and transmission context. The simple procedure of attaching a JPEG of Martyn Rooney in action in Australia, China or Japan to a press report, in the knowledge that it would be on the screens of the Croydon sports editors within seconds, gives me a huge buzz of satisfaction every time and will continue to do so in the years ahead.

The only action shot of the secretive Zola Budd at Norman Park, Bromley, 1985. Did I miss a fortune here?

See Figure 90 – Mike and Gerry Cranham "Maestro" photographer of the 1960s

Spectating and supporting

My draconian dismissal as chief athletes' assembly steward, together with the team of Shirley High School boys and girls, after years of dedicated service at the big Crystal Palace meetings, was at the time a huge disappointment. This came about when it was falsely alleged by the meeting organiser that one of the young stewards had broken the strict rules by seeking the autographs of a star. In truth, the boy had personally been asked by Steve Cram to look after his wallet. Cram, in gratitude, signed his race number and gave it to the delighted lad. No explanation was accepted and we were summarily dismissed to be replaced in later meetings by police cadets.

See Figure 92 – Mike with Shirley High School Big Match Kit Stewards Crystal Palace

It was something of relief to be clear of a regime whose pressure could, at times, reflect the kind of "dictatorship" usually reserved for recruits being knocked into shape on a military parade ground. The silver lining was that I now found myself free to watch top class athletics regularly again. Away from strict time-tabling and not having to worry about television sight-lines or the threat of wayward javelins, one could absorb the skills and thrills from the stand, take photographs of the action and even encourage accompanying youngsters to go to the trackside and ask stars to sign their programmes! One could mostly also avoid the extremes of rain and sun which previously, as an official, had to be "taken on the chin" or more often than not down the neck!

I suffered most in my pocket as I became, once again, a member of the paying public. On one unforgettable occasion when undercover seats were not available, a deluge which I recall as a "Niagara" had to be endured by the sodden spectators, that is apart from cold water survival specialist Dr Martin Collis, my old school friend visiting from Canada, into whom I had literally "bumped" at the Montreal Olympics in 1976. Spaceman-like in his patented survival suit, he alone remained dry. The match was diluted into insignificance, but I will never forget that downpour which penetrated all protection I threw at it, before cascading down the terraces to soak the track.

In retirement, membership of the British Athletics Supporters Club has enabled the renewal of old friendships and given birth to new ones. I would never have expected to re-encounter David Gardener, the rugby fives star and President of the Loughborough Students Union in the late 1950s, as a devoted follower of athletics, nor with respect could I have imagined what other fascinating folk there were to be found cheering behind the Union Jacks which had been so proudly waved during my stewarding days.

And talking of "Jack", what an education it has been spending time with Jack Miller, one of British Athletics biggest fans in more ways than one. Hugely knowledgeable, eloquent and enthusiastic Jack, former Chairman of the British Supporters is a key contributor to the UKA with the Athletics Hall of Fame, and together with luminaries like Stan Greenberg, Peter Lovesey, Peter Radford, Mel Watman and Peter Matthews has been instrumental in the establishment of the National Union of Track Statisticians Library and Archive at the Cobham Hall School near Gravesend in Kent. It has been my pleasure to contribute to the enterprise alongside these athletic legends, and what good fortune it was for me to collect volumes donated by 1956 Melbourne Olympic silver medallist John Disley, not only to meet his Olympian wife Sylvia, née Cheeseman, but then to notice that several of the books loaded into my car bore the inscription:

Christopher Brasher

his copy

The Navigator's House
River Lane
Richmond
Surrey

Here was the legacy, together with other volumes, of the 1956 Melbourne Olympic Games steeplechase champion and prime mover behind the establishment of the London marathon to the archive.

Whether viewed from the towering heights of the Stade de France, the hardly evident ones of the City of Manchester Stadium or from outside the fence at the track on Tooting Bec Common, the fascinating variety which is our sport always entertains.

On trips abroad it has been intriguing to observe Jack using his contacts and experience to gain access to places to which no other mortal would contemplate, thereby obtaining documents and publications normally only reserved for the ranks of the press. Jack and his kind can be expected to attend most major international events, enjoying the action cheek by jowl with proud parents at lower age group championships, while on other occasions every fourth year watching intently when Olympians strive for the ultimate athletic glory, a gold medal. I have been lucky enough in recent years to benefit from his company, expertise and friendship.

Not proud, he even sportingly joined me for an auction at Stevenage Town Football Club to witness the sale of most of my boyhood collection of soccer programmes, highlighted by twenty "Tasty, well sought after West Hams" which subsequently sold for an amazing £950. Unfortunately we were not available to attend the second sale at which an even bigger surprise was in store. This was revealed when eighty "Interesting non-league Whitstables", with a reserve of £80, sold almost unbelievably for £1,200! These were the highlights from the sale of some five hundred programmes carefully collected in my early teens, and provided the funding for the publication of this book.

The common ground interest shared by the British Athletics Supporters brings together an amazingly diverse group of individuals, who must surely be the most knowledgeable and well behaved fans to be found at any track and field meeting.

Among them I have encountered:

- Sports minded philanthropist Barry Wells who supported Katerina Thompson on a trip to the 2010 European Championships in Barcelona for experience;

- former top athletes like ace walker Bob Dobson turned travel guru; former Comrades Marathon and London to Brighton aficionado Don Turner; and Tom Richards Junior, whose father finished second in the

1948 London Olympic marathon;

- highly experienced officials like Janet Bensley, Jeanne Coker, and Mike and Sandy Forrest;

- regular family supporters like the Maceys from Canvey Island; the Rooneys from South London, but with deep Irish roots; the Shakes-Draytons from East London; the Simpsons from Cornwall; the Tobins from the Isle of Wight; and Sheila Parsons – who travel to enjoy events featuring their sons and daughters.

Such is the fascinating human tapestry which makes up our great British athletics family.

Not for this cosmopolitan group is the thoughtless, seemingly non-stop flag-waving of the fanatical Finns, nor the bucolic behaviour of some Swedes, and certainly not the all too often extreme "let your hair down" antics from the followers of other nations notching gold. They simply exude strong knowledgeable support for, and recognition of, any top class performance, with a bit of extra gusto reserved for our somewhat sombre National Anthem. Even a proud rendition of "God Save the Queen" sadly pales behind my out-and-out favourite, the thrice re-written Russian rival; the zest of "The Marseillaise"; the regal tones of "Deutschland, Deutschland Uber Alles"; and dare I even add, the emotion conveyed by Uncle Sam's "Stars and Stripes Forever"! I say bring on "Land of Hope and Glory" suitably updated for a triumphant London 2012.

Looking back, I still chuckle at the man who expected the marathon to take place round the track and who wondered aloud where the runners were going as they exited the stadium after the opening lap.

I remain amazed at the Japanese fellow who slept through the session which included the finals of the men's 1500m and the relays in Montreal, and I am still incredulous at the up-market couple who were bored by a morning of predominantly multi-event action in Munich and who left to go to watch the sailing near Hamburg some 380 miles distant, and I continue to wonder about the wealth and wisdom of the family whom I know to have at least twice been accompanied to major meetings by a young girl, who appears never to have watched any of the action, preferring to play computer games, and of course eating and drinking!

International spectating is highly sociable and to be thoroughly recommended, as Nicola and I have found to our delight on many an exciting tour to distant and not so distant lands during the past 20 years. Such travel not only opens a wider window on athletics, but also opens doors to unusual tourist opportunities; furthermore it provides great scope for informal people-watching.

See Figure 93 – Mike, Nicola and a Beijing volunteer with the "Bird's Nest" Stadium behind

13

Thanks to Athletics...

Throughout my sporting life, I have, thanks in particular to athletics, encountered a wealth of uplifting experiences and encounters, certainly none of which I would have missed. Our global sport offers so many opportunities. Here are some of mine and I urge every reader to seek his or hers.

...I flew: in a Vickers Viking, formerly of the Queen's flight, hair-raisingly over the Alps to Bulgaria; in that pioneer of the jet passenger age, a de Havilland Comet to attend the Independence Ceremony of Uganda; a creaking Tupolev 124 within the air space of the then Iron Curtained USSR; an Ilyushin 18 from Budapest to London, and experienced the spectacular rarity of a jumbo jet hop from Vancouver Island to Vancouver City en route for England for fuelling up after watching the 1994 Commonwealth Games in Victoria.

...I have had the opportunity to pay my respects: at the astonishing Airborne Cemetery in Arnhem; at the Munich Olympic Stadium memorial to the Israelis who were killed by terrorists at the 1972 Games and at the epicentre of the Hiroshima atom bomb blast.

No impressionable eighteen year old could fail to have been moved as I was when visiting the Oosterbeek Airborne Cemetery as part of a Croydon-Arnhem link athletics exchange in 1956. The ranks of 1,754 neat headstones, each commemorating the life of a serviceman of similar age who died in just eight months in 1945, were seemingly endless. It was humbling as one who had survived World War II in childhood to win my first "international" 800m within yards of where so many young men of my age had fallen in the cause of our freedom.

...I chose and have never regretted taking the opportunity to take time off from the 2007 Osaka World Championships and travel by bullet train to Hiroshima. No normal person could fail to be shocked at being reminded of the appalling devastation and loss of life wrought by the A bomb in seconds and by the head in sand intransigence of the Japanese whose concurrent clearance of inflammable wooden buildings by schoolchildren, students and women hugely added to the loss of life.

On August 6th 1945 the detonation of the 9,700lb "Little Boy" uranium bomb killed some 70,000 people on the day, with some 70,000 others suffering lingering deaths. A little boy riding his tricycle was, instantly, turned to cinder. His distorted machine remains as a poignant memorial to him and to so many other innocent children whose lives were terminated in a flash.

See Figure 99 – The poignant Hiroshima Atom Bomb Memorial

One could not start to imagine the searing heat which struck down so many desperately unfortunate souls more than fifty years before. The 20º+ temperature generated by the sun on the day of my visit simply paled into insignificance.

Stunning too, but in a totally different natural and awesome context, were the Niagara Falls which I visited over thirty years earlier after the Montreal Olympics. The sheer spectacle of thousands of tons tumbling thunderous water; the constantly contorting cloud of spume and the seemingly minute tourist ship "Maid of the Mists" sailing enthralled tourists into the watery whirlpool were almost too much to take in.

There was a flicker of awareness as I recognised the striking white track-suited young woman, who emerged unobtrusively from the haze of sparkling spray, rising from the roaring watery tumult nearby.

"That's Annegret Richter" I almost thought aloud.

"Ja, it is she" her proud chaperone confirmed, as they passed.

Clearly a kindred spirit in the context of making the most of ones sporting travels, the star was capitalising on the opportunity, as I would advise athlete abroad to do in the future

A few days earlier the German star had been on the rostrum 371 miles away receiving her 100m gold medal having won in 11.08sec, following a brilliant 11.01sec world record in the semi final.

See Figure 100 – The awesome Niagara Falls, one of the Wonders of the World

Similarly no-one could have been nothing but stunned by the major terrorist attack launched in the Munich Olympic village in the autumn of

1972 when the sinister Black September Group took a group of Israeli sportsmen hostage. The Olympic movement had been caught off guard. It all began on the morning of my departure, and at the time I was totally unaware of such sinister developments until I called on some of my German friends to say "Auf weidersehn". I was surprised when they said I was lucky to be leaving the buzzing Bavarian capital! Further explanation left me relieved to have used up my ticket allocation. They told me that big trouble was brewing back at the Games Village. They spoke of terrorists and gunfire, so I did not delay my drive, and headed promptly north out of the city, listening to my radio to the sensationally unravelling events and noticing considerable helicopter activity. The unravelling mayhem gradually became clearer, and as the miles increased between Munich and me, so too did my sense of relief.

Later I was shocked and saddened to learn of the death of Amitzur Shapira, the athletics coach whom I had met at a Loughborough Summer School, and with whom I hoped to arrange a Croydon Tel Aviv exchange. With so much violence in the world one becomes partially anaesthetised, but I will never forget my desperately unlucky friend, the only member of the Israeli team whom I knew personally, nor the shock of learning that he was no more.

These were the most significant experiences which athletics brought to me, emphasising the value of life and the value of life in a peaceful world; happily my interest in athletics also provided a wealth of events, both serious but none the less significant and humorous, which I would not have missed for worlds.

See Figure 94 – Amitzur Shapira

...I played football against the late great former England football manager Sir Bobby Robson, learning a few subtle tricks from him like shouting loud and closely in an opponent's ear when challenging for a high ball. Sadly such tricks were encountered too late to enhance any pretence I might have had of becoming an exponent of the great game.

See Figure 95 – International Athletes Club charity football team and All Star XI. Bobby Robson back row centre, Mike back row second from end R

...I have swum: in the Indian Ocean alert for the great white sharks; the Eastern and Western Pacific Oceans; in the Bass Strait and in an upstairs pool of a Beijing hotel. In the latter, signs decreed "No Smoke, No Run, No Frolic and No Photo!" I am the proud possessor of a photo taken of me by the young son of a Russian tourist to prove it. I must add thanks to the sporting Chinese lady in charge who had kindly given her consent!

...I had the honour of broadcasting with the legendary Harold Abrahams, and while I can confirm I appeared on the programme "What makes an Athlete", the great man predominantly held forth while I was mainly restricted to nodding in approval of his expressed wisdom and therefore not appreciated nationwide for my contribution!

...I distributed (thanks to one-time British Universities team mate John Holt, then International Amateur Athletics Federation General Secretary) agendas and cups of tea to the bemused British delegates at the IAAF congress during the Montreal Olympic Games, eliciting quizzical glances from Sir Arthur Gold and Marea Hartman with the former unable to contain his curiosity asking with emphasised stammer:
"Mmmike wwwhat a surprise ttto find you here, wwwhaat are you dddoing here?"
"Good to see you Arthur, I am the official IAAF tea boy, one sugar or two?" I responded smugly.

...I experienced the exhilaration of running round the brilliantly lit Lloyd Park in Croydon one winter at midnight with an awestruck group of athletes. The full moon and accompanying thick blanket of fresh snow created the catalyst for this one-off experience.

...I trained with hurdles hero David Hemery and his Croydon Harrier colleague Alan Carr-Locke in Richmond Park. We enjoyed a hill repetition session a few weeks before Hemery's 1968 Olympic 400m hurdles triumph. I participated, albeit at considerably lower intensity. The experience reassured me that my pre-Perth sand dune session wasn't too far off the mark after all.

...I confidently told Jeffrey Archer, author and ex-athlete, that we most definitely had not been in the same Great Britain team together. He made the claim before, as announcer at the Achilles Schools Relays Meeting, I introduced him as the Honorary Meeting Referee.

"What does the role entail?" he asked.

I explained that the honour required the incumbent to acknowledge the successful, sympathise with the less successful, arbitrate in disputes and finally make the presentations.

"Oh I can handle that," he stated confidently and strode out purposefully onto the grass beside the home straight where he dutifully stood for a long while.

At one point my very good friend and latter day running partner Chris Scott, who was there to watch his son Anthony run, came to me in the Iffley Road track announcer's box:

"That poor chap Archer looks pretty lost out there. Do you think he'd like a cup of tea?"

I agreed and, by the look on his face, Jeffrey then had the possibly novel for him, experience of imbibing the national beverage in public from a polystyrene cup!

...I once light-heartedly chided Lord Coe for obliterating my 1:48.7 UK age 30 best 800m mark, of which he coolly claimed to be totally unaware!

...I have enjoyed the honour of dining at the House of Commons, courtesy of Speaker Lord Bernard Weatherill, and more personally of sharing a lift with him and Lady Weatherill from ground floor to banqueting hall en route to a Croydon Harriers dinner.

See Figure 96 – Mike with Lord Weatherill, Mary Berkeley and Don Faircloth at "The Speakers House"

...I much more recently and nervously shared a very small lift in Portugal with the huge former World and Olympic discus champion Lars Riedel (110-115kg, or in our language 242-253lbs!), his almost as huge coach and another very large German thrower. It says much for the overworked lift that it kept going throughout the week we were there together!

...I have sadly, and even more nervously than facing any athletics starter, experienced the front line of British justice at the Old Bailey, when appearing as a witness before the Recorder of London in a rape case.
"Mr Fleet, study the site plan before you, and tell the court how long in your expert opinion it would have taken the accused to walk from the scene of the alleged crime, from behind the female changing room door to where you say you were coaching him at 7.30pm?"

"I don't know whether he walked, my Lord."
"You are to answer the question"…
Not a good experience, but with the charge proved, justice was done and the accused sentenced.

…I have met so many fascinating characters from whom two stand out. First, Dave "The Running Dustman" Smith who escaped his mocking colleagues for running at work, by becoming a dedicated Croydon Harrier, "I like running with no shoes on through all the people in the Whitgift Shopping Centre," he would announce cheekily. One can only speculate at the effect that Dave's teak-like limbs and determined tooth baring grin had on the little old ladies and pram pushers in central Croydon.

…and then break-dancing "Big Eric" Campbell, my gardening adviser, seven-minute miler, sprinter, hurdler and steeplechaser.
"Was that a new BP[26]?" is often Eric's question to the timekeepers. Although an unusual but readily understood intrusion for Croydon-aware timekeepers, they prefer this to athletes who constantly cross the line taking their own times.
"Got your runner beans in yet, Mike?" he helpfully asks each year just at the right time.
After all his competitions the likeable fellow states questioningly:
"I done all right, didn't I?" followed up by, *"How did you like my race?"*

…I learned from old Herne Hill Harrier Edgar Lloyd's informal history lessons, while giving him lifts, about the Old Surrey Iron Railway from Merstham to Croydon, Croydon Central Railway Station and the Croydon canal from the Thames to the West Croydon Docks. Yes, there is still evidence to be seen, and without the welcome chattering of that near ninety year old, I would have been none the wiser, nor would my all-suffering wife and probably hundreds of Croydon Harriers over the ensuing years, as I give similar travelogues when driving around the borough.

…I had the good fortune to serve as Chief Assembly Steward at Crystal Palace over many years, dealing with, and hopefully helping hundreds of high class athletes, ranging from the aspiring to golden Olympians en route from warm up to the cauldron of competition. That role gave me a rare insight into all sides of the sport. During that time I had the chance, tongue in cheek, to appear unaware of the identity of the impressive and readily recognisable American athlete who queried.

---

[26] Eric always reverses the letters; he might be better understood in Germany!

"Say mister, when's the broad jump?"
"Who are you?"
"Lewis!" he exclaimed incredulously.
I made out as if to check the call list. Carl Lewis stood by bemused.
"C. Lewis USA?" Everyone burst out laughing.
"Call time 2.15pm, and please remember your number Mr Lewis, and the best of luck. You did mean long jump, didn't you?"

...I was rebuffed by the dour Russian coach whom I stopped entering the Crystal Palace arena, before trying to appease him by offering a jelly baby. Was he serious, or was he winding me up when he strongly rejected the peace offering. *"No, no, drugs,"* he grunted in rich Russian/English. Maybe it was because it was black and not red! British officials were most definitely not stopped smilingly all those years before in Volgograd with the offer of Chuk Chuk to sweeten them up!

...I witnessed a large wad of sterling notes therapeutically waved under the nose of a snuffling female Olympian who claimed to be too ill to run in a major meeting. The "prescription" effected the most astonishing, seemingly magical cure for the flu suffered by the conniving big name competitor, who then strode off purposefully to race and "surprisingly" win.

...I was told of the large world-class athlete who took the pair of size five and a half Adidas long jumping spikes intended for a female athlete whom I was helping to train for the Commonwealth Games. An enquiry was held subsequently at the British Board headquarters where I was greeted by the smiling miscreant and his girlfriend before being ushered in front of the sport's bosses to give my side of the story. After presenting my case I was quietly informed, *"Sorry Mike, we hear what you say, but we need athlete "X" to compete in the Olympics in a couple of months' time!"*

See Figure 84 – Who forgot his vest? Henry Rono, "The Croydon Harrier!"

...I had the opportunity to lead many people to believe I had recruited the great Henry Rono as a member of my club after I had "conjured up" a Croydon Harriers vest for the Kenyan, otherwise deficient just before his 5000m. I remain ever grateful to a then very young Noel Moyston for loaning his vest in return for the promise of it being signed afterwards by the great athlete….. well away of course from the warm up area. I never saw that famous item again, although a colour photo of it in international action appeared on the cover of Runners World magazine. I can only assume that it is now a treasured family heirloom. What a club record we would have had if such a signing had really taken place, not that Australian David Chettle's 13:46.9 is anything other than high class!

...I was introduced to a somewhat non-plussed Lord Mayor of Birmingham at the Alexander Stadium as "the Surrey man in charge of girls' knickers," by highly respected official, Jill Wright, the mischievous President of the English Schools' Athletics Association. In these days of CRB checks and much more, this has to be explained. The boring truth was that I had been delegated the responsibility by less thick-skinned Surrey School's management colleagues, to run the gauntlet of the daunting Jill. My duty was to gain clearance for Surrey girls unable to fit into team kit, to wear non-regulation but otherwise decent shorts in which to compete!

...I have deputised for Dame Mary Peters, the 1972 Olympic Pentathlon gold medallist on a question and answer panel at the National Union of Track Statisticians 50th anniversary. I felt a mere mortal among legends John Disley CBE, 1956 Olympic silver medallist, and co-London Marathon Founder and former world 200m record holder Professor Peter Radford. This provided me with the unique opportunity to congratulate John on heading me in the 1958 half mile rankings by a tenth of a second.
"Now I didn't know that," he whispered, *"I was never a NUT!"*
I further admitted that at my sprinting best I would have finished fifteen or more yards behind the "Peter the Whippet" in any head to head 200m race!

...I have happily become an accredited British Athletics Supporter via some fascinating Centresport Tours trips led by the likeable "Tall Thin Man" Graham Botley, counted as a friend despite his allegiance to Blackheath Harriers. Great bonuses have been making the acquaintance of the hugely knowledgeable and enthusiastic "Big" Jack Miller, and re-encountering athletics and student-day friends Eric Thompson, formerly a Surrey AC rival, and David Gardener, one time superstar of the Rugby Fives World and Chairman of the Grove Hall of residence at Loughborough, which we shared with among others, Mike Ellis, one of Britain's greatest hammer throwers.

...I have developed the highly rewarding hobby of athletics photography, thanks to inspiration from star sports cameramen Gerry Cranham and the late Ed Lacey. I have also greatly benefited from studying their outstanding work and that of current top athletics photographer and Croydon Harriers Vice President Mark Shearman. Mark, like all too many of my running rivals, is more often than not a step ahead of me, thus providing the opportunity to learn from the master.

Thanks too to their skills and advice, many of my efforts on film have been expertly reproduced to proudly appear in this book alongside their contributions.

...I have similarly developed my enthusiasm for press reporting, again albeit at local level in the wake of top men like the late James Coote of the Daily Telegraph, John Rodda of the Guardian and Neil Allen of The Times, whose graphic accounts still embellish my archive. It is to John though to whom I forever owe a debt of gratitude for referring to me as *"The Barrel-chested Fleet"*. I have always liked that! Once, way after my competitive days I had the pleasure of meeting Neil again, in the unlikely environment of the Henley Regatta. There, thanks to an invitation from my rowing friend Bernie Regan, my wife and I were enjoying the world famous event. I was being kindly escorted through the famous Stewards Enclosure by Aileen Regan when Neil came into view.

"*Mike Fleet,*" he exclaimed enthusiastically, as he connected me with my faded 1962 Commonwealth Games blazer, taken out of retirement for the day...

...*"and what a pleasure it is to meet your lovely wife,"* he continued effusively to Aileen, at something akin to half-miling pace – that is if one can compare the speed of speech with the recalled speed of running! He gave me not the slightest chance of introduction to put him right. When at last I managed to intervene and explain, Neil continued the conversation unabashed, proudly proving that there is life well after sixty by showing us a photograph of his recently born little boy.

...I had the good fortune to meet the endearing veteran Sikh, multi-event athlete Jahlman Singh, who fell at least three times in the hurdles in the National Veterans' Championships at Sheffield in 2002, on each occasion compounding the fractured arm sustained in the first tumble.

I can still clearly recall the incident.

"*Stay where you are,*" I shouted "*you've broken your arm!*"
"*Oh dear me I think I've broken it,*" he cried with a rich Indian accent, scrambling to his feet and trailing an S shaped arm, stating, "*I must finish*".

The same happened at the next two hurdles before even this Spartan masochist was persuaded that discretion was the better part of valour and called it a day.

I would love to have someone like Jahlman Singh to inspire my athletes with his courage, determination and experience, but perhaps not by demonstrating his technique!

...I have been privileged to meet two very different national war heroes from different eras. The first sadly, an almost unsung civilian from the mysterious code breaking days of World War II at Bletchley Park, and the second a widely acclaimed young soldier relatively fresh from heroic action during the recent Anglo American campaign in Iraq.

Tenuous though it may seem, had my wife not been Nicola, the athlete, I would never have met her uncle, the fascinating Shaun Wylie, a Wellington College schoolmaster in 1940, who later become an eminent academic, and had been one of the elite group of cryptanalysts who broke the German Enigma cipher at Bletchley Park. I will always remember the gaunt, top-hatted elderly gentleman going up to the Chivers' coach, more commonly used for Croydon Harriers trips, but on 19th October 1991 provided free for our wedding day transport, and exclaiming,
"*My oh my, a charabanc don't you know, I haven't happened upon one of those since before the War.*"

"*I'll have you know, sir, this is a luxury coach,*" retorted the indignant driver Alan, with the importance of one wearing a tie specially for the occasion.

Shaun was a delight to talk to and modest in the extreme. I only wish I could have learned something at first hand of his vital wartime work with the great Alan Turing in Hut 8 at Bletchley Park or even of his experiences as a Scottish hockey international, but opportunities were few and far between and as far as I was concerned and many others too, he kept such things close to his chest.

The other hero was a VC whom I met one day, as one does, at the Croydon Lexus Car Sales Centre when discussing the company's sponsorship of the Croydon Charity 10K Road Race.

"*Spare me a few minutes, we're just discussing a sale with that young military man over there*" said my valued contact, the After Sales Manager, adding, "*He holds the Victoria Cross.*"

"*Who is he?*" I enquired.

"*Mr Behari,*" I heard him say, which immediately rang a bell.

"*We used to have a good athlete of that name in our club,*" I replied, "*may I just check if he is one and the same?*"

Having been given the go ahead I introduced myself as the Croydon Harriers senior coach and asked the uniformed fellow if he had ever been a member of our Club.

"*Sadly not,*" he replied, asking "*How did your athlete spell his name?*"

"*Behari, John Behari.*"

"*Certainly not me, I am Johnson B-E-H-A-R-R-Y, but from the same roots in India. My group of the family immigrated to Grenada from India.*"

"*What made you think of buying one of these fine Lexus vehicles?*" I asked by way of damage limitation for my intervention.

"*Most black people buy BMWs and I want to be different!*" flew back the response from the smiling Beharry.

I later learned of the extraordinary selfless heroics of this astonishing young soldier four years earlier while under fire in Iraq.

With the benefit of hindsight and the knowledge of the £1 million deal for his autobiography, "The Barefoot Soldier", I should perhaps have asked, "*Why are you not buying a Lamborghini?*"

...I had the opportunity to try wheelchair racing, to my cost, against disabled boys at the Thomas de la Rue School near Tonbridge. It saw me humiliated, sporting bloodied knuckles and blistered hands, and gave me a new-found respect for these athletes. David Weir, Croydon's and one of the world's best, graduated from unnerving little old ladies including my mother when, as a lad he raced his wheelchair around our local Roundshaw shopping precinct in his wheelchair. This successful Paralympian still owes Mrs Fleet Senior a visit to apologise for his youthful exuberance, and to sign his autograph for her!

...I have encountered numerous tempting and not so tempting culinary delights all over the world, starting with a wonderful ten course meal for 10/- at the Lake Victoria Hotel in Uganda in 1961. Since then the curd cheese and rough bread of Bulgaria has been followed by many a welcome "nosebag" world wide.

For visitors to Lithuania I can thoroughly recommend many of their, to us unusual and mouth watering dishes like "Anykstenu Gaspadoriaus Sonines Kepsnys" otherwise "Anyksciai Town Masters Flank Roast" or "Anukeles

Blyneliai Su Bananais Ir Obuolais, Trintu Uogu Padazu" being clearly one serving, "Grandaughter's Pancakes with Banana and Apples and Mashed Berry Sauce". My favourite dish, by name at least, was "Gimnaztiko Vistienos Troskynis", "Gymnasium Boys Chicken Meat Stew".

"*Is it,*" I asked "*delicate chicken-like meat carved from young male gymnasts or more likely a meal in the style of that served for the benefit of young gymnasts in training?*"

During the Beijing Olympics, I was not persuaded to try Bull's Penis Balls in gravy, for I was feeling justifiably uncertain about the type of gravy they might have used, but the Hot Chilli Bull Frog Casserole offered a more readily identifiable delicacy, although I do concede that it might have been cunningly concealed toad! If you have the luck like I have to savour food universally, I thoroughly recommend going for the more unusual, for more often than not it will prove to be memorable in one way or another. The choice is yours.

See Figure 93 – Mike, Nicola and a Beijing volunteer

...I have even been asked if I am still alive while visiting the wonderful V&A Olympic poster exhibition in Sutton. I overheard a chap pestering a librarian about a particular poster. No wonder she was having trouble: he was confused between 1896 and 1904. The gentleman in question turned out to have been a runner in my hey-day in Surrey, who had suffered many a hasty opening lap of mine.

"*Did you know that fellow Fleet?*" he asked.
"*Bit of an oddball,*" I responded.
"*Is he still alive do you know?*"
"*Shouldn't think so, probably ran himself out long since,*" said I, straight-faced.

At that point, Nicola, my wife, unable to stand it any more, intervened. One time Bank of England athlete John Gibbins, a former Bank of England athlete, shook hands and we exchanged email addresses.

...and above all, thanks to athletics, I met Nicola, my wife, for she it was who (as Nicola Murray) was that eye-catching young Woking Athletic Club sprinter whom I noted way back in the 60s, with her trade-mark mini velvet cushion to protect her knee from the deleterious effects of track ash.

The retro-clad Nicola returned to competition in the early 90s and her immediate success caused consternation among many of her lycra-adorned rivals. Unluckily, she sustained an injury which cut short a veteran career that promised much.

Subsequently, she took up officiating and reached National level as a timekeeper (which really keeps me on my toes!) enabling us to work together and enjoy the ensuing banter. She now officiates at all levels in several disciplines and acts as referee for our annual Lexus Croydon 10K. I would like to think the balance we achieve between humour and efficiency enhances the officiating experience.

Doubtless many a reader, can out-do some of these instances but I defy anyone to muster a more fulfilling experience than mine. Feel free to try!

14

A Glance or Two Over My Shoulder

Never having succumbed to such a physical temptation during my competitive days, I crave my readers' indulgence to glance back now.

Regrets beyond the unfulfilled Olympic ambition, yes indeed!

Not to have beaten the long-haired youth who headed me and others at Liverpool in 1975. It was the only 800m in which I competed against Steve Ovett, then aged 19, who won in 1:52.3.! I was 37 at the time and finished 5th in 1:54.2, noting in my records that I had the new experience of running the first bend in lanes.

I would love to be able to say that I had run against those Great British track legends Roger Bannister and Seb Coe but I was the filling in the golden sandwich between their historic careers.

I regret that I never ran a marathon. The madman in me says that I would have relished a run in the great London event, just once of course, ideally in 2:59:99! I am not at all sure that he's right. The few 20 mile training runs I tried were really rather more than tough! The extra 6 miles 385 yards would probably have had me climbing an overhang, let alone a wall!

...and I will always wonder if, had I been blessed with some of today's experience way back in the late 1960s, I might even have achieved my Olympic dream. Hindsight remains an eternal frustration.

So how do I see my almost life-long involvement in the great sport of athletics? It has all certainly been an extraordinarily worthwhile journey, both for the wealth of wonderful experiences it has provided and for the great number of long-lasting friendships made along the way.

My advice to anyone who is "Also Running", is to make sure that you really enjoy your athletics to the full. It is a truly wonderful sport with challenges for everyone. You should justify each challenge as a test, from which to gain experience. Individually we learn young, find expression and mature – fulfilment will normally follow.

There is of course a double-edged legacy. For me it is to be found in my stiff joints, sore knees and scars, but the experiences encountered while running along my "Memory Lane" remain richly rewarding. They almost anaesthetise the pain and leave me more than happy that I ALSO RAN.

Appendix A

880yd/800m Personal Best Progression

See Figure 101 – UK 800m Number Ones 48 years and 4 seconds plus apart. Mike with Michael Rimmer 2010. Nicola Fleet photo.

This table shows my progression from schoolboy to international status

Note: All race times are as run.
To compare 800m times (denoted by 'm') with 880yd times, 0.7sec should be added.
ht = heat, sf = semi-final

Time	Pos	Event	Venue	Date
2:44.9	2	Whitgift Middle School Sports	North End, Croydon	15/3/50
2:20.5	1	Whitgift Middle School Sports	North End, Croydon	—/–/53
2:18.2	1	Whitgift Middle School Match	North End, Croydon	—/–/53
2:16.2	1	Whitgift Middle School Match	North End, Croydon	—/–/53
2:16.7	1	Whitgift Middle v Shooters Hill	Shooters Hill	—/6/54
2:14.0	1	Whitgift Middle School Match	North End, Croydon	—/–/54
2:08.5	1	Whitgift Middle School Standards	North End, Croydon	15/3/55
2:05.0	1	Whitgift Middle School Sports	North End, Croydon	23/3/55
2:04.7	1	Time Trial	North End, Croydon	19/4/55
2:01.2	2	Whitgift Middle School v Selhurst	North End, Croydon	09/5/55
2:00.8	2 ht	London Athletic Club Meeting	White City, London	20/4/55

Time	Pos	Event	Venue	Date
1:59.6	1	Whitgift Middle School v Colfes	North End, Croydon	31/5/56
1:58.5	1	Surrey Schools Championships	Motspur Park	30/6/56
1:54.8	5	Inter City Match	Croydon Arena	28/7/56
1:53.6m	3	Croydon & Commonwealth v England	Croydon Arena	15/8/56
1:54.0	4 ht	Inter Counties Championships	White City, London	16/5/59
1:52.2	3	Surrey Championships	Motspur Park	30/5/59
1:50.8m	5	Invitation International	White City, London	04/6/60
1:50.9	4	Southern Championships	Motspur Park	25/6/60
1:50.0	3	Southern Championships	Motspur Park	25/6/61
1:49.9	3	London v Rhineland Cities	White City, London	28/6/61
1:48.9	1	Inter Club Brighton v Croydon	Withdean Stadium	01/9/62

*Mike's best time replicated on watch which was used
when he ran 880yds at Brighton 1:48.9 in 1962*

Appendix B

My Top Hundred
880yd/800m Times

Note: All race times are as run.
To compare 800m times (denoted by 'm') with 880yd times, 0.7sec should be added.
ht = heat, sf = semi-final

Time	Pos	Event	Venue	Date
1:48.9	1	Inter Club, Brighton v Croydon	Withdean Stadium	1/9/62
1:48.7m	1	Great Britain v Sweden	White City, London	14/9/63
1:48.9m	6	International Invitation	White City, London	3/8/68
1:49.7	2	Surrey Championships	Motspur Park	30/5/64
1:49.1m	1	Great Britain v Russia	Central Stadium, Volgograd	28/9/63
1:49.2m	2	Great Britain v Hungary	Nep Stadium, Budapest	2/10/63
1:50.0	3	Southern Championships	Motspur Park	25/6/61
1:49.95	5	Commonwealth Games	Perry Lakes Stadium, Perth	26/11/62
1:50.0	3	Inter Counties Championships	White City, London	18/5/64
1:49.3m	4	International Invitation	White City, London	7/8/61
1:50.1	1	Brockman Trophy	Wimbledon Park	20/7/63
1:50.2	2	BUSF v AAA v Combined Services	Gosling Stadium, Welwyn	8/9/61
1:50.2	1	Fulham Borough Meeting	Hurlingham Park	22/9/62

Time	Pos	Event	Venue	Date
1:49.5m	2 sf	World Student Games	Vassil Levsky Stadium, Sofia	1/9/61
1:49.6m	2	International Kanguro Meeting	Vallehermoso, Madrid	7/6/64
1:50.4	4	AAA Championships Heat	White City, London	13/7/62
1:50.5	4	Welsh Games	Maindy Stadium, Cardiff	23/7/64
1:50.5	2	Surrey Championships	Motspur Park	25/5/63
1:50.6	1	Inter Club Match	Tooting Bec	15/8/62
1:50.7	3	Inter Counties Championships	White City, London	3/6/63
1:50.7	1	Southern Invitation	Battersea Park	26/6/63
1:50:0m	3	International Invitation	White City, London	4/8/62
1:50.0m	3	International Invitation	White City, London	21/8/63
1:50.8	1	Inter Club Meeting	Carshalton	12/8/64
1:50.8	2	Welsh Games	Maindy Stadium, Cardiff	27/7/68
1:50.9	1	Southern Championships	Motspur Park	25/6/60
1:50.9	2	Arena Trophy	Withdean, Brighton	20/7/68
1:51.0	1	Fulham Borough Meeting	Hurlingham Park	23/9/61
1:51.0	2	Welsh Games	Maindy Stadium, Cardiff	28/7/62
1:51.0	1	International Meeting	Ibrox Park, Glasgow	3/10/62
1:51.0	2	Loughborough v AAA	Loughborough	30/5/63
1:51.0	1 ht	Inter Counties Championships	White City, London	16/5/64
1:51.0	4	Southern Championships	White City, London	20/6/64
1:51.1	3	Southern Championships	Motspur Park	23/6/62
1:50.4m	1	England v Italy	White City London	14/8/63

Time	Pos	Event	Venue	Date
1:51.2	3 sf	Commonwealth Games	Perry Lakes Stadium, Perth	24/11/62
1:51.2	1	Southern Championships	Gosling Stadium, Welwyn	22/6/63
1:51.2	5 ht	AAA Championships	White City, London	12/7/68
1:51.3	3	Surrey Championships	Motspur Park	2/6/61
1:51.3	4	AAA Championships	White City, London	13/7/62
1:50.6m	3	Great Britain v Hungary	White City, London	5/8/61
1:50.7m	4	Great Britain v Switzerland	Wimbledon Park	12/8/61
1:50.7m	1	London v Munich	Dante Stadium, Munich	13/6/63
1:50.7m	7	International Invitation	White City, London	14/8/65
1:51.4	1	Rosenheim League	Wimbledon Park	15/6/66
1:51.4	5 ht	AAA Championships	Crystal Palace	23/7/71
1:51.5	2 ht	Commonwealth Games	Perry Lakes Stadium, Perth	24/11/62
1:50.8m	5	Invitation International	White City, London	4/6/60
1:51.6	1	Jack Lewis Trophy	Croydon Arena	15/6/68
1:51.8	2	AAA v Cambridge University	Milton Road, Cambridge	7/5/63
1:52.0	1	Arena trophy	Withdean, Brighton	22/7/67
1:52.1	1 ht	Southern Championships	White City, London	19/6/64
1:51.5m	3	Birchfield Floodlit Meeting	Perry Barr	3/10/59
1:52.2	3	Surrey Championships	Motspur Park	30/5/59
1:52.3	4	Loughborough v AAA	Loughborough	8/6/61
1:52.3	4 ht	Inter Counties Championships	White City, London	27/5/67
1:52.4	1	Loughborough v Army	Loughborough	17/5/61

Time	Pos	Event	Venue	Date
1:52.4	5	Southern Championships	Welwyn Garden City	26/6/66
1:51.7m	1	BAAB Invitation	Paddington	11/8/62
1:51.7m	2	Surrey Championships	Motspur Park	30/5/70
1:51.7m	6	Southern Championships	Crystal Palace	26/6/71
1:51.8m	2 ht	Surrey Championships	Motspur Park	7/6/69
1:52.5	5 ht	AAA Championships	White City, London	14/7/61
1:52.5	1 ht	Southern Championships	Welwyn Garden City	21/6/63
1:52.5	4 ht	AAA Championships	White City, London	9/7/66
1:52.6	2	Loughborough v Camb.v Lond	Motspur Park	4/5/60
1:52.6	2	U.A.U Championships	Nottingham	21/5/60
1:52.6	2	England v Wales v Scotland	Withdean, Brighton	20/10/62
1:52.6	4 ht	AAA Championships	White City, London	9/7/65
1:52.7	1	Bracknell Invitation	Bracknell	22/8/64
1:52.7	1	Jack Lewis Trophy	Croydon	11/6/66
1:52.7	2 ht	Southern Championships	Motspur Park	/6/68
1:52.1m	5	World Student Games final	Vassil Levski Stadium, Sofia	1/9/61
1:52.1m	2	National League	Iffley Road, Oxford	16/5/70
1:52.8	9	AAA Championships final	White City, London	13/7/63
1:52.9	1	Inter Club	Wimbledon Park	13/6/62
1:53.0	1	Loughborough Championships	Loughborough	18/6/60
1:53.0	1	Croydon Harriers Championships	Croydon	23/5/62
1:53.0	1	Inter Club	Croydon	25/8/65
1:53.0	1	East Surrey League	Ewell Court	2/7/66

Time	Pos	Event	Venue	Date
1:52.3m	4	Club Tour Match	Eskilstuna, Sweden	1/9/70
1:53.1	5	AAA Championships	White City, London	10/7/64
1:53.1	4	Graded Meeting	Withdean, Brighton	10/8/67
1:53.1	2	AAA v Combined Services v British Universities	Portsmouth	7/8/68
1:52.4m	1	Midweek Trophy	Crystal Palace	17/9/69
1:53.2	2	Loughborough v Cambridge University	Milton Road, Cambridge	25/5/60
1:53.3	2 ht	Southern Championships	Motspur Park	18/6/65
1:53.3	1	Croydon Harriers Champs	Croydon Arena	17/7/68
1:53.4	4	Loughborough v AAA	Loughborough	4/6/59
1:53.4	1	Graded Meeting	Withdean, Brighton	28/8/65
1:53.4	2	Brockman Trophy	Wimbledon Park	21/7/62
1:53.4	4	Welsh Games	Maindy Stadium	10/9/66
1:53.5	1 ht	Southern Championships	Motspur Park	21/6/62
1:52.8m	2 ht	Southern Championships	Crystal Palace	25/6/70
1:52.9m	4 ht	AAA Championships	White City, London	14/7/67
1:53.6	4	Invitation Meeting	Aldersley Stadium	8/8/64
1:53.7	2	Surrey Championships	Motspur Park	2/6/62
1:53.0m	1	Croydon v Arnhem	Arnhem, Holland	2/9/64
1:53.9	1 ht	Southern Championships	Welwyn Garden City	24/6/66
1:54.0	1	Crump's v Sage's	Ewell Court	13/5/64
1:53.6m	3	Croydon & Commonwealth v England	Croydon Arena	15/8/56
1:53.6m	1	National League	Croydon Arena	19/9/70

Appendix C

My Top Ten Male Athletes (11!)

...Actually eleven with a certain Mr Bolt staking a late and totally outstanding claim impossible to overlook!

Emil Zatopek

The astonishing triple Olympic champion at the 1952 Helsinki Games for 5000m, 10000m and Marathon, and many times world record holder.

It is claimed that he famously asked the Helsinki marathon favourite Jim Peters if they were going fast enough, and having been told "yes", sped away en route to an astonishing victory on his debut over the distance.

Another version is that, although wondering about the wisdom of the early pace, he was challenged by a Swede to overtake the Briton and shortly after they caught up with him at 15k he invited the tiring Peters to *"Come with us, it's much easier when there are three together"*.

Zatopek went on to win in 2:23.03. The unfortunate Peters failed to finish. This was in my humble opinion, a clear example of self-belief and no fear of reputation.

The young Emil's first race was a wartime Bata shoe advertising event in the town of Zlin, but he was so unenthusiastic that he tried to feign knee injury to avoid participation. His hostel doctor was having none of it. *"That's nothing! You can run quite safely!"*

...and run he did – though not before he had tried to avoid the race by disappearing into his hostel reading room, only to be quickly discovered by one of his friends and, reluctantly, sent on his way to the start.

Once there he remembered what his wise father had tried to drum into him. "A thing worth doing, is worth doing well". He did his best, and his innate talent took him into second place and won him a fountain pen. Others noticed and the pressure was on to train and to continue.

So we have to thank a combination of circumstances, including the astuteness of a doctor who wouldn't have the wool pulled over his eyes by the reluctant Zatopek, for the incredible athletics career which evolved.

Zatopek often ran circuits in deep winter snow to create his own running track and also ran to the point of collapse when holding his breath, the latter was an innovation perhaps not to be recommended!

The other most important side of Emil Zatopek away from the glare of publicity was that he displayed great humanity and modesty.

He was, we are told, an essentially happy and seemingly carefree man of youthful spirit, who displayed impeccable behaviour and was a fine companion.

I first became aware of the great man in 1952, when the photograph of Chris Chataway's tragic fall appeared in the press, in which the ungainly contorted Zatopek featured, storming round the final bend vainly pursued by Alain Mimoun and Herbert Schade. The Czech's final lap of 57.9sec guaranteed him the second of his three Helsinki gold medals.

The basis of Zatopek's terrific achievements can be traced to his rigid daily training routine. Do we hear echoes of Alf Shrubb? Come wind, rain, frost or snow, and no matter where he was, he kept to a routine which featured a huge work load, but it was the one which suited him and the one which produced the results.

I was fortunate to attend a question and answer session with him at Crystal Palace in the 1960s. He exuded charm, modesty, patience and enthusiasm. He was a truly great ambassador for athletics

His personal best times include: 3000m 8:07.8; 5000m 13.57.0; 10000m 28.54.2.

Peter Snell

Double Olympic Gold Medallist in 1964 at 800m and 1500m, this super strong New Zealander had come from being a possible tennis star to an athlete who thought nothing of running 100 miles per week in training, several times in the year.

At one time Snell held eight World and two Olympic records.

Peter was an athletic "iron man" who set a string of world records and showed me a clean pair of heels on the three occasions we met in competition!

Echoes of the paternal Zatopek mantra... *"if a thing is worth doing at all it is worth doing well"* was part of the young Snell's psyche when he "walked the course" of his school steeplechase several times, and his attention to detail was rewarded by a 16 second improvement on the record.

He went to the 1960 Rome Olympics as a virtual unknown. So much so that when his heat was announced, the BBC commentator failed to forecast Snell as one of his three to progress. It was just the right time for him to produce a personal best of 1:48.1 to qualify in second that afternoon. He improved dramatically to 1:47.2 to win his semi final.

It was only with 20 yards to go in the final that Snell felt he could win. He drove hard for the finish and did not know the result until runner-up Roger Moens congratulated him. He had improved for the third time to an amazing Olympic record of 1:46.3.

It was probably my luckiest break when I was called up as a late replacement to run against him at the White City in 1961. It proved to be a salutary experience from which I learned that youthful exuberance and enthusiasm cannot match world class.

The reigning 1960 Olympic champion won with consummate ease thanks to a decisive burst with 40 yards remaining, during which he stretched to more than a second ahead of Paul Schmidt who narrowly beat me for second.

My recall of the Perth Empire and Commonwealth Games is slightly at odds with that recorded in Snell's book "No bugles No Drums". In that he wrote... *"Approaching the bell, in 54sec, I shifted to Fleet's shoulder to duck any chance of boxing... This slowish pace was made to order for George[27]."*

At that point he says he made his break *"...It was a dreary job,"* he continued!

My memory is that he came alongside me in the back straight, assessed my flagging form in a split second, and made his successful dash for gold, with the Jamaican in hot but vain pursuit. I finished a disappointing 5th 2.4sec adrift.

---

[27] George Kerr.

Snell ran his then fastest 800m in 1:45.1, just at the right time in Tokyo in 1964, for it won him his second Olympic gold over the distance. Fierce heat times in the 1500m which followed contributed to a winning time of 3:38.1 but it was achieved off a last lap of 53.2sec and earned him his second Olympic double.

His personal best times include: 800m 1:44.3; 1500m 3.37.6; 1 mile 3:54.1.

Gordon Pirie

Gordon was my local boyhood athletics hero.

Pirie, having tried to mix it with the best in the 1952 Helsinki Olympics, tried similar tactics in the 1956 Melbourne Olympic 10000m when he was the only athlete to stick with the relentlessly surging Russian Vladimir Kuts. He eventually succumbed and fell away, but bravely bounced back after his dramatic collapse, and followed up a few days later with courageous 5000m run to win a well deserved silver medal.

He displayed the indestructible spirit of a truly great competitor, showing that one can quickly overcome adversity and the disappointment of defeat.

Gordon was self confident to the point of apparent big headedness, but he genuinely believed in himself as all successful athletes must.

This aspect of the great gaunt athlete from Coulsdon can be clearly appreciated from his reported approach to venture into the realms of miling and in particular his brash challenge to American star Wes Santee in the inaugural, and to become classic, Emsley Carr Mile in 1953.

Pirie, noted as a swashbuckling front-runner, typically led at the bell, only to be passed by the American whom he then tucked in behind until, with 150 yards remaining, our man visibly gathered his resources and gaining momentum, passed the waning Wes with 60 yards to go, breaking the tape in the modest time of 4:06.8 and yet, for the upper distance man, a personal best.

But who cared about the time? It was the manner of the execution that made Gordon a hero with the big White City crowd that famous day.

Sydney Wooderson, Britain's legendary miler, commented that, *"Pirie had clearly shown that distance work, properly carried out, did not impair speed".*

As a wide-eyed schoolboy at the time, I had seen with my own eyes that Gordon's distance work incorporated plenty of impressively fast solo running, hence his ability to run his final lap in under 59 seconds.

He was famous for his recovery mattress, his custom-made two foot high stopwatch, his work ethic and huge capacity for training, whether on the track with interminable sessions of "Quarters", or in army boots on the Farthing Downs. This prepared him for numerous world record attempts, several of which were successful.

Gordon set the following world records: 3000m (7:55.5), 3 miles (13:16.4), 5000m (13:36.8), six miles (28:19.4), 10000m (29:17.2=) and 4x1500m (15:27.2). A non-world record breaking time he possibly enjoyed the most was when he ran under 4 minutes for the mile, and was heard to exclaim, *"I've done it, I've done it,"* when told his time of 3:59.9.

Haile Gebrselassie

Behind the most famous smile in the world of athletics lies a man of steel.

Such is the astounding range, talent and athletic longevity of this eternally smiling human dynamo, that one would need a separate book to do him real justice.

His childhood spent living on a farm, requiring him to run to school and back, 20km per day, clearly stood him in good stead for his amazing string of athletic achievements in later life.

It is encouraging to note that he more often than not overcame the privations of asthma during his outstanding career, but being a sufferer, and fearful of the air pollution for which Beijing is notorious, the cheery little man unfortunately decided against running in the 2008 Olympic marathon. When later aware of the good job the Chinese had done in cleaning up the environment for the Games he expressed understandable disappointment at not having been involved in the classic event.

I can vouch for the astonishing Chinese pre Games clean up, sharing amazement with locals at an almost unique view from Beijing of distant mountains and a glorious sunset.

He recently announced his retirement after the New York marathon, from which he was forced to withdraw through injury. A few days later he let it be known that he had changed his mind and hopefully he will be seen in London in 2012.

He broke 26 world records and won two Olympic and nine World titles. Astonishingly, he was 35 when he won the Berlin Marathon in which he achieved the world's best time of 2:03.59.

His range of talent extends from a 3:31.76 1500m (I), through a 10000m in 26:22.75 to the world's fastest marathon in 2:03.59.

He won four consecutive 10000m World Championships.

Sebastian Coe

News that we in significant part owe the existence of one of Britain's greatest athletes to the humanity of a wartime German sea captain, Otto Fein, commander of the battle cruiser Gneisenau, adds a new dimension to the Seb Coe story.

Seb's father-to-be, Peter, adrift in an open lifeboat in the Atlantic in 1941 with other survivors from his sunken ship, was rescued by Fein.

Fifteen years later baby Sebastian Newbold was born. History records that he grew up to be an athlete of the highest quality, whose analytical father and coach Peter, maximised a unique combination of both mind and body to produce Olympic glory.

A very single minded athlete, Seb set a string of world records from 800m to 1 mile between 1979 and 1981.

Clearly benefiting from similar knowledge of the type of progress I made through rivalry with my club colleague Bob Harvey, Coe capitalised on competition with his great contemporary challenger Steve Ovett. Inevitably their battles for success, sharpened by the presence of heir apparent Steve Cram, stretched all three in the quest for supremacy.

At eighteen his 800m personal best was 1:53.8, 0.2sec slower than mine at the same age. I can only surmise how my athletic fortunes might have progressed had someone of his father's prowess overseen my training. Knowing me, not much, for I guess that I might well have rebelled at such strict control.

Had I run my best 800m time during his world record run in 1:41.73, I would have been admiring his achievement some 50m adrift back down the home straight!

That incredible time set in 1981 remained unbeaten for sixteen years.

I first personally encountered him during my time as Chief Assembly Steward at the big Crystal Palace meetings. On those occasions he was so focused that he was always on hand for the final call, when he would ease in line in response to a nod, while others less experienced would dash up nervously, often at the last minute.

Coe would remain seemingly ice cool throughout.

In contrast at the other end of the scale, a relaxed and apparently unconcerned Steve Ovett would be waiting in one of the furthest corners of the warm-up area unresponsive to urgent calls, but always finally willing to fall in line when fetched by one of my pretty young schoolgirl helpers!

Now The Rt Hon Lord Coe, Earl of Ranmore KBE, he is very effectively using his huge reputation and experience to drive the London 2012 Olympic project to a successful conclusion.

His other personal bests include: 1500m 3:29.77; 1 mile 3:47.33.

Roger Bannister

See Figure 103 - Roger Bannister completes the first ever sub 4 minute mile. Iffley Road Track Oxford

The first sub-4 minute man over the mile in 1954 was still involved in full time study at university.

One of the last true blue athletes, he evolved a plan in collaboration with colleagues and friends Chris Brasher and Chris Chataway and guided by coach Franz Stampfl to crack the elusive barrier early that May in order to thwart the concurrent challenges of shrewd Australian John Landy and brash American Wes Santee.

On the due day, with the tension mounting, officials at the Iffley Road track at Oxford nervously eyed the flag as it flew somewhat too stiffly for confidence on the nearby church. Then it miraculously drooped to a flutter and the starter capitalised on the moment, and the master plan swung smoothly into action.

The field of seven was called to its marks, and steadied. Starter Mr R.C.Barkway fired his pistol...

...Brasher burst eagerly into the agreed early lead, peering intently though his spectacles as he concentrated on setting the Stamfl prescribed early pace.

Bannister, spikes specially sharpened on a grindstone, tucked in behind, slipstreaming.

Brasher pacing perfectly covered the first lap in 57.5 sec and reached the half mile in 1:58.0, with Chataway taking on the critical third lap, passing the bell in a finely poised 3:0.7.

Then, like the final stage of a space rocket, Bannister shot on alone into unknown territory, before reaching the target almost oblivious in 3:59.4; mission accomplished, history had been made.

Bannister, classic mile apart, did have a very respectable athletics career. He declined the chance of becoming a "possible" for the 1948 Wembley Olympics, but he did become an Olympian four years later in Helsinki, when he ran himself to the limit, to finish fourth in the 1500m in 3:46.0.

Four months after his carefully-orchestrated record breaking Oxford run, he proved himself to be an outstanding competitor when he out-thought and out-kicked Landy to win the Empire Games mile in Vancouver in 3:58.8.

Now turned 80, and still physically active, Sir Roger Bannister is equally well known in medical circles – following an eminent career in that field – as he is through his relatively brief time in athletics.

See Figure 97 – 1995 MFG Re-union dinner

Usain Bolt

Usain is truly quite something when it comes to sprinters, for it is he alone among sprinters since the silky speed of Rhodesian[28] Seraphino

---

[28] Now Zimbabwe

Antao during my active days, who has completely captured my attention. Bolt's impressive physique at 6' 5", encompassing 198 lbs of lean power, more often than not places him head and shoulders above his rivals. As well as being a brilliant athlete, he is a modest man who displays a zanily endearing personality. His very presence at the start of a sprint generates an electric atmosphere in anticipation of the bolt of human lightning he becomes when he flashes across one's vision.

A lesser known fact about him is that he has been making a habit of starting his summer season with a more than respectable 400m and he has already run a "mouth watering" personal best of 45.28sec. Michael Johnson's 43.18sec world record will surely be in Bolt's sights soon.

Currently the fastest man on earth, Bolt, with more crowd-pulling power than a top Premiership soccer match, looks set to remain in pole position. Prehistoric man, living some 30,000 to 40,000 years age, stimulated by the need to survive by hunting some animals and by escaping others were, it is claimed, clocking speeds of 23mph without the benefit of springy rubberised tracks, scientific or super lightweight running spikes. There are no films and no records beyond fossilized stride patterns and the calculations related to them to validate the claim, but the Jamaican world record holder living in a far more cosseted world is thus in my opinion very special indeed. Probably along with millions of others, Usain Bolt is for me THE business when it comes to man and speed. I've witnessed his stunning world record-breaking achievements at the Beijing Olympics and the Berlin World Championships.

His personal best times include: 100m 9.58; 200m 19.19.

Jesse Owens

He was the "black thorn" in Hitler's flesh at the 1936 Nazi Olympics, when he won four gold medals. He "cocked a snook" at racism in a two-tier American society, and more significantly in the cauldron of the Berlin Olympic stadium when he beat the great white German hope Lutz Long in the long jump.

He quietly refused to become involved in any of the unsavoury pre-Olympic political carrots which were being dangled in front of him by American officials and in particular Avery Brundage, whose ambitions of Olympic power led him close to the wind on more than one occasion.

Jesse, derived from his initials J.C. became his name when he was nine.

His still shining personal bests are: 100yds 9.4s; 220yds 20.3s; Long Jump 8.13 (26'8¾"); 220yds Low Hurdles 22.6s, first to break 23 seconds.

Alf Shrubb

Although I am of fairly advanced years, I have no personal recall of Alf Shrubb, the Horsham Blue Star Harrier who, sadly for me, set up home in Canada in 1928 where he died in 1964.

I am hugely impressed by his recorded exploits which I researched further, ever since being given a copy of the book he wrote in 1908, "Running and Cross-Country Running", by former Croydon Harriers coach and pre World War II athlete Les Rickett.

Shrubb said, "Of all forms of pedestrianism and indeed of all the branches of athletics, there can be nothing superior to cross-country running for either pleasure or health", a sentiment with which I fully concur.
He also wrote, "Of all athletic forms running is perhaps the most taxing and the most exciting; that is; when carried out to the extreme."

Shrubb was recognised as a prolific "Shamateur[29]" athlete and keen student of the sport.

He won 1,000 of his 1,800 races and broke all the amateur records from six to eleven miles, and all the professional records from eight to eleven miles, the last record remaining unbeaten until 1951.

His astonishing performance at Ibrox Park, Glasgow, on November 4th 1904, saw him break the one hour record, as well as all amateur and professional records from 6 to 11 miles. His distance of 11 miles 1,137yds covered in the hour stood until 1st June 1951.

In all he set 28 world records.

See Figure 104 – Prolific record breaker Alf Shrubb

Michael Johnson

---

[29] 'Sham amateur' who appeared to be an amateur but was understood to have received payment during his career.

An amazing latter day "mirror" of Jesse Owens in terms running of style and cadence, Michael was as outstanding in his time – some ten years ago – as Owens was way back in the 1930s.

Having a high school record of 20.41sec for 200m in his very first race, he then became injured and was forced to miss the Seoul Olympics in 1988, but three years later he won the World title by .33sec which was the largest margin of victory since the great Owens in 1936.

Johnson is the only man to win Olympic gold in both the 200m and 400m during the same games. Those two events, which he won at Atlanta in 1996, contributed to his impressive Olympic and World Championship tally of twelve, three being won as a key member of United States 4x400m squads. His 19.32sec 200m clocking stayed as the world record for 12 years.

I find it incredible that my 200m best even doubled, would be slower than Michael's world record 400m time of 43.18sec, which he set in 1999.

Very fortunately for contemporary athletes of his with ambitions like mine, he stuck to his guns and never moved up to 800m or else we might well have seen the world's first sub 1:40.0 800m runner, so the door is still open for Martyn Rooney.

Johnson voluntarily returned his 2000 Olympic 4x400m gold medal in 2008 feeling that it had not been won fairly following Antonio Pettigrew's admission in 2007 of drug taking.

Johnson is now one of the most respected athletics broadcasters and analysts on the circuit.

Sydney Wooderson

The diminutive, bespectacled Englishman set the World mile record at 4:06.4 in 1937, and his 1:48.4 800m best in 1938 was the last English-held 800m World record until a certain Seb Coe came along in 1981 with his 1:41.73 epic.

It seems strange today that in the 1938 race, Sydney beat both the world 800 and 880 yard records but did not cross the line first. The explanation is that the event was a carefully planned handicap race won by his brother who, with other non-scratch men, ran in lane 2, to allow the chief contender a free passage. Brother Stanley was off 85 yards, with five others spread between him and Sydney.

He was undoubtedly a great talent, with a top class range of performances from 440 yards to 5000m on the track. We can only surmise what he might have achieved but for the intervention of World War II. He might even have beaten Roger Bannister to break the four minute mile barrier.

His distinguished competitive career extended from running in the 1931 Public Schools Championships as an unnoticed sixteen year old Sutton Valence schoolboy, to his final race "easing down" for the first time, in fourteenth place in the 1949 English National Cross-Country Championships.

Wooderson, AAA mile champion from 1935 to 1939, won the European 1500m title in 1938, the year of my birth, and he won the European 5000m championship in 1946.

Running lame in the 1936 Olympic 1500m he had further Olympic disappointment when, expected to be the final torch bearer at the 1948 London Games, he was sidelined in favour of the unknown, hardly talented but physically more impressive, John Mark.

I hope, when it comes to the selection of the final torch-bearer for London 2012, that it will be Roger Bannister who walks slowly up to ignite the flame; to receive the acclaim he justly deserves; and maybe some too on behalf of the small bespectacled man who preceded him as British holder of the world mile record.

Sydney ran at international level both before and after World War II and proved that size and age could be overcome.

During the war, excused active service abroad because of his poor eyesight, he endured the horrors of the Blitz on London, possibly alongside my father, as a member of the National Fire Service. Later he transferred to REME.

British team manager Jack Crump was a guiding light at that time and Sydney was a key member of a group of athletes who continued running despite many difficulties raising money and morale for the war effort.

In 1944 he developed rheumatic fever which might have put paid to the aspirations of many lesser mortals. One athletics correspondent of the day wrote that Wooderson was finished. He decided otherwise!

He recovered so well that, in a close run race in 1945, against the fit looking war-time neutral Swede Arne Anderson, Sydney by contrast wan and looking undernourished, held on magnificently and was only beaten in final strides by 0.4sec in 4:09.2, his fastest since 1939. Watching that day was a schoolboy called Roger Bannister.

Had the seeds of sub 4 minute ambition been sown?

In 1969, when he was in his mid 50s, he ran for his beloved Blackheath Harriers in their Centenary 100x1mile relay and such was his preparation, having specially come out of retirement for the occasion, that many a reasonable athlete, myself included, did not dare take it easy for fear of the regenerated hero of the 1930s and 1940s showing us up. He was clocked at 6:14 that day and what a thrill it was to see a legend in latter day action.

"He was a wonder, – fearless, super fast and rarely beatable," says David Thurlow, in his biography of Sydney Wooderson.

This is an arbitrary and subjective list. Please feel free to use the space which follows for your own favourites!

See Figure 72 – The great Sydney Wooderson setting a new mile record of 4:06.4 at Motspur Park In 1937

Appendix D

My Top Ten Women Athletes...

Lillian Board MBE

A lovely athlete with seemingly unbounded talent, Lillian won the Olympic 400m silver medal at altitude in Mexico City in 1968, ran 2:01.5 to take the European 800m gold and won a share in the British 4x400m World record set in the same championships in 1969.

Tragically cancer crept up on her in 1970, when she was understandably planning two years ahead to the Munich Olympic Games. She died that December aged 22. Ironically the young star had finally faded away in the city of her athletic dreams.

Lillian had been a highly motivated yet modest athlete who found it hard to relate to those who failed to set their ambitions high enough.

She could however empathise with others, as I once personally experienced during a training session at Crystal Palace, when her father unceremoniously set up camp at the 100m start and suggested that I took my young sprinters elsewhere.

"You know who this is, don't you?" he queried pointedly.
"Well, yes, Lillian is very well-known," I responded.

Clearly sensing something of a confrontation brewing, Lillian gently intervened, pointing out that we could do starts alternately or even together, which is just what we did thanks to her thoughtful intervention, hopefully to everyone's advantage.

Best performances: 400m 52.12sec; 800m 2:01.50

Donna Fraser

In my humble opinion, Donna is the greatest ambassador for British women's athletics, still competing at international level aged 36.

I am proud that she is a member of my club, Croydon Harriers, for whom she first competed as a twelve year old. So good was she way back in

1985 that her two sprint records of 12.7sec and 25.9sec still grace the archive. Overall she holds twelve club records.

Fourth in the 2000 Sydney Olympic 400m when closing fast in the final 50m she ran out of track, substantiating my theory that she could have been the next great British "half miler" after Ann Packer. One is left wondering whether an individual Olympic medal would have come her way had she cast caution to the wind and tackled two laps seriously.

Donna is a great example to younger athletes as a modest, ever smiling lady who always has a word for young and old admirers alike.

Having retired from the top level at the "grand old age" of 35 there still might be the happiest of endings coming the way of this lovely lady. An Olympic bronze 4x400m relay medal is highly likely to come her way from way back in the Athens Games following an American drug-taking confession. When it is presented I predict a world record breaking smile from the delightful and thoroughly deserving Donna.

Best performances: 200m 22.96sec; indoors 23.05sec; 400m 49.79sec; 800m 2:09.7

See Figure 105 – Donna Fraser supreme Croydon Harriers female sprinter in full stride

Dame Kelly Holmes

Kelly's fantastic first women's double Olympic Gold medal winning runs in Athens in 2004 over 800m and 1500m and her incredulous expression on realisation of her achievement are etched on my memory. She is a great example of a hugely patient athlete, overcoming much adversity, both personally and in athletics, to achieve an ambition.

Kelly was a key player in the successful London 2012 Olympic bid, and it was a thrill too to witness her obvious delight when the announcement was made.

Now splendidly inspiring aspiring male and female athletes through her "Camp Kelly" initiative, the dashing Dame continues to contribute to the sport in a very positive way. Camp Kelly "graduates", while continuing to benefit from the wisdom of their home coaches, clearly benefit too from what their golden mentor has to offer.

Current beneficiaries include: Dani Christmas, Charlotte Best, Hannah England, Charlotte Purdue, James Brewer and Simon Horsfield.

Best performances: 800m 1:56.21; 1500m 3:57.90

See Figure 122 – Kelly Holmes with Loulou Rowlands

Yelena Isinbayeva

When athletic brilliance and beauty go hand in hand on the end of a 15 foot fibreglass pole there is truly an athlete well worth watching and that is the Russian "Queen of the Vault", Yelena Isanbayeva. So graceful is her vaulting that she would not look out of place on a ballet stage rather than at the top end of a dramatically bending pole!

From a male point of view she is a joy to behold, except when she retreats under her trademark blanket between attempts. As a former Loughborough PE student for whom participation in pole vault was mandatory and who could only manage flying pole-assisted a mere metre into space, I view all vaulters with awe and admiration.

Such is the ability of the former gymnast that she cleared 4.00m in only her third competition at sixteen years of age. In 2005 Isanbayeva became the first woman to break the 5.00m "barrier". Since then she has remained the world's top ranked female pole-vaulter. Interestingly she also holds the rank of captain in the Russian army.

This hugely talented athlete shrewdly follows the flight path of her Russian millionaire mentor Sergei Bubka, nibbling away, centimetre by centimetre, at the world record to maximise her income. She has bettered the record on almost thirty occasions and we are told that she has also beaten it more than once in training.

Her current personal best and world record height of 5.05m is good enough to have won the men's Olympic pole vault title from 1896 until 1960 and would have shared silver in 1964. Isinbayeva has been IAAF World Athlete of the year on three occasions. She has won seven World Championship titles and two Olympic titles.

There was a curious glitch in the 2009 World Championships when she "blew out" in Berlin. It was a strange echo of what happened to that other great Russian exponent Sergei Bubka at the Barcelona Olympics. Even the greatest have the fragility to succumb to pressure at times. We are all human after all.

Best performance: 5.06m

Judy Oakes OBE

A prolific record breaker for athletics achievement, team captaincy and international appearances, Judy is among the greatest of British field events exponents, having amassed 87 international appearances and 45 national titles.

She started club athletics at my Croydon club as a semi reluctant girl half miler, accompanying her then more highly rated sister Hazel, who became a junior international, but did not continue as a senior. Judy meanwhile persisted, gradually developing an appetite for athletics, changing discipline from running to shot putting and the rest is history.

Judy, who was frustratingly deprived of an Olympic medal by Australian Gail Mulhall who was later uncovered as a user of performance enhancing drugs, competed tenaciously against all comers, acutely aware of sharp practice. Now well after retirement from the sport, she understandably remains steadfast in the cause of clean athletics.

She competed in four Olympics with a pinnacle performance when placed fourth in Los Angeles in 1984. Three times Commonwealth Games champion, Judy also won a silver and a bronze and she still holds the UK women's shot put record. At age 40 after final Commonwealth success, Judy who admitted to feeling her age, was innocently asked by a Malaysian press man,"*How many grandchildren do you have?*"

Her reaction is unreported, but one might reasonably guess that Judy threw back her appropriately golden embellished hair (the patriotically requested red, white and blue fringe had failed!) and roared with laughter.

Following her eminent athletics career, Judy embarked on a new one in power lifting, at which, hardly surprisingly, as a supremely strong athlete standing at 5'4", she excelled, to become world champion three times.

Best performances: Shot 19.36m: Discus 53.44m

See Figure 106 – Judy Oakes Commonwealth joy 1994 Victoria BC

Dorothy Odam-Tyler MBE

As a sixteen year-old, Dorothy Odam proved that where there is talent, youth is no barrier to major success when she won Olympic high jump silver at the 1936 Berlin Olympics. Not at all put out by a "Heil Hitler" when shopping after the games, she patriotically responded with a "God Save the King".

Like Sydney Wooderson's, her career spanned World War II, after which she competed in both the 1948 and 1952 Olympics. Dorothy won an Empire and Commonwealth Games high jump gold medal at Sydney in 1938, and again in Auckland in 1950. She made 38 international appearances and won 12 national titles. Technically she was among the elite of "scissors jumpers" and converted brilliantly to the Western Roll under the tutelage of Arthur Gold in 1951 prior to placing seventh in the 1952 Olympics before bowing out internationally, winning a silver in the 1954 Vancouver Empire and Commonwealth Games.

Dorothy was a versatile athlete who did not limit herself solely to the high jump as evidenced by her WAAA title winning performances in the long jump and pentathlon in 1951. The latter was won with a British record-breaking performance. Now Dorothy Tyler, having spent many post Olympic years as a coach, still exudes enthusiasm and strongly argues against over training.

A great advert for participation in sport at nearly ninety, her offer to appear in Tom McNab's thought provoking play "1936" recently, had to be politely declined in favour of the significantly younger actress otherwise far less appropriately cast in the role of a high jumper! In the interests of health and safety, I presume.

She once famously said, *"When I cease to be amazed, I will quit!"*, and clearly she has no intention of quitting yet.

Best performance: high jump 1.68m

See Figure 110 – Dorothy Odam-Tyler practising post war Western Roll

Ann Packer

Ann started her relatively short but exciting athletics career as a sprinter/hurdler, and her international career as a long jumper. Shrewdly she realised that it would be hard for her to become a world beater in those events so she stepped up first to the 400m, and it was my good fortune to be present when she notched a dramatic win in 53.3sec in Volgograd in 1963.

Her first 800m in 1964 was a modest 2:11.1. A little later, she caught the eye when she ran the 800m, 400m and 200m at the White City over the Whitsun weekend, and won all three!

She ran the two longer events at the Tokyo Olympic Games where, having narrowly missed out on 400m gold – maybe a victim of her own enthusiasm in qualifying fast, Ann moved on to the 800m with a wiser head on her shoulders and qualified comfortably.

The ensuing final was the story of legend in which the relaxed and confident Packer trailed until entering the home straight, where her finishing strength and speed made the opposition appear to be treading water. Her storming win, proved that relative novices can stun the experts so long as they stay calm and dig deeply into their resources. Her winning time of 2:01.1 was a new Olympic and world record. She also took silver in the 400m in 52.2sec, just .2sec behind the winner.

With Ann retiring from the sport at the age of 22, we are only left to speculate on what further advances this astonishing athlete might have achieved.

Best performances: 400m 52.20sec; 800m 2:01.1

See Figure 107 – Ann Packer wins at White City

Dame Mary Peters

Mary was one of the greatest late "developers" in athletics crowning her multi-faceted career with an Olympic gold .

Like several of my other selections, her story is one of dogged perseverance. In 1961 she set the highest UK score for the pentathlon and showed her competitive worth with a dogged 4th in the 1964 Tokyo Olympics. She took a deliberate rest in 1971 and returned refreshed when it really mattered.

A hard-earned loss of 3 stones of the weight she had gained to accommodate international shot putting, an event in which she set a UK record, led to a more finely honed Peters journeying to Germany for the

1972 Olympic Games, where in Munich she had to face the massive vocal support for the local heroine and hope Heidi Rosendahl. The epitome of calm in the steady rain, Mary was seemingly uninfluenced by the mayhem around her. She did exactly what was necessary when she squeezed out every remaining ounce of energy to run her 200m in 24.08sec, thereby clinching victory and setting a world record into the bargain.

She is another athlete who is repaying society by raising essential funds for the athletics community in Northern Ireland.

Best performances: pentathlon 4,801 points (world record 1972); shot 16.40m

See Figure 108 – Mary Peters

Paula Radcliffe

Whether it is for Olympic marathon failures or fantastically fast world record achievements elsewhere over 26 miles 385 yards, one simply cannot ignore this extraordinarily dedicated runner.

A promising young runner from a sporting family, Paula had a distinguished track career including fifth in the 1995 World Championships 5000m, and frustrating fifth in the 1996 Olympic event, and did even better on the country, winning her first world title at the eighth attempt. I can definitely relate to that, having experienced a similar wait for my county half mile gold.

She made her marathon debut in London in April 2002, and in 2003 Paula was the fastest British marathoner with all the red faced men wallowing in her wake. In 2005 she became the first Briton, man or woman, to win the World marathon title.

Her resilience and talent are legendary, and few if any British athletes have pushed to the limit as hard as Paula, but I do believe that on occasions she has been her own worst enemy. An anaemia and exercise-related asthma sufferer, she is however a great example to others who suffer similar conditions over which to achieve.

But who am I to talk, having only "raced" (endured!) about a third of her chosen distance ten times in the National Cross Country Championships, and run twenty miles plus, twice in training! She is an astonishing athlete, who along with her advisers seems to be taking an interminably long time to learn that, with a reduced workload, her body might be more responsive. But the body and mind of a natural long distance runner are extraordinarily special and complex and often have to be given their head.

Paula might even yet improve over the classic distance to win that oh so elusive Olympic gold which she craves, but with gritty knees and a rebuilt ankle myself on a fraction of the mileage, I wouldn't wish years of that kind of pain on one who so clearly accommodates pain in the pursuit of perfection.

What does surprise and disappoint me in this context is that British men have not been inspired to greater things themselves when they have such a talent in their midst.

Best performances: 5000m 14.29.11; 10000m 30.01.09; marathon 2:15.25

Mary Rand[30]

Pin-up Olympic long jump gold medallist at the 1964 Tokyo Olympics, Mary won with a world record of 6.76m which she so closely matched eleven days later in Japan when she finished a mere two centimetres shy. Her Tokyo performance totally made up for her confused failure in Rome four years earlier.

Mary's winning jump beat the previous record by 6cm, and her record remained intact for a further four years when a Rumanian with an unpronounceable and unspellable name added a further 6cms. Her positive impact on the British team at the time was put down to her "bubbling enthusiasm and sense of humour" which played a key part in the successes which followed.

In 1966 she had achieved all of Britain's top thirty all time long jumps. She also ranked first in the pentathlon, second in 80m hurdles and was also fourth in the high jump. More than an "inspiration" to many a male athlete in my time, Mary was a fantastic and athletic role model to an incalculable number of girls entering the sport in the 1960s.

A truly great all round athlete whom I greatly enjoyed being with, and who played a more than respectable game of squash, as I discovered to my pleasure and cost!

---

[30] Maiden name, Bignal.

Best performances: Long jump 6.76m; 80m hurdles 10.8sec; pentathlon 4,578/5,035

See Figure 109 – Mary Rand. White City action

As with the men, you are free to compose your own list of outstanding female athletes in the space below!

Appendix E

Now for Some of Britain's Brightest Prospects

With Martyn Rooney[31] Croydon Harriers, and Stephanie Twell[32] Aldershot Farnham and District, already established at almost the highest level as young Olympians, but clearly with much more talent "in the tank" to unleash, I put my neck on the block and list my predictions for more future stars of our sport, again presented in alphabetical order to avoid bias or controversy and with apologies to many more who live just around the corner!

See Figures 111 and 111a – Rooney and Twell
See Figure 112 – Stephanie Twell Young Olympian

Of course one's crystal ball cannot reveal distractions, alternatives or, perish the thought, mishaps which might lurk ahead to dilute the future.

Having enthused over the athletics potential of rugby players George Chuter, Danny Cipriani and Shane Roiser, one can only reluctantly concede that outstanding exponents of the Webb-Ellis code have to be very athletic these days, and that without it they would certainly not have become stars. What a pity for us It is that athletics did not have the attraction for them that their chosen sport did.

See Figure 113 – George Chuter javelin potential (Inset MF photo) now
England rugby star
See Figure 114 – Danny Cipriani, huge athletics potential is rugby union
gain

When at school, Cipriani would frustratingly clear the high jump bar at 1.80m plus, having been told not to because jumping in ordinary clothes and shoes were not allowed. Chuter, whose broad shoulders were so powerful at eighteen that he could threaten school windows with misguided shots at a hockey goal from 200m, was an accomplished javelin thrower, while Shane Roiser was a national standard, powerfully

---

[31] See other entries elsewhere.
[32] UK rankings 2010: 1500m, 2nd, 4:02.54; 3000m, 1st, 8:50.89; 5000m, 1st, 14:54.08.

silken sprinter cast in the Jesse Owens and Michael Johnson mould.

Likewise emerging soccer star Victor Moses delighted in mocking his Whitgift School athletics classmates by comfortably zig-zagging ahead of them with frustratingly arrogant poise and control during sprinting sessions. Moses at 20 is currently the £3 million property of Premiership Wigan Athletic FC.

Karen Brown and Alison Cummings were promising young Croydon Harriers athletes who moved on very successfully to other sports. Karen a county standard middle-distance runner gave up in favour of hockey to become outstanding as a Great Britain Olympian and top goal scorer, while Alison, a really promising javelin thrower, transferred comfortably to take on the world of women's squash in which she excelled.

One can only conjecture how they and hundreds of others throughout the country might have progressed had the attraction of athletics prevailed over the lure of another sport, or had illness or injury not intervened. For example, heroic rugby star and 400m hurdler Andy Ripley who, despite the discomfort of serious illness, found solace in rowing; or youthful sprint prodigy Theo Walcott, who turned to professional football.

It is my belief that we in this marvellous sport of ours do not make it anywhere near as attractive as we could. With London 2012 fast approaching, radical action urgently needs to be taken to ensure that the nation's athletics talent is fully tapped.

Babatunde Amosu (Croydon Harriers)

While declaring my interest, or rather my confusion, over this athlete's complex and illogical event, the triple jump, being on the athletic schedule, I have nothing but admiration for his achievements within it. Apart from Jonathan Edwards, this slightly built young man is the most exciting exponent of the demanding activity who I have had the pleasure of watching in action.

He is so fast, light and springy that at the tender age of 16 he cleared nearly the same number of metres with his best of 15.22m. Such is the progress in his event since my active days that had he been competing then, his best performance of 15.74m would have been 36cms ahead of John Vernon, his international coach, as the 7th British performer of all time!

Injury is a particular concern with young triple jumpers and Babatunde has not been immune. The hope is that as he matures and acquires natural strength, he will be able the follow the beckoning road of progress with fewer obstacles.

Oliver Bradfield (City of Norwich)

Oliver is a dynamic fifteen-year-old javelin thrower, who has improved an astonishing 17.99m in two years, from 47.86m to 65.87. Unbeaten in his speciality for three seasons, he is several times English Schools Champion, Athletic Association of England Champion and McCain's Young Athletes' Cup final winner. Developing well, he has moved on in 2010 to an U15 UK Age Group record making an amazing hat trick alongside those achieved as an U13 and U14 athlete.

See Figure 115 – Oliver Bradfield

Coached carefully in his formative years by his sports master father, Oliver now trains under the watchful eye of Tony Newenham, the England Athletics javelin mentor. This young athlete certainly looks the part, and he competes with a maturity which belies his youth. Size apart but surely still growing, he exudes the attributes of a high quality thrower, co-ordinating good technique with speed and power.

Oliver is a student at Gresham's School, where he is a key member of their successful rugby fifteen and he has already been recruited to the elite player development squad at Leicester Tigers. It will be interesting to see which sporting path this talented young man will finally follow. Let's hope it will be athletics.

Beth Carter (Aldershot, Farnham and District)

Physically cast in the mould of Liz McColgan, this quietly determined young lady displays competitiveness at a high level which promises much. She has achieved good times from 800m to 3000m and runs equally well on the country. As an U17, Beth ranked 2nd in the UK over 5000m and 3rd over 3000m. She achieved her 3k personal best of 9:39.52 unluckily losing out only in the dying strides of a gripping race in the UK School Games in Bath, having done most of the leading.

She also finished second in the England Open Championships and the English Schools Championships. In 2009 Beth won the Southern Cross Country Championship and took creditable 3rd places in the McCain Cross

Challenge and the Italica International Cross Country Race.

Like many hard-training current young athletes, Beth has endured more than her fair share of injuries, but her underlying steely nature has helped her to overcome all such stumbling blocks so far, revealing her as one with the determination and desire to succeed. Recovering from a long injury-enforced lay-off, her 2010 season revealed encouraging signs and her positive approach in the English Schools' senior girls 3000m Championship earned her second place in 9:46.81. In common with her contemporaries, Beth is accommodating the demands of school examinations which when completed will surely give her added freedom to develop her athletics potential.

After formative years with Invicta East Kent, Beth has recently moved to Aldershot, Farnham and District. In 2011 she made a great advance in the 2011 English National Cross Country Championship to take 4th place 45 sec behind international winner Charlotte Purdue.

See Figure 116 – Beth Carter

Peter Chambers (Croydon Harriers)

This very exciting student at my old school Trinity Croydon, is an intelligent, race-hungry sixteen-year-old with a shrewd competitive brain and is a key young member of my training squad too!

Peter won his races in the London Borough's Mini Marathon in 2008, 2009 and 2010, and has already run 800m in 2:02.8, 1500m in 4:08.6 and 3000m in 8:59.08.

See Figure 117 – Peter Chambers Lexus Croydon 10k Runner-up age 15 2010

A high achiever on the country too, Peter was a close up, but slightly disappointed bronze medallist in the 2009 English Schools Junior Boys' Cross Country Championships. He had beaten the winner earlier in the season and later gave a strong indication of his outstanding competitiveness when he overcame indisposition to achieve a memorable victory in the junior boys' race in the English Schools team finals at Newquay.

A first year U17 on the country in 2011, Peter has mixed it well with his older rivals as evidenced by a fighting 30th in the English National

Championship. When this hugely talented young athlete becomes entirely relaxed and accepts that one does not always need to train hard or race when unwell or suffering a growing phase, he will have moved on significantly from an already eye-catching level.

Peter is similar in many ways to Croydon club forerunner Don Faircloth, whom I first encountered as a young teenager in the 1960s. Both revealed a seemingly insatiable desire to train at high volume, a quality which can in my opinion be counterproductive for the development of a young athlete. Don, partially "controlled" by coach Brian Proctor, his parents and myself, went on to win the Commonwealth Games marathon bronze medal at Edinburgh in 1970, and to finish in the London Marathon top ten three times, and it is my hope that Peter will progress to emulate and surpass the achievements of his famous predecessor.

Watch this space, but you will probably have to wait at least seven years or so for the real big time performance!

Emelia Gorecka (Aldershot, Farnham and District)

Tenacious and talented, this slim, smiley young lady takes on a totally different persona as soon as she gets into racing mode. She throws down the gauntlet against contemporaries, while hanging on limpet-like, much to the disquiet of older rivals in open races. Emelia is clearly quick with an 800m best of 2:11.84, but her ability and aptitude for competition over longer distances is very clear to see. A first year under fifteen in 2009 she has achieved a clean sweep of championship titles both on the track and the country.

As a Surrey Schools and South East England team manager, it has been my good fortune to see her preparation and racing ability at first hand. Her capacity for calm competitiveness is a pleasure to experience. Her 2009 3000m best was 9:24.79 which ranked her top UK U17 and twenty-fourth overall, was achieved in adult competition at the St Mary's Classic, while her majestic but slower English Schools' victory was earned by a brave front run. A week later she won the SIAB International 3000m again in blustery conditions.

Into 2010 and Emelia confidently showed her heels not only to her contemporaries, but also to many older challengers. She proved good enough but was not old enough for an international U20 selection, and took the English title by a massive margin from her very talented club-mate Ruth Haynes who had a similar distance between her and the third finisher.

See Figure 118 – Emilia Gorecka/Ruth Haynes

At sixteen Emelia grasped a World Cross Country Championship selection with great maturity and her 23rd place finish, although ending an unbeaten streak, was outstanding on a much bigger stage, at a much higher level as second finisher for the 5th placed Great Britain Junior team.

Early in the track season she successfully made the predictable step up to 5000m and was rewarded with a 15:56.87 clocking. Her 1500m and 3000m bests have been excitingly advanced to 4:16.79 and 9:13.93. At the end of 2010 Emilia led the GB team to victory in the Junior European Cross-Country Championship and impressively, for one so young, won the individual bronze medal.

Her winning form continued into 2011 with a totally dominant victory in the Surrey Schools Championship followed by a hard-fought SEAA U17 Cross-Country Championship win and a similarly impressive victory by 30 sec over Jessica Judd on the 5K National Championship course.

I am confident that Emelia, characteristically sporting the red white and green of her club on her cheeks, will be right at the forefront of UK women's distance running very soon, and for many years to come.

Twinelle Hopeson (Croydon Harriers)

Here is an established young sprinter who, having shown great form over the shorter distances, has taken the transition to the 400m like a duck to water.

Twinelle is the younger of two sisters who have greatly benefited from the shrewd management of their cheerful, caring father Joseph[33] whose successful involvement with Twinelle and Joselynn has disproved the theory that fathers can seldom successfully coach their offspring.

Twinelle is a delightful and ambitious eighteen year old who clearly takes challenges very much in her stride. She caught the attention of experts when at thirteen she became Surrey 100m champion in 12.84sec, a time which she improved to a wind-assisted 12.46sec to take silver in the

---

[33] aka Guiseppe!

South of England Junior Championships and she also clocked a highly promising 25.5sec for the 200m the same year. At U15 level she reigned virtually supreme over 100m and 200m.

Four of her five outdoor "defeats" came in major championships. One was her superb silver medal spot in the AAA 100m in 12.14sec which saw her ranking 3rd in the UK in 2006.

The following year Twinelle showed up well as a first year U17 and took a creditable third in the European Youth Festival in Belgrade in the 200m in 24.52sec and she won 100m bronze in the England Athletics Open Championship. Predictably she enjoyed a better season as a second year U17. A 38.98sec 300m county championship win saw her ranked third in the UK and gave a clue as to what might be lying ahead.

2009 was another season of consistent high quality from her with a really encouraging unpressed 400m debut of 57.0sec while her best UK ranking was as 6th placer in the U20 200m.

With her 400m best down to 55.41sec in 2010, plus the retention of fine basic sprint form honed to 11.91sec over 100m and 24.13sec for 200m, which earned her World Junior Championship relay selection. The years ahead promise much for Twinelle.

See Figure 119   Croydon's quadruple Olympian Donna Fraser welcomes emerging star Twinelle Hopeson to "Wall of Fame!" mural by Jeanne-Marie Cars and Susan Beresford

Freya Jones (Team Southampton)

With a serious interest in javelin coaching, the performances of two girl throwers, sometimes at first hand, have regularly caught my eye, and I first noticed Freya when she was fourteen. This bubbly teenager just wins my vote for future fame over similarly outstanding, slightly older North Devonian Izzy Jeffs (48.90m) and Tesni Ward (48.49m).

The clear number one in her own age group in 2008, Freya, who threw her 600g spear a prodigious PB of 44.23m to win the English Schools U15 title, ranked second in the U17 category and twelfth among all ages, where she remained a year on.

The ambitious Freya, hurled her spear out to 49.66m as a first year U17, a distance which headed the UK list and placed her 4th overall.

She won the 2010 Youth Olympic Games Trials in Moscow, and soon after with a hike of over 1.5m on her personal best, Freya joined the elite band of 50+m plus practitioners with a 51.28m best to take Inter County silver in senior competition, a 6m cushion ahead of the second throw. This effort ranked her 6th in the UK Women's list.

She has a fine physique which will surely strengthen as she gains muscular maturity, and her already excellent technique will be honed to perfection in the years ahead.

Jessica Judd (Chelmsford)

This slim sixteen-year-old is not just another of a fine crop of emerging female distance runners but one whose swashbuckling approach to competition and the results achieved are thrilling in one of such tender years. I admire this youngster hugely and not least because she dragged one of my ambitious fifteen-year-old training squad athletes to a 1500m PB at Watford in 2007!

"What are you doing letting that little girl beat you!" I yelled at the unfortunate Scott Fanner, a keen young fellow, who try as he might was unable to make any impression on the then flying female. He was however persuaded to go over to the bemused Jessica after the race to thank her for towing him into new territory!

In 2008 Jessica ran nearly fifty middle track distance races, winning all but twelve of them. In one "losing" race against older opposition she made an impressive 3000m debut with a time of 9:53.43.

Runaway winner of the 2009 English Schools Junior Girl's Cross-Country Championship, Jessica showed that she is as focused against hundreds of her young female contemporaries, as she is against faster and older athletes in mixed races. Similarly dominant on the track, this sylph-like young athlete exuded confidence and talent when she soloed way ahead of all comers in the 2009 junior girls South of England and English Schools Championships 1500m events. Jessica seems to revel in one of the toughest aspects of the sport and her consistent domination is truly exciting in one so young. Her 4:21.03 1500m best would have topped the British women's rankings in my racing days in the early 1960s!
Continuing successfully into 2010, Jessica is seemingly irrepressible with majestic English Schools and English National Cross Country Championship victories and on the track too.

Her win in the 2010 English Cross Country Championship on the testing terrain of Roundhay Park Leeds was a lesson in confidence to many a senior athlete and unbeaten throughout that winter, gave a hint of what was in store on the track. Taller and stronger, the Chelmsford athlete has advanced her 800m best to 2:06.95, her 1500m to 4:18.38 and her 3000m to 9:08.47, the last achieved by a huge margin and representing 15 second improvement in a year.

Jessica impressed again in the 2011 English National Cross-Country race when she finished a strong second although a year younger than winner Emilia Gorecka.

At this early stage of a hopefully long career, she definitely displays all the characteristics of what it takes to become a champion. Her range of top quality results from a 42.0sec 300m to a 9:15.61 3000m speaks for itself. I hope that she retains her hunger for athletics success and matures into a future Olympian.

See Figure 120 – Jessica Judd win SEAA title by a "straight" Ashford.
Inset Victor characteristically waits for vanquished to finish

Lawrence Okoye (Croydon Harriers)

The 2003 Whitgift School intake welcomed the arrival of the youthful, long-limbed Lawence aged eleven. At my first coaching session with him I was immediately impressed by the young boy's potential.

After a few runs, jumps, shot puts and some ragged but well above average novice discus throws I was more than excited at the thought of what might lie ahead.

"What's your name, young man?" I queried.
"Lawrence Okoye, sir," came the polite response.
"Lawrence, I think that if you worked on it, you could become a very good multi-event athlete."
"What's that?"
"A decathlete like Daley Thompson or Dean Macey," I told him.
"No Sir, I want to be a rugby player," he said.

Clearly in a school like Whitgift with its huge rugby reputation, a long and torsuous road stretched ahead!

Six years later and lying eighth in the ESAA Senior Boy's Discus final with one throw remaining, a seemingly satisfied Lawrence was listening to his music while the other finalists worked towels, rehearsed technique and chatted with coaches. Breaking his "sound barrier", I was struggling to convince him that some similar action might be productive when Eric Scott, the lead Surrey team manager, arrived, clearly heaven sent.

I briefly explained my dilemma, and the dynamic, virtually incomprehensible Glaswegian ex decathlete worked the oracle. Obviously stunned into far more effective action, Lawrence despatched his discus over 58m to snatch second place at the last gasp. He did seem pleased, which was encouraging.

Another year on and with fewer than ten serious competitions to his name, the six foot six, almost 20 stone Okoye sits solidly second in the UK All Time U20 Rankings with a 63.92m throw which won him the UK World Junior Trials and earned him his ticket to the 2010 World Junior Championships in Monckton, Canada.

Just before his trip there, he overcame any disappointment at being sidelined to a downhill rear field for the ESAA final, by winning to the acclaim of a large, often in more ways than one, crowd who enthusiastically acknowledged his final and winning throw of 61.22m.

Latterly coached by Ian Briggs at Croydon, he has now moved on to the care of former international, and now coach, John Hillier. Lawrence was unable to repeat his 60m plus form in Canada, but his 59.77m effort for 5th place on the World stage was still very good indeed in his first really serious season.

See Figure 121 – Record breaking Lawrence Okoye, Croydon Harriers at Bedford 2010

Edward "Ned" Quiney

I first happened upon Ned Quiney whilst coaching at Whitgift School when he was fourteen years of age. Then a wiry and not altogether well co-ordinated teenager, he nevertheless nervously exuded talent across the board, and application which suggested a great future.

Since then he has graduated from being an able and versatile enthusiast, to becoming a very competent high jumper at 1.93m and more excitingly into the realms of pole vaulting where he has competed well and having cleared 5m and narrowly missed at 5.11m, looks set to be moving onwards and upwards, very soon.

Ned, now over six feet tall and seemingly getting stronger by the day, is also a raw but quick-armed thrower and competent hurdler, and has in addition maintained a respectable level of all round skills as evidenced in his first decathlon, in which he scored 5,308 points. There could well be a big future for him as a multi-eventer.

Now dear reader, I present you with the *"We can do better than Fabio Capello team challenge"*, to name young athletes who may vie with my predictions to achieve world status by 2012 or 2016! The exciting fact remains that there are many hundreds of other extraordinarily talented young athletes throughout Britain, similar to these right across the range of athletics. My hope is that their potential will be tapped and carefully nurtured within our sport and not just used as stepping stones by unscrupulous coaches, some of whom dare I say are marketing themselves rather too aggressively.

See Figure 124 – Ned Quiney breaks the 5m barrier at Crystal Palace 2010

Loulou Rowlands (South London Harriers)

A sixth former at Caterham School, Loulou looks as though butter wouldn't melt in her mouth, but... put her in a race, and this highly focused and able South London Harrier reflects the steel and former speed of her coach Mick Firth. Loulou has made astonishing progress on the country since the 2008 Intermediate English Schools' Cross-Country Championships when she finished a respectable 17th. She won the 2009 ESAA Senior Cross Country title in convincing fashion, with her closest challenger 15 seconds adrift. A month earlier she finished runner-up in the Inter Counties Championship and was otherwise unbeaten.

Here is a quiet and versatile young lady whose immediate impression does not reveal her inner steel. Already she has endured an extended spell of injury, patiently working well within herself to achieve the recovery. This was confirmed after many months of rehabilitation, in her winning come-back in a high class south Eastern England Inter Counties cross country event.

An athlete has to be made of stern stuff to successfully overcome such a long spell of enforced and very restricted activity and Loulou has clearly shown that she is made like that.

Loulou displays a good range of performances on the track, from 200m to

1500m, the speed of which will surely stand her in good stead over much longer distances in the future. In 2010, she ran a best of 4:28.63 for a well-earned 4th place in the ESAA Championships.

See Figure 122 – Kelly Holmes with Loulou Rowlands

Katarina Thompson-Johnson (Liverpool Harriers)

Already firmly established as a young star in her own right, Katarina has all the attributes of a world class heptathlete in the making. She is a tall, strong, competitive and highly motivated individual.

At sixteen in late 2008, she ranked first in four events, and to U19 level in two of them, the high and long jumps. Katarina won most of the titles she tackled that year, and while representing Great Britain in a combined events match early in 2009 she set four personal bests.

Her top high jump is 1.81m (1.82 indoors) and her furthest long jump is 6.31m.

She ranked seventh against all ages in the UK heptathlon rankings and is currently 5.16m behind Kelly Sotherton in the javelin, and looks good to overtake the Olympian in that discipline soon.

She has progressed to an indoor UK Heptathlon best and with the gods on her side the world is surely her oyster. Her championship and highlight details occupy twelve lines on her "Power of 10"[34] entry and I defy anyone to find a longer and more impressive section for any young athlete.

See Figure 123 – Katerina Thompson

---

[34] The 'all singing and dancing' athletes performance database.

Appendix F

Foot Soldiers beat Falsifiers by a Furlong

It was my original intention to highlight my "Victor Meldrew-like" hatred of drug cheats here in a list of "My Bottom 20 Athletes". Following advice, wisdom has prevailed and I decided to avoid the risk of litigation. The creation of this chapter in praise of the unknown and unsung foot soldiers of athletics is in a truly positive vein.

Much more comfortably, I take this opportunity to feature the front-line action of just a few of athletics' unpaid and unsung heroes, past and present, whom I know and without whose generous involvement our sport would be in a very poor state.

Hail my chosen few representatives of this wonderful unpaid workforce, who guarantee the smooth running of athletics in perpetuity. Eat your hearts out glory-seeking cheats; this is where many of the real rewards lie, in creating opportunities for, and ensuring that, genuine enthusiasts enjoy fair competition.

Mine is only a sample study, for the limitations of which I apologise, but if I succeed in directing acclaim across athletics to the many hundreds of honorary unsung heroes to whom the sport owes so much, I will have no regrets.

Here are my heroes, presented in alphabetical order to reflect fairness.

David Barrington (Kingston AC and Polytechnic Harriers, Surrey County AA, Downs League)

David is currently best known beyond his club in Surrey as the "Hurdles King of the County Championships!" where each year he co-ordinates his team of young helpers to ensure smooth transition from one event to the next.

That however is just the very public tip of a great iceberg (more appropriately perhaps showcase of dedication), with the seemingly tireless senior citizen of athletics officiating in numerous key areas of administration, while still enjoying the buzz of personal competition.

A long time lynch pin of his club's organisation, David started in the sport in 1956 with North Staffs and Stone AC, and became a very successful 400m hurdler, peaking with an inter-county bronze proudly behind such luminaries as John Cooper and Peter Warden.

"They were the bane of my hurdling career," he said.

He was a regular AAA Championship competitor, but reflects ruefully on the intrusion of too many foreigners, a sentiment to which I can subscribe as one time fourth placer behind an American winner.

Not even the shock of moving to the allegedly inhospitable south could derail David from his highly productive journey in the athletics world.

He subsequently struck European silver as a veteran in the 1980s, five years after becoming General Secretary of Polytechnic Harriers. Such is his dedication that he remains in that key post with the merged Kingston AC and Polytechnic Harriers.

David is also the man behind the Downs League, a children's Sunday morning cross-country event, which is enjoyed by hundreds of youngsters annually at Epsom.

The British Athletics League has had the benefit of his input from the start, and he fills numerous roles on the domestic front, most important among them being that of general "Dogsbody".

See Figure 125 – David Barrington beats computer results!

Ian Briggs (Surrey Beagles/Croydon Harriers)

Contrary to spurious legend, the infant Ian was not talent spotted when hurling his rattle from the pram. His evolution in the sport was in reality far more gradual.

"Herr Brigand", as I jokingly call him, is indeed completely the opposite of one's first impression. Behind the gruff exterior of this former PE teacher is the caring, conscientious discus coach.

Ian was a child of post-colonial India, where his family lived. On the establishment of Pakistan, his father, with job prospects in mind, sent him to England. Although he had won the Victor Ludorum at school in Rawalpindi, he had little grounding in athletics, hence his rather delayed development.

The relatively short spell in the Royal Navy which followed held mixed athletic blessings, with Ian capitalising on shore time to compete and to qualify as a coach. Undeterred when at sea, on calm days Ian and other enthusiasts launched shot and other modified impedimenta from the flight deck of an aircraft carrier, wisely when planes were not taking off!

The navy was compassionate in 1952, allowing Ian the opportunity while in port to attend the Helsinki Olympics, when as he says, "The triple gold medallist there, Emil Zatopek, fired up athletics in my mind".

Ian rapidly developed an eagle-eye for the best discus techniques, being enthralled at the skills of the "technically brilliant" Al Oerter, gold medallist in three Olympics, and the "physically perfect" Ludovik Danek.

As a successful competitor and devoted coach, Ian peaked in the Veteran 50 ranks as 2nd in the U.K and 14th in the World. Generous in competition, Ian was regularly in discreet "coaching" action, which I can confirm as recipient of his wisdom, giving rivals technical tips in between his throws.

Ian delights in advising young athletes too, prominent among whom has been Lawrence Okoye, now UK number two all-time U20 thrower at 63.92m. He and dozens of aspiring discus throwers each have Ian to thank for pointing them in the right direction, whilst he continues to develop the technique of established athletes.

Devoted to the Surrey Beagles club until its recent sad demise, he has continued, completing the landmark fifty summers of coaching at Croydon in 2010. Ian is a fascinating coach, some of whose unusual techniques, evolved over many years, painlessly break the ice on the way to full understanding.

He has not limited himself to coaching in retirement and is regularly to be seen, during the summer months, officiating in field event competitions from school to county level.

Jeanne Coker (Highgate Harriers, Middlesex County AA)

Jeanne, it is fair to say, is among the most knowledgeable and even-handed top British athletics officials whom I have had the pleasure of meeting and working alongside. She has an aura of severity about her, but not far underneath there is a lady of compassion.

Jeanne took up athletics for endurance training while a county netball player. She found herself immediately drafted into the cross-country team and the 440 yards on the track. Jeanne ran in the first London marathon and was a founder member of Veteran Women's athletics in the UK.

During five years teaching at Holland Park School she conditioned the boys' football team with circuit training and clearly won their respect, being affectionately known by the nickname "Thunder legs".

Jeanne took up officiating in 1970 at the instigation of Vera Searle, one of the greatest champions of the cause of women's athletics.

Well-versed in the minutiae of athletics rules and regulations, Jeanne is one of the first whom I would recommend anyone to contact for patient and clear clarification. Willing to work and advise almost beyond the call of reasonable duty, Jeanne, still an active athlete in her seventies, prepares the ground, does the job, and leaves no doubt that it has been well done.

She is always highly organised, if seemingly a little dogmatic, and has, over many years of officiating, won the respect of colleagues and competitors alike.

See Figure 126 – The fair and knowledgeable Jeanne Coker

Jeanne's pet hates, doubtless shared by many, are the pre distance-race actions of male athletes who use bushes and trees rather than toilets (shades of an athlete in need, who alienated a certain Duke before a Windsor to Chiswick marathon – the castle wall was not an appropriate convenience and a tongue-lashing from the royal Land Rover driver was the miscreant's reward); and the finishing-funnel spitters, whose unwelcome waste products often find their way onto the shoes of unsuspecting officials.

On the subject of drugs in athletics, and the fallibility of testing, Jeanne recalls one occasion, when a tester attended a Southern Men's League match. He asked for a position in the 200m and the athlete was indentified. The tester stayed at the finish and Jeanne pointed out that the individual was returning to the start.

"*Shouldn't you follow?*" she suggested.
"*No,*" he said, "*I will catch him later.*"
"*I doubt it,*" Jeanne replied knowingly, "*he will be out of the back gate and into his car before you can catch him!*"
She was right.

Jeanne does not limit herself to where or in what standard of meeting she works. Happy to serve club and county through to national and Commonwealth level, Jeanne regularly champions disabled events too. Nor does she restrict her grass roots efforts to the North of the Thames, and sorties south have more often than not been to "lend a hand on the land" notably in the recent Lexus Croydon 10K.

Ken Crooke (Croydon Harriers/Veterans AC/Surrey County AA)

I would defy anyone to have produced more paperwork in the interest of athletics and cross country and road running in particular, or to have spent more hours striving in the cause of the sport than Ken. The list of clubs and organisations he has served would fill many a page, and his roles have ranged from club and league secretary, treasurer and team manager to well-deserved election as club and current Surrey County President.

An active athlete into his eighties, Ken has never lost his all-round enthusiasm for the sport to which he remains truly devoted.

Recent recall of him in action belies a very capable athlete of yesteryear, who way back in 1952, despite being what I would describe as an upper middle-distance man, having heard of Rudolph Harbig the great German "half-miler", was inspired to break two minutes for the one and only time, amazingly on the six laps to a mile grass track at Salisbury.

The "Lost Ken" situation in the 2008 Surrey County Veterans pentathlon 1500m raised considerable concern for his well-being, but clearly made of stern stuff, our hero disregarded his first impulse of "I'm staying here" where he had fallen by the trackside hose. He rose (Monty!) python-like from the yellow coils, and finished briskly to "the inspiring cheers of the crowd".

That he was more suited to longer distances is evidenced by his record of fifteen or so cross-country wins for Southampton AAC and his National cross-country competitive record which extended from 1950 to 1989. On one occasion as the incumbent English Cross-Country Union (Association from 1992) Championship Secretary, he suddenly realised that his job was done 30 minutes before the start, and that he could go and race! Ken served in that role from 1988 to 1997.

Ken's service in other administrative roles for the Surrey AA, East Surrey League, Croydon Harriers and more, totals well over 100 mind-boggling years.

Austin Fox (Croydon Harriers)

Austin, an athletics enthusiast, true club man through and through, and keen student of the sport, has followed a long successful career as a competitor and continues as a dedicated club and county official.

As a war-time schoolboy deprived of sports opportunities, he soon afterwards discovered athletics in 1946, and was an immediate success as a plimsoll-shod racer on his works' sports day. He was inspired by the great Jamaican duo of the 1948 Olympians: the powerful Herb McKenley and the contrasting smooth running Arthur Wint.

See Figure 126 – The Magnificent Arthur Wint. 440yds start at Motspur Park 1946

Thereafter Austin developed what was to become his abiding interest in the sport: he moved rapidly to join Croydon Harriers and happy action in the open handicap scene in vogue at the time. He was limited, with the exception of one sortie to the hallowed Motspur Park, to running on grass, until 1952 and the opening of The Croydon Sports Arena.

He explained that running on grass tracks then always required walking the course to check for manhole covers and drains! Easily recognisable in the beautiful badge be-decked sweater knitted by his wife Dorrie which he favoured to a tracksuit top, Austin was also recognisable when racing, for his early speed and progressive lean, and while training for recording his repetitions on a knitting gauge.

His fondest racing recall was of his sole sub two minute half mile achieved in the County final when a desperate home straight dash and a clash of elbows left a rival sprawling and Austin safely home in 1:59.0!

Season in and season out Austin has devoted most of his weekends, plus many weekdays too, to officiating. Even into his late seventies, he endured all kinds of weather to work as a knowledgeable clerk-of-course and cross-country course marshal. I recall one bleak, wintry occasion when I had to rescue him from the threat of frostbite in a hoar-whitened field as he was vainly trying to hammer marker flags into the rock-hard ground.

Over the years, he has famously driven to athletics venues, Del Boy-like in a series of Robin Reliants. On one memorable occasion when Croydon Harriers President he kindly offered to pick up a then-aspiring Yacin Yusuf en route to a County Championship.

Imagine the excited lad's deflation when the Club President rolled up not in a luxurious Lexus "limo", nor a V.W. Fox or even a dated Austin, but in one of his favoured fibreglass Robin Reliant three-wheelers! The boy's "Street Cred." was in tatters, but athletically un-phased he did go on to win the county title.

Nowadays, with walking difficult, Austin still contributes significantly, happily hiding himself away from the action under stands and in gloomy sheds, weighing and issuing equipment and checking all items back. He is also key in checking field cards with his long-time friend Don Webb.

Austin still retains a good sense of humour despite the discomfort he experiences when walking, smiling when urged over the PA to attack his 17sec best for crossing the track, or hopefully to get to his post before the meeting is over. What a star!

Carolyn Franks (Cheltenham and County Harriers)

Recognised as one of the country's most knowledgeable and effective javelin coaches, Carolyn started on her career helping throwers way back in 1960. Working tirelessly since then helping many throwers to progress, her significant contribution was recognised with the 2009 Gloucestershire Outstanding Services to Sport award.

Carolyn, modest in the extreme, said of her award:
"It's nice to be recognised, but there are a lot of people out there doing a lot of hard graft. It is something for which I would like to see them being recognised too."

Her interest in the sport "kicked off" in her first year at secondary school, when the headmistress inspired her during early morning sessions and she was even allowed the freedom of an un-caged discus circle in which to train.

She joined Cambridge and Coleridge AC in the early 1960s when the girls' athletics section was somewhat peripheral, but as good fortune had it, further inspiration was on hand when the great Australian Herb Elliott paid a visit to her school.

Training to be a PE teacher followed, and then it was out into the demanding world of teaching. There another significant situation haltingly evolved. Unwilling to follow advice to vote for her school's area committee nominee Cliff Franks, then little known to her, she could have deprived herself of a husband, and the sport of her significant and ongoing contribution.

Happily, thanks to those who knew him better, Cliff was elected anyway, and Carolyn's subsequent compassion in offering him a lift one day may well have set the ball rolling for her future happiness. The rest is history.

Her most outstanding recent outstanding athlete has been James Campbell, who threw the javelin 73.00m at the Beijing World Junior Championships, when he finished 8th. He has since moved to Commonwealth Games status, representing Scotland as the UK number one ranker in Delhi in 2010. Carolyn is currently nurturing two exciting girl shot put prospects in an enthusiastic and diverse group of throwers.

The offices she has held, the committees she has served (and in many causes still serves) are legend, and her 30,000 a year mileage by car speaks for itself. One of the jobs this tireless lady inherited from her husband is that of Secretary of the Birmingham and District Invitation Cross-Country League, a post in which she continues to hold in parallel with being their President.

Her inter-personal skills have also been recognised in the many team management posts she has held from schools level to UKA Small Team status.

Carolyn lists among her many qualifications that of a Chief Timekeeper and on finding herself to be beyond Seiko's athletics needs at the Barcelona Olympics, she changed sports, and worked with their rowing team at the 1500m mark. This became known notoriously as the "Piddle Point" due to the extra-curricular activities in the vicinity of some of the returning oarsmen.

Clearly not among them, the British Searle brothers, allegedly "blown", by Carolyn, to victory after she had recorded their time, were not only excellent practitioners of their sport, but apparently rather gorgeous into the bargain! So much for the Barcelona memories of this heroine.

See Figure 126 – Carolyn Franks discussing finer points of javelin throwing with Wilf Paish

Linda Harrison (Croydon Harriers)

Here is an insatiable veteran athlete who has put so much into the sport through her efforts in providing refreshments year in and year out that she wins my accolade as Queen of Athletics Club Tea Ladies.

Linda like so many outstanding servants of the sport arrived on the scene as a parent of young athletes whose careers were short-lived. Their legacy, as it has often been with numerous young athletes, is that their parents stay after they move on.

Her athletic inspiration, Colin Oxlade, is not a household name in the sport except in Selsdon, but one would be hard pressed to find another so devoted, with such a sensible and rewarding approach to senior participation.

No natural athlete, Linda has become an invaluable team player who sets a fine example with her willingness to cover almost any event. She is happy to go for points, where many younger athletes would baulk for fear of "making themselves look silly". She is one of those relaxed latter-day athletes whose realism when it comes to achievement is refreshing. Linda delights in a finish, smiles happily on hitting the sand when completing a triple jump and is positively radiant when she clears a modestly raised high jump bar. Her proudest achievements have been with her beloved heavy hammer with which she won a World indoor bronze medal in 2008. Two years later she struck gold on her World Veterans 4x200m relay rush with the Great Britain team in Kamloops, Canada with her team including Colin and the indefatigable Andy Del Nevo.

On the catering front, Linda is an Olympian of self-challenge and competitiveness who has worked tirelessly with her team to raise essential funds to help to keep the Croydon Harriers solvent. She bakes cakes and makes sandwiches, persuading others to provide similarly;

then she and her team cheerfully serve behind refreshment counters and tables, both inside and out, on training nights and at club, county and schools events all the year round, having always arrived well in advance with her car well stocked from regular visits to the wholesaler.

As well as being one of the key welcoming smiling faces at the Croydon Arena, she also holds the important post of Club Welfare Officer for girl athletes, is a key committee member and a Past President.

See Figure 129 – Linda Harrison enjoying her athletics!

Derek Hayward
(Loughborough Colleges AC, English Schools AA & Kangaroo Club)

Most of Derek's working life has been devoted to the cause of sport, not just athletics alone but, significantly, swimming too.

His appetite for athletics began at school, thanks to an astute PE teacher at Buckhurst Hill who spotted his jumping potential and inspired the 15 year-old Hayward to ESAA selection at Southampton in 1951. From then on the die had been cast.

Derek was the first official alongside whom I was privileged to work. During my early student days at Loughborough, he steered a very steady ship as a secretary of the Colleges' AC. I learned a great deal from him about organisation, in those formative days. The Colleges' Athletics Club naturally benefited as did the wider world of athletics.

His love for the horizontal jumps was infectious and clearly advanced their cause over the years in the UK. In 1959 he founded the Kangaroo Club and is in his 44th year as its Secretary/Treasurer. Derek and his wife Jackie are highly qualified field judges, with both reaching Referee status, and they still work to the great benefit of the Shropshire County AA, Shropshire County Schools' AA and beyond.

A PE teacher himself for ten years, Derek then became the Shropshire PE Advisor, and remained in that post for a further eighteen years. His sixteen years in retirement have been used generously in numerous honorary capacities.

Derek has been a key English Schools AA committee man for twenty-five years, served as their combined events secretary for eighteen of them, and most recently for a further ten he worked as their extremely helpful and effective press secretary, ably assisted by his wife. He contributed as advertising secretary (1981-99), advancing the cause of ESAA Track and Field Championships, other related athletics events and significantly helped to raise £30,000 for the association. He is still their race walking secretary, and his major contribution in that context has now been acknowledged by the Race Walking Association.

Active on the team front too, Derek has founded three athletics clubs, Bridgnorth, Oswestry and Telford, and he has assisted in the re-formation of two others in Shrewsbury and Much Wenlock.

See Figure 130 – Dedicated Derek Hayward on ESAA duty

Ron Jewkes (Ealing and Southall AC/Middlesex County)

Throughout one of the sports longest careers, Ron gained respect and admiration far and wide from fellow officials and starters in particular. He came into the sport as a young competitor in 1933 and was still actively involved as a starter well into his nineties. Always a firm and friendly exponent of the art, Ron was equally fair and professional whether he was firing his 45s at club or international level. His qualities were acknowledged way beyond athletics when he was made a Freeman of the City of London In 2007.

So vast was his positive influence on athletics that one could not presume to do it justice here, but I urge readers and especially starters should you feature among them, to delve a little deeper into the story of a fascinating man.

For a start, dare I say, no pun intended, I would recommend a visit to the NUTS Athletics Archive at the Cobham Hall School in Kent, where Ron's scrapbook dating from the 1930s is a prized exhibit, providing a wonderful insight into the man and those distant days. I feel honoured to have been guided by him.

Matthew Kiernan (Croydon Harriers)

Matthew is first among many members of my club in their twenties, who are worth more than their weight in gold!

Modest in the extreme, Matthew describes himself as having been "Useless at ALL sports at school", but one who benefited from making the great leap into club athletics to run slowly over long distances without embarrassment.

He recalls from that time, "A tall gangly chap," who turned out to be Martyn Rooney!

A tail-end finish in the London Mini-Marathon of 2003 hooked him, and in just five years he proved what dedicated young athletes can achieve, when at the age of 20 he achieved his dream of a London Marathon finish. His "gold" was won in 22,000th place.

A recent university graduate and an athletics enthusiast "par excellence", Matthew has, since then, become a towering ideas man in my club, and has established himself as the popular and extremely effective right-hand man for me with my MFG training squad.

While I went to the Beijing Olympics, I confidently left Matthew in charge of my training squad and he justified my confidence in him by dispensing the schedules which I had set in a flexible and most productive fashion. Not being satisfied in that role alone, he is a tireless team manager and "athlete for all events".

Never afraid of drawing attention to himself in the quest for team points, he is famously recalled carefully descending the steeplechase barrier on the wet side, before pushing off to the shoreline. There was thus no need to shake himself dry, dog-like, and he trotted home weary but comfortable with points secure.

He is a huge inspirational asset to his team, with the one fault of maybe exhausting himself in the interest of the cause.

See Figure 131 – Valiant team manager Matthew Kiernan prepares plunge in pursuit of points

Matthew, now a promising journalist, has also made a major contribution not only on the committee, but also making promotional films and developing the Croydon Harriers's website alongside "young" veteran athlete Martin Rowe, another innovative enthusiast, more of whose kind our sport urgently needs.

Terry Lapins (Croydon Harriers/Surrey County AA)

Terry is the second of those valuable, rare young and gregarious enthusiasts, still in his twenties. He is the kind of man for all roles, whom every club longs to have in their ranks.

He is the most willing of club athletes, committee man, official, team manager and volunteer handyman all rolled into one. Often spontaneous, spotting faults and correcting them without prompting, he can, at other times, be seen making storage boxes, re-attaching dislodged book cupboards, attaching curtain rails and easing doors. He applies his energy with infectious enthusiasm, which was recognised in 2007 when he was the deserved winner of the UK/England Athletics London Young Volunteer. As a carpenter by trade, is skills are readily on call.

With a solid school athletics background behind him, Terry's first true success came when he finished the Great North Run. An admirer of Hicham El-Gerouj, Haile Gebrselassie and Paula Radcliffe, he is the first to admit that he could not aspire to their achievements, but is more than happy to gain inspiration from them, and to follow in their footsteps at a respectful distance.

Terry's love for steeple-chasing is printed boldly in gold on his club vest, but it has not restricted him to that discipline, and during many a summer match he often has to be advised against running or even jumping himself into the deck by tackling too many events.

Always ready to suffer for the cause, Terry's face was etched with disappointment when he failed to gain a place in one of Harriers' London Marathon ballots, but ever the sportsman, he was the first to wish successful colleagues the best of luck.

It is my hope with London 2012 fast approaching, that his infectious enthusiasm will be caught by more and more young men and women up and down the country.

See Figure 132 – The "Chippy and the Pedagogue" Terry Lapins and Paul Weston with their England Athletics Officiating and coaching Awards

Jeff Manson (Oxted County School/Surrey Schools AA)

On being invited to supply information for his inclusion in this "Anti-rogues gallery", the modest Jeff proclaimed himself to be honoured, although jokingly he added a request that should any pictures of him be published... *"please darken my hair!"* Photo? Sorry Jeff you must be joking!

Jeff "Mr Surrey Schools' Cross-Country", is possibly the most infectiously effervescent, enthusiastic of leaders with whom I have had the good fortune to work with: team manager and motivator extraordinaire, he has the trick of relating to, and working with young, athletes in such a way that they really want to achieve for him and his teams.

Jeff's school coaching/management career started at Oxted County School in January 1982 in the cross-country context and extended to the Surrey Schools' Championships that summer. Since then, Jeff has nurtured a seemingly endless string of talented runners at his central Surrey School; selecting county squads, organising training days and managing teams at summer and winter English Schools' Championships.

The buzz of Oxted boys' successes readily compensated for the decline of his own half-marathon and marathon career, as Jeff devoted more and more of his time to their cause. Predictably with progress, tougher challenges were accepted and more illustrious individuals encountered.

His success in the role of master in charge of cross-country running at Oxted County School is reflected year in and year out in the size and success of the teams which he regularly turns out.

Jeff acknowledges local and national "legends" Ursula Blanchflower and Frank Horwell as having greatly enhanced his skills in the sport. The latter's involvement with early county developments was, he says, instrumental in their establishment, and which are now regularly attended by a hundred or so eager candidates. He is still happiest working to develop the talents of boys at his beloved Oxted School, but it is the good fortune of boys and girls beyond its boundary that he still willingly devotes a large amount of his time and energy to their interests in inter-county and English Schools competitions.

Peter O'Brien (Wallington Grammar School/Surrey Schools AA)

Now regrettably retired from the sport, Peter served athletics as an energetic and knowledgeable PE teacher for thirty-seven years at Wallington Grammar School for Boys. Peter proved himself an adept master in charge and among his early protégés was team captain and proficient miler Chris Woodhead who, possibly with academic foresight, abandoned the road to track stardom for one which led him to peak elsewhere as Her Majesty's Government Chief Inspector of Education.

Peter became, in my opinion, one of the best announcers to ever to preside over athletics events. He spread his skills between the frenetic two days of the County Schools Championships at the much missed Motspur Park, to the "Seat of pants" open competitions at Crystal Palace. He treated each with the same meticulous preparation, and produced the same controlled and informative delivery, unmatched by many a current incumbent.

Ever vigilant, Peter seemed aware of any key action in the stadium which merited introduction, and his subsequent clear and timely call for respect from the spectators always generated a good response. Way before the golden days of Jonathan Edwards, triple jumpers especially loved him for the slightly biased way in which he drew attention to their discipline. One has happy memories of his clear cheery and well informed delivery as an announcer.

He was for many years too, an efficient athletics administrator, dealing with the popular, late lamented Three Star Award Scheme, which was ineffectively replaced by an anaemic and somewhat gimmicky alternative. Always one to acknowledge the contribution of others, Peter, having read my tribute to Tommy Thomas, described him perfectly as "a true gentleman of the sport!"

Lack of acknowledgement of Peter's skills and industry, and the favouring of media men as announcers at the time, plus his own increasing interest in "Matters Folk" (US Music) while he was also producing his own magazine "The Omaha", led disappointingly to his premature departure.

Peter Radford (Trinity School of John Whitgift, Croydon Schools AA, Surrey Schools AA)

Namesake of Peter "The Whippet" Radford, former 200m world record holder, this Peter Radford is one of the famous Millfield School's athletics sons. He later carved his own significant niche contributing significantly as coach, organiser, team manager and official, first while teaching at Millfield and later at Trinity School in Croydon.

Inspired, like so many connoisseurs of athletics, by Mary Rand, Peter soon developed as a competitor to become a speedy sprint hurdler, setting an English Schools Best performance in 1966.

Thanks, dare I say, to relatively short legs and the increasing height of hurdles as he progressed through the age groups, Peter moved comfortably into multi-tasking as coach, official and organiser. During his

Trinity based years, he presided over many highly successful athletics teams and I was luckily on hand for his final fifteen to witness his good work. In that period, the school produced twelve ESAA Champions, two of whom, 400m hurdlers, Tom Haynes 1st and Jason Davenhill 2nd, were Peter's personal charges. Their achievements were the product of his meticulous approach to hurdles preparation. If only he would take on some of today's aspiring Akabusi's or Hemery's (simultaneously a colleague at Millfield).

Peter's thirty seven years as master in charge of athletics at Trinity School say much for his professionalism, endurance and love of the sport. A seemingly tireless committee man, he continues to contribute elsewhere, notably as secretary/team manager treasurer at Borough and County level.

See Figure 133 – "Grass Roots" multi-tasker Peter Radford

His trademark orange jacket and generally jaunty presence, plus plenty of repartee, are always welcome on competition days, especially cloudy ones, when they go some way to brighten up the gloom.

Mike Scott (Woking AC/Surrey County AA)

Mike suffered an incurable attack of timekeeping addiction with Newport Harriers in 1980. Fortunately for athletics from then in Wales, to the present day in Surrey, he is still gripped by the condition.

For the next ten years Mike acted as Vice-Chairman and Young Athletes' Team Manager, concurrently progressing to regional level at both timekeeping and track judging.

He chaired Gwent County AA in 1986, and moved to Stockport five years later, again raising his head above the parapet, now elevated to national grade track judge. He returned to Surrey in the early nineties and again had his services snapped up, this time the lucky club was Woking AC, so adding to his self-inflicted workload with the South of England AA.

Mike initiated the key bid for photo-finish equipment funding in 2001, while insatiably taking on secretary-ships; those of the Surrey County AA Development and Coaching committee, plus serving as an Active Sports and South East Region Council Member. 2002 saw him promoting and operating the Surrey photo-finish system and he is currently recognised as the definitive Surrey County photo finish guru, who seldom sees the action first hand, but is more often than not the best informed person in the stadium on any of the track activity.

Before competitions he can be seen clambering, like Spiderman, up and down ladders, dashing back and forth attaching wires, and setting up finish line beams and the electronic clock. Out of public view he busies himself with screens, keyboards and many more metres of mysterious wire, to ensure that demanding present day track athletes can be judged and timed to the nearest millimetre and hundredth of a second! Under Mike's management, race control and results provision in our area have become the envy of many.

Mike clearly predicts the end of the world in 2015... I quote *"2015 Give it all up!"*

Sue Shilling (Kingston and Polytechnic/Surrey Schools AA)

Due to Sue's modesty, much of what follows has been provided by her husband Peter, himself a significant "player" on the athletics scene from schools to international level.

Her competitive claim to fame at least as a Surrey athlete might reasonably be seen as her run in the inaugural ESAA Cross-Country Championships at Rochdale when she was the first Surrey girl home.

Sue, a teacher by profession, is another ex-athlete turned official, who has served her club from Surrey A C days to Kingston and Polytechnic guise, and the Surrey Schools' Championships. In particular she became Championship Secretary in 1985 when she had her arm gently and effectively twisted by another great servant of the sport, Bernard Apps. Thus one of the biggest county schools' championships in the land continues to be healthy.

In addition to that time-consuming role, Sue has been a key member of the county schools team management for many years, specialising in the monster job of kit issue and more importantly in its safe return.

The reputation of her lemon drizzle cake, always much in demand at Kingsmeadow Championship meetings, is only matched nationally in my experience by the astonishing Victoria sponge cakes of a wonderful Devonian, a gentleman timekeeper, even more senior in the sport than I.

Mark Steed (Kelly College, Berkhamstead School)

Mark is the public school Principal who goes the extra mile in the interests of athletics as the almost single-handed organiser of the prestigious Achilles Schools' Relay Meeting, the organisation of which he took on in 1991.

Another self effacing contributor to the sport, he claims to have developed his interest while bouncing pebble-like along the bottom of a challenging academic stream. The change would then perhaps allow him to leap salmon-like from the flow to shine elsewhere.

Never coached, and not allowed to compete on Sundays, shades of Olympian Eric Liddell, Mark persevered and won a place at Cambridge with "the sole ambition of winning a Blue". I wonder if he had his priorities right then, but I have to admit to remaining envious of his "Joseph-like many-coloured blazer".

It is hard to imagine the now almost sylph-like Mark, as a 15 stone high jumper with little technique, but that was how it was as he progressed in the teaching profession as master in charge of athletics, alongside the demands of the class-room and career development. His early coaching career in schools ran alongside his competitive one, and was especially productive during his time at Oundle School.

Three years into his reign as meeting organiser, Mark was presented a major boost, when the 40th anniversary of Bannister's break-through fell on 7th May 1994 and he was faced with moving the meeting, away from Iffley Road, Oxford, immortalised by Roger Bannister's ground breaking sub 4-minute mile.

Ever the entrepreneur, Mark negotiated the integration of the Celebration Pentland Veteran's Mile into his programme, and the schools' competitors were treated to seeing several of the world's greatest athletes in action. Maybe some of the stars were a shade or two slower than in their heyday, but has such a prestigious field ever been amassed before or since?

See Figure 134 – Achilles Relays "Anchor Man" Mark Steed centre at Iffley Road with John De'ath, and fellow blue Alan Sexton

See Figure 135 – Bannister First Sub 4 minute mile Anniversary Achilles Relays Programme

The programme read:

1.45 p.m   EVENT 1
THE PENTLAND VETERANS' HANDICAPPED MILE
Sponsored by G. T. Law

Filbert Bayi	Tanzania	40
Chris Brasher	Great Britain	55
Eamonn Coghlan	Ireland	41
Kipchoge Keino	Kenya	54
Jim Ryun	U.S.A.	47
Peter Snell	New Zealand	55
Bruce Tulloh	Great Britain	54
Pekka Vasala	Finland	46
Thomas Wessinghage	Germany	42

SIR ROGER BANNISTER
Will make a presentation to the winner ...and he did!

*See Figure 102 – Sir Roger Bannister congratulates Kip. Keino after
Pentland Anniversary mile at Iffley Road, Oxford 1994*

I was listed as announcer in the programme that day, but was not deemed worthy of such an occasion, dare I say by authority beyond Mark, and I was replaced by the more experienced Tony Ward. My demotion turned out to be a blessing in disguise, offering me the best opportunity to meet the stars, and in particular to reminisce with the greatest of my former rivals, Peter Snell.

If my memory serves me correctly Chris Brasher won, cannily making the most of a realistic handicap, while Eamonn Coughlan fell short of his aim be the first man over forty to beat 4 minutes for the mile. I was delighted that my Trinity School 4x800m team won that day, to make it the more memorable for me.

Now nearing its half century, the Achilles Schools' Relays Meeting has happily expanded and features a healthy diversity of schools, all displaying a serious interest in this important technical side of athletics.

Mark took on the organisation of the event In his early days at Oundle School, continuing even when he moved on to be headmaster at Kelly

235

College in distant Cornwall, when he could easily have relinquished his valuable control of the historic event.

To his great credit he has never claimed distance and pressure of work as a get-out clause and accordingly thousands of boy and girl athletes have benefited. Such is his devotion to the cause that he remains at the helm despite having moved further up the academic ladder to be Principal at Berkhamstead School.

No man with airs and graces this, Mark is very much a hands-on event organiser and can often be seen, blues blazer removed, sleeves rolled up, helping stewards at the ever popular event, which may now be unique, featuring 4x100m shuttle hurdles relays in the programme.

To quote the man who significantly keeps The Achilles Show on the road, Mark endearingly describes relay running as "The quintessential team running event".

Many of the young men and women who have enjoyed competing at Iffley Road thanks to Mark's efforts have certainly contributed to the quintessential nature of the occasion. May many more have the opportunity in years to come.

"Tommy" Thomas (South London Harriers)

"Tommy" Thomas, otherwise "Mr South London Harriers", MR Thomas to his face, was one of a wonderful league of gentleman who graced the sport for years following World War II. Almost to the end of a very long and chequered career he addressed me as "Fleet" both in the written form, finishing with "Yours faithfully, Thomas", and in conversation.

He had an endearing stammer and a captivating manner, and was always willing to advise and help, especially in my early days as "rival" club secretary in the mid 1960s.

I have two lasting memories of Tommy, a seeming Methuselah even in my early days: one concerns the "The Emsley Carr Mile" Trophy and the other epitomised him as a seemingly indestructible pillar of the sport.

In the first instance, I contacted him about the signature of the late Peter Driver missing from the vellum bound and lavishly illuminated tome which was the Trophy.

"Can you help, Mr Thomas?" I asked timorously.
"Leave it to me, Fleet," was the reassuring response.

Although I was confident from his reputation that there would be a positive outcome, I must confess to feeling some doubt when after a month I had heard nothing, but I did not have the temerity to phone him to check. I need not have feared! I received a call from the AAA office to say that "Tommy" had come up with a letter from Peter Driver, and that the signature could be transferred. Job done!

Towards the end of his life, I encountered Tommy for the last time, then well into his eighties, sitting stoically in a snowstorm, in the unbelievably bleak finishing field near The Fox Pub at Coulsdon. Uncomplaining, he was squinting through the snowflakes, cheering his athletes on by name, as they finished in the Surrey Cross-Country Championship.

"Good to see you Mr Thomas; how are you?" I greeted.
"A bbbit bbbloody ccccold!" came the climatically unsurprising response.

I must confess that I was surprised by the strong but realistic response from the old gentleman who had in fairness been static in his "Arctic grandstand seat" for over an hour.

What a classic old school club servant he was! "Tommy" worked as SLH secretary seemingly for ever. He remained interested right up until he crossed his own finishing line.

See Figure 136 – Tommy Thomas long time South London Harriers
secretary photographer Ed Lacey Centre

Don Turner (Epsom and Ewell Harriers/Surrey County AA, Southern Men's League, NUTS)

Don was first fired up athletically by Britain's Tom Richards who won the silver medal in the London 1948 Olympic Marathon.

He simply revelled in notching up the miles, both in training and racing, moving on smoothly to a distinguished career as a long distance runner to become, in the 1960s, one of Britain's best ever long distance racers.

He was second finisher for the triumphant Great Britain team in the 1962 Comrades Marathon in South Africa, in third place, closing fast on second, with friend and rival John Smith the winner.

"Smithy and I regularly ran 180 miles a week in training," he once recounted casually.

The classic London to Brighton Race was taken comfortably in the Turner stride several times. He finished second twice and third once.

Ever modest, details of this enduring servant's life in the sport have proved hard to prise from him, but steadfastness of purpose is a recurring and happily ongoing theme.

Don has thankfully stayed on in the sport to pass on his experience and become one of its most respected officials and enduring timekeepers.

Naturally he helped with the organisation of the London to Brighton Race which, because of police restrictions, is now but a fond memory. Don became Surrey County Secretary in 1990 and retains that post. For many of those years he served too as Championships Secretary and the Southern Men's League Secretary.

Quietly efficient, Don has also dedicated much of his time to Surrey AA and his Epsom and Ewell club, as treasurer/auditor, as well as auditing the accounts of other clubs and leagues. He now walks a great deal, leading fellow officials on Mondays for four or more hours, often appropriately in the company of Tom Richards junior (Surrey official and medal engraver) whose father it was who inspired Don over 60 years ago.

One would be hard pressed, to find another former top class athlete, who has put more back into his sport than Don Turner.

See Figure 137 – Don Turner presents Surrey gold to Shirin Irving, one of Britain's brightest multi event hopes

Don Webb (Croydon Harriers/Surrey County AA)

Don, like so many long time servants of the sport, owes his father a great debt of gratitude for introducing him to it at a very young age.

Father Webb, a PT instructor with the Boys Brigade in the early 1950s took twelve year old twins Don and Doug to the Coombe Lodge grass track in Croydon for athletics practice.

There the fortuitous interface between club and schoolboys occurred, and both boys joined ultimately to become county standard athletes. At first, contrary to his current physique, Don recalls starting out as a sprightly young high jumper happily landing on coir (coconut) matting. What would the Health and Safety Executive think of that today? Don became proficient in many events over the year and this led to success in the demanding decathlon. Brother Doug, a sharp sprinter in his active days, later specialised as a starter and became one of the best in the land.

Now a highly respected field official and committee man, Don has served club and county in many capacities, deservedly recognised by both, which have honoured him as their President. The South of England AA awarded him a 40 years long service badge, but how many of the general public know of such recognition or of similar un-headlined accolades for his many "twin brothers and sisters" throughout the land?

See Figure 138 – The dedicated Don on duty while awaiting a hip
Replacement

His experience and sound judgment, plus his ability to collect, collate and polish club trophies, have made him unchallenged first choice as my club chairman for many years. Other clubs need not enquire. Any transfer fee would be prohibitive!

Paul Weston (Croydon Harriers)

Despite the fact that he is a West Ham United fan, and I support the Wolves, Paul and I have worked happily, and I like to think successfully, for over 20 years as the joint managers of the Croydon Harriers Young Athletes team!

Paul's athletics launch-pad was the Mexico 1968 experience, with Jim Hines, Bob Beamon, the Dick "Fosbury Flop" high jump sensation, David Hemery, plus Tommy Smith and the eye-opening Black Power protest.

Paul was, he said *"A child of the Cold War, wanting the western nations to win…. Naïvely believing we were all clean, while the commies were all on drugs!"*

As a keen PE teacher in the mid 1980s he had already stepped into North Croydon Schools' management, to ensure continuity at a time of shortages and disputes.

Paul, who features among the best speed coaches I have ever met, generously claims that he caught the coaching bug from me when he came soon after our first encounter, to the Croydon Arena, where he has coached with charisma and success ever since.

His long time achievements were recently recognised by England Athletics London Region with the award for Participation (Sprint) Coach of the Year. He fits his highly organised coaching activities in smoothly, besides being a family man and senior teacher at Warlingham School from which, due to his influence, a regular stream of talented girls and boys comes into club athletics.

Paul's favourite day each year is the Saturday of the English Schools' Championships.

As he says *"Pure, relentless sport at its best, BRILLIANT."*

See Figure 132 – The "Chippy and the Pedagogue" Terry Lapins and Paul Weston with their England Athletics Officiating and coaching Awards

Now kind reader, I ask you to spare some time to pinpoint similar pillars of the athletics fraternity in your domain, whose works all too often go unnoticed.

The time is right to pick up the phone, to tell them that they too have been added to a list of Foot Soldiers, yours, worthy of much more publicity and appreciation than many athletes who "sail far too close to the wind" and who bring discredit on a wonderful sport.

Long Live the Foot Soldiers!

Appendix G

Olympic Recall

1948 At age 10 unaware of competitive athletics, I was excited to learn that there was an Olympic soccer match featuring Egypt at Selhurst Park, home of Crystal Palace FC just 20 mins walk from home. For some good reason I am certain, my father didn't take me.

1952 "Unknown Luxemburger" Jose Barthel beat Roger Bannister, 4th in the 1500m by 0.8sec in Helsinki.

1956 Melbourne. The glorious Gordon Pirie "failure" against Russian Iron Man Vladimir Kuts, and similarly Derek Johnson's valiant "nip and tuck" losing 800m "effort against American Tom Courtney. On the victory front who could not have been thrilled by dashing Irishman Ron Delany's golden 1500m run.

1960 Rome. Shocked pigeon escapes flattening from beneath the speeding foot of Italian sprinter Livio Berutti.

1964 Tokyo. Sadness at not "making" MY Games but delight for my four gold medal winning contemporaries, Lynn Davies long jump, Ken Matthews 50k walk, Ann Packer 800m and Mary Rand long jump.

1968 Mexico City. THE Colemanballs comment during David Hemery's epic Olympic 400m hurdles victory "...and who cares who's third?" shouted the excited commentator David Coleman or was it dear old Ron Pickering? Well, I think every British athletics fan did care, for it was none other than our own John Sherwood, magnificently winning the bronze medal.

1972 Munich. Having put my 1964 disappointment to rest, I drove alone to Munich to watch my first Olympics. The pentathlon triumph of Mary Peters over local heroine Heidi Rosendahl came at the end of an enthralling tussle which left the Brits with strained vocal cords from incessant cheering. What might have been the occasion of a lifetime, fell victim of the terrorists who targeted the Israeli team, killing several, one of whom was my friend, coach Amitzur Shapira.

1976 Montreal. Thanks to Canadian Olympian Thelma Wright I shared a just-vacated and spotlessly clean former construction worker's apartment within easy walking distance of the stadium. Shame they had not been able to finish its spectacular retracting roof.

The seemingly non-stop salesman's nasal intonation of "Hot Dogs, Cold Beer", the prompt departure of the American who sat beside me expecting to watch the marathon unravel in the stadium, and physically bumping into old schoolfriend Martin Collis, a converted Canadian, were notable non-athletic memories.

In the cauldron of competition how could one forget Edwin Moses' annihilation of the 400m hurdles field with his 47.63sec win. It was great to see two personal Canadian friends, Thelma and Lee Wright representing the host country, and there was some much needed national pride too when Brendan Foster won 10000m bronze.

1980 Moscow. The US boycott and the subsequently shallow Allan Wells 100m sprint gold for Great Britain, but I have to admit too, that I really enjoyed watching the Coe and Ovett 800m double more than once on television!

1984 Los Angeles. Seb Coe's 1500m triumph plus 800m silver was enhanced by Steve Cram's 1500m silver, but sadly one could hardly overlook Steve Ovett's tragedy. Tessa Sanderson, my late friend Wilf Paish's protégé, also shone to win the women's javelin with Fatima Whitbread further raising British spirits behind her in bronze medal position.

1988 Seoul and the awful anticlimax of the Ben Johnson drugs scandal.

1992 Barcelona, and the sensational Sergei Bubka blip in the pole vault. The "King" sat out for 90 minutes, failed 5.70m twice, and moved to 5.75m where failure hastened his departure from the hushed Montjuic Stadium.

1996 Atlanta hosting the Centennial Games movingly nominated Mohammad Ali to light the flame and added to the poignancy of the occasion by presenting him with a replacement for the gold boxing medal which he won in 1960.

2000 Sydney, when great British oarsman Steve Redgrave became a member of the very select "Club " of athletes to win five Olympic gold medals.

2004 Athens. Thank heavens for Kelly Holmes and her golden 800m and 1500m double. Without it the athletics could have been even more seriously tarnished by the incomprehensible antics of Greek sprinters Konstantinos Kenteris and Ekaterini Thanou who staged a motor scooter accident to avoid a drugs test.

2008 Brilliant Beijing, with the increasing warmth of our Chinese hosts, the exciting Martyn Rooney 400m runs, and universal sympathy for the stunned Chinese at the withdrawal of their great high hurdles hope, Liu Xiang. It was hard to believe that the pageantry of the Opening Ceremony, for which I could not afford tickets to attend, exceeded that of the Closing Ceremony which enthralled me.

Olympic Miscellanea

When London won the 2012 Games bid nobody could have been more thrilled than me. Immediately I resolved to make my celebratory mark by creating a scheme which would involve schoolchildren throughout Britain "Leaping for London". It would be mass participation at a basic level, with lots of fun, involving minimum administration.

I worked on the idea for several months, running it past teaching colleagues and expert coaching friends Tom McNab and Wilf Paish. I welcomed their advice, and encouraged by their interest circulated a draft to all county managers at the English School's Championships for return and comment. It must have been good, for it generated a 10% response! Heartened, I tweaked it further, incorporated the idea of fund raising for the Paralympics through it…they were pleased at the prospect… and having paved the way on the phone, I forwarded it to Lord Coe's secretary. The eagerly awaited response was not long in coming.

"…thank you for your interest. Please find enclosed promotional CD…!

There was no reference to the scheme I had sent and my modest dream will doubtless remain gathering dust in a drawer….

…so now for the THE GREAT BRITISH SPORTING DREAM and the 2012 LONDON OLYMPIC GAMES with, I hope, Jessica Ennis, Jenny Meadows, Martyn Rooney and Stef Twell topping the Olympic podium in London… plus optimistically, ten others making the medals!

See Figure 139 – Jessica Ennis at full stretch in Long Jump

Postscript

Walking ever-watchful, as any self-respecting tourist must be on Barcelona's famous Las Ramblas thoroughfare, during the 2010 European Championships, I recognised a familiar young face in the crowd.

Katerina Thompson: yes, I had identified the outstanding multi-eventer correctly.

"Hi Katerina, I'm so glad to have spotted you. You feature in my book which is nearly finished. I hope you and your parents are happy with that," I said.

I continued turning to seek approval from the man in the group whom I wrongly assumed to be her father.

"You must be Dad; I am Mike."

"Mike who?" he asked, inadvertently earning himself a place in the postscript of this book by referring to the title.

"Yes, that's me," I replied, shaking his hand.

With lunch beckoning in the nearby plaza, I bade them farewell and left the philanthropic Barry Wells (as I later discovered) looking distinctly bemused as I strode off, golden-socked and white-hatted into the lunchtime throng.

Acknowledgements

This has been a massive undertaking for me and a huge number of people have made valued input. It's just not possible to thank everyone here, but I am immensely grateful to you all, including the following:

Zoë Alsford	Graphic Designer extraordinaire
Daisy Collingridge	Original illustrations
Gerry Cranham	Photographs and photographic advice
Fritz Emmert	German language advice
Beryl Fleet	Family information and photographs
Nicola Fleet	Scanning/technical support
Chris Garrett	Russian translation
Ian Gillett	Photograph
Vicky Jover	Tommy Jover information and photographs
Peter Lovesey	Historical information
Robin Macklin	Proofreading and editorial advice
Emmett McGowan	Scanning photographs
Neil Millard	Croydon Advertiser
Jack Miller	British Athletics Supporters Club/NUTS
Annie Morley	Trinity School Croydon Archivist
Bernie and Aileen Regan	Proofreading
Martin Rowe	Photographic archive research/ technical support
Chris Scott	Aeronautical advice and proofreading
Karolin Scott	Swedish start instructions
Alan Sexton	Proofreading - Athletics
Mark Shearman	Photographs
Eric Thompson	Loan of archive Athletics Weekly Magazines
Don Turner	Proofreading

To the best of my knowledge, everything in this book is correct. I have made strenuous efforts to check dates, times, names etc to ensure accuracy.

Inevitably, these are edited highlights and it is, of course, impossible to include all the fascinating people and anecdotes from the past 70 or so years. You are very much part of this book even if your name doesn't appear!

Book References

Bannister, Roger: - The First Four Minutes (Putnam 1955)

Booth, Dick: - Gordon Pirie the Impossible Hero (Corsica Press 1999)

Coe, Sebastlan with Miller, David: - Running Free (Sedgwick & Jackson 1981)

Emery, David: - Lillian (Hodder & Stoughton1971)

Freud, Gideon (Ed.): - The Games of the XVIII Olympiad Tokyo 1964 (International Olympic Institute 1965)

German Sport Aid Foundation: - Munchen72

Huxtable, Andrew & NUTS: - British Best performances of All Time (NUTS 1956)

Kozik, Frantisek: - Zatopek The Marathon Victor (Artia 1954)

Lovesey, Peter: - The Kings of Distance (Eyre & Spottiswoode 1968)

McAllister, Peter: - The Science of the Inadequate Modern Male 2009

Ovett, Steve with John Rodda: - Ovett an Autobiography (Willow Books 1984)

Peters, Mary with Ian Wooldridge: - Mary P (Hutchinson 1974)

Pirie, Gordon:- Running Wild (W.H.Allen 1961)

Radcliffe, Paula with David Walsh: - Paula: My Story So Far (Simon & Schuster 2004 & 2005)

Rand, Mary: - Mary Mary (Hodder & Stoughton 1969)

Rowe, Warren: - Front Runners; The First Athletic Champions 1857-1875 (Book Guild 2002)

Shrubb, Alfred: - Running & Cross-Country Running (Health & Strength 1908)

Snell, Peter & Garth Gilmore: - No Bugles, No Drums (Minerva 1965)

Thurlow, David: - Sydney Wooderson – Forgotten Champion (1989)

Turnbull, Simon: - Steve Ovett, Portrait of an Athlete (W. H. Allen 1982)

Watman, Mel: - All Time Greats of British Athletics (2006)

Watts, Dennis: - Tackle Athletics This Way (Stanley Paul 1964)

West, Douglas: - Portrait of a Seaside Town (Emprint 1984)

List of Illustrations

(in order of appearance)

Cover photos
"Mermaid" emerging from Sea (© Pathe News reproduced with their permission)
Commonwealth Games
World Student Games
Surrey Championships
Schoolboy break-through

Mike and Chris have post race chat 1956.

The only action shot of the secretive Zola Budd at Norman Park, Bromley, 1985. Did I miss a fortune here?

Tissot split time stopwatch used for my 880yds PB

The Inspirational Alf Tupper every boys athletics idol. Image D C Thompson.

Tommy Jover (left), the speedy Dulwich Hamlet winger.

Gordon Pirie, characteristically in the lead. Photo Gerry Cranhan.

Mike and Pirie biographer Dick Booth on Gordon's memorial seat, Farthing Downs.

Mike in the footsteps of Milo de Cretona.

John Fleet.

"Chain He". Illustration by Daisy Collingridge.

The Legendary Jesse Owens blasts out of blocks in Berlin. Photo Courtesy of the Library of Congress.

Mike with Russell Coffin, 92, son of the late head mistress, at the Aberdeen house school entrance 2011.

"The Shrimping Boy". Illustration by Daisy Collingridge.
"Corgi Record Chase". Illustration by Daisy Collingridge.

Joan Pick beats the bus. Paul Matyniuk photo.

Dick Fosbury pioneering the successful "Flop" Mexico 1968 Mark Shearman photo.

Aerial view of Whitgift Middle School.

"Did I get out of that?!" Upside down on Barham Down. Young Mike R.

Surrey School's Long Jump Certificate.

Art master to be, Sub Lt Tony Renouf emerging from below decks.

Scene of subterfuge revisited. Mike and Derek Cooper at Motspur Park 56 years later. Nicola Photo Courtesy Fulham FC.

School quarter-mile champion.

School long-jump champion.

Inspired Chris Chataway beats Vladimir Kuts.

The start of Mike's schoolboy records

LAC Schools at White City Brian Linke leading.

White City Stadium panorama Senior boys 880yds.

It's not WHAT you know, but WHO you know. Jack Crump business card.

Penultimate School Half Mile with Phil Collins, 2nd & 3rd L.

"It's Fun being Trinity School Athletics Captain!" Mike front row 3rd from left next to master i/c Arthur Mapp.

1956 Croydon Arena mid straight 880yds start in London Inter Old boys Match.

Programme for Croydon International Meeting Arena Big Match.

Big Break Through. Chris Chataway Race Finish. Mike, 27 Chris, 18.

"The event the never was!" Ponomareva discus details from "the match that never was" programme.

Friends for life. (From left to right) Jean Luc and Chantal Cescina, Marty and Henk Boersbroek, Mike Fleet, Yvonne and Ferdi Koch.

The start of over 50 years plus as a Croydon Harrier.

Friends of influence in the fifties – Austin Fox, Frank Turk and Ken Fuller.

Coach Bill Coyne on wind gauge duty.

RAF Friends and Rivals. 800m with Frank Di Rienzo.

Start Ausweiss TSV Germania, Wilhelmshaven.

Winning RAF Jever Team HQ 2TAF Munchen Gladbach. Team captain Mike, centre, with trophy.

What Health and Safety? Loughborough XC. Hurdling a stile in style.

21st Birthday Southern Cross Country Championship XC Aylesford, cheered on by Frank Turk.

Disputed Loughborough dead heat Mike (L) and Wynne Oliver.

Anchoring Barker's and Derry and Toms to historic victory over Harrods at Wimbledon.

First Athletics Weekly cover appearance and first AAA vest partnering winner Mike Rawson (3).

Loughborough Athletics Team 1959/60.

"Not bad after a swim" First Sub 1:50.0 800m Mike (1) leading Peter Snell.

International Debut GB v Hungary. A disappointed third. Gerry Cranham photo.

World Student Games 1961 Fisu I/D.

GB Athletics Team Sofia. John Holt (End right, second row) later to become Secretary General of the IAA. Menzies Campbell (Top left) later to become leader of the Leberal Party. Mike (third row, centre).

"Cross-sport inspiration" Olympic diver, Liz Ferris' MF photo. Inset – Gerry Cranham photo.

Ron Delany wins World Student Games 800m Mike 5th second from right.

Leaving our trusty Viking behind at Gatwick. Mike and trilby-hutted Menzies Campbell with others.

White City Whitsun Games. Cover Boy Mike in the lead!

1962 "Welsh distraction" Janice Catt in action.

1962 AAA Championships 4th, 3rd English. Mike behind 10 and 17.

1962 Happy Harriers Quartet White City, Mike Fleet, Bob Harvey, Michael Soubry, Doug Webb.

1962 Welcome information from fellow NUT. Updated UK All-Time Rankings.

East African Airways Comet 4B.

1962 Commonwealth final. Mike unusually chasing Kenyan with Peter Snell waiting to strike.

Peter Snell holds off Geoge Kerr for Perth Gold. Mike 5th. Cerca 1963.

Personal best page from the record book MF photo.

Southern 880yds title winner Welwyn.

Win in controversial shorts v Sweden White City.

Volgograd "World Record" in lane three. Soviet Sport Photo.

Volgograd letter re Photos. MF photo.

Russian poster exchanged for a bar of Cadbury's Dairy Milk chocolate! MF photo.

Selhurst Grammar School Team.

Brightwell Inter Counties "Bombshell." Robbie Brightwell, 40, Mike, 30 and John Boulter, 7. Gerry Cranham photo.

London v New Crystal Palace match York Menu. MF photo.

John Le Masurier's dreaded "Kiss of non selection" list.

1964 Olympic Gold Medallist Lynn Davies. Welcome home poster donated by Stan Levenson of the Daily Worker.

In the bag!... The oh so elusive Surrey title 1967. Photo Ron Linstead.

Nicola in ESAA 200m Championship. MF photo. Nicola timekeeping (blue cap) at Olympic Trials with "Stan the Man" Burton (top right).

The great Sydney Wooderson setting a new mile record of 4:06.4 at Motspur Park in 1937. Corbus Photo.

Mike with sister Judy. Photo Croydon Advertiser.

Something tells me it's all over. MF looking back down track.

1974 AAA silver in 4x400 Mike to Roy Fox.

Mike with Fritz and Gudrun Emmert at the rain-soaked Munich European Championships 2002. NF photo.

Tanja Granig Croydon Harriers' Austrian hurdler visitor.

Decathlete Lloyd Maloney javelin throwing in Aden.

The Indestructible Jahlman Singh with admiring sympathisers, at UK Veterans Multi- event. MF photo.

Mike presenting Wilfried Spronk the Munich Olympic Stadium director with a Croydon Harriers tour T Shirt, 1986. NF photo.

Janko Stamoff guide to GB students team during 1961 World Student Games, Sofia Bulgaria.

Mike with Helmut Weinzierl in Freising 1978.

Croydon Harriers and guest stars in Germany for Freising Stadium Opening.

A youthful Steve Ovett shows the way. Mike (L) in vain chase after youthful Steve Ovett (R) in British League 800m.

Generous Dalton Grant's Eberstadt medal. MF photo.

Grange Hill TV "English Schools sprint final!"

Mike taking Selhurst Grammar cross-country boys for a five miler. Croydon Advertiser photo.

Bob Benn racing bend at Wimbledon Park. MF photo.

Yacin Yusuf Post European U23 1500 ESAA 3000m Victory. Mark Shearman photo.

Martyn Rooney and coach Mike after UK Junior 400m win. Chris Carter photo.

Who forgot his vest? Henry Rono "The Croydon Harrier!" Mark Shearman photo.

Now I know how mother felt! NF photo.

Timsbury Manor Group world record hammer thrower Harold Connolly USA (L), Mike at back and Oliver Cutts (R).

"Galleann" Organ, CPFA. Sporting Salt of the Earth.

Loud hailing. 2009 Lexus 10k Mike with his personal mike. Ian Gillett photo.

Announcing at 2010 Inter Services Championships "Mike with the Mike" with Squadron Leader Jason Davenhill at RAF Cosford.

Mike and Gerry Cranham "Maestro" photographer of the 1960s. Mark Cranham photo.

Mike (L) Official Shepherd accompanying Glen Cohen, David Jenkins and Bill Hartley to the Europa Cup 400m Start at Crystal Palace.

Mike with Shirley High School Big Match Kit Stewards Crystal Palace.

Mike, Nicola and Beijing Volunteer with "Bird's Nest" Stadium behind.

Amitzur Shapira. Photo Israeli Embassy.

International Athletes Club Charity Football team and All Star XI. Bobby Robson back row centre, Mike back row second from end Right.

Mike with Lord Weatherill, Mary Berkeley and Don Faircloth at "The Speakers House".

MFG re-union photo at Croydon Harriers 75th Anniversary Dinner 1995.

MFG 2010. Graeme Fanner Photo.

The poignant Hiroshima Atom Bomb Memorial. MF photo.

The awesome Niagara Falls, one of the Wonders of the World. MF photo.

UK 800m Number Ones 48 years and 4 seconds plus apart. Mike with Michael Rimmer 2010. Nicola Fleet photo.

Sir Roger Bannister congratulates Kip. Keino after Pentland Anniversary mile at Iffley Road, Oxford 1994. MF photo.

Roger Bannister completes the first ever sub 4 minute mile. Iffley Road Track Oxford. PA photo.

Prolific record breaker Alf Shrubb.

Donna Fraser supreme Croydon Harriers female sprinter in full stride. MF photo.

Judy Oakes Commonwealth joy 1994 Victoria BC. MF photo.

Ann Packer wins at White City. Gerry Cranham photo.

Mary Peters. Gerry Cranham photo.

Mary Rand. White City action. Gerry Cranham photo.

Dorothy Odam-Tyler practising post war Western Roll. Inset Dorothy age 91, 2011.

Martyn Rooney in very tight 400m Beijing Olympic final chase, second from left. MF photo.

Martyn Rooney's (3rd L) home straight dash in Beijing Olympic 4x400m final. MF photo.

Stephanie Twell Young Olympian. MF photo.

George Chuter javelin potential (inset MF photo) now England rugby star. Getty image courtesy RFU.

Danny Cipriani, huge athletics potential is rugby union gain. Getty image courtesy RFU.

Oliver Bradfield. MF photo.

Beth Carter. MF photo.

Peter Chambers Lexus Croydon 10k Runner-up age 15 2010. Peter. MF photo.

Emilia Gorecka/Ruth Haynes. MF photo.

Croydon's quadruple Olympian Donna Fraser welcomes emerging star Twinelle Hopeson to "Wall of Fame!" mural by Jeanne-Marie Ears and Susan Beresford. MF photo.

Inset, Twinelle Hopeson the club athlete. MF photo.

Jessica Judd win SEAA title by a "straight" Ashford. Inset Victor characteristically waits for vanquished to finish. MF photos.

Record breaking Lawrence Okoye, Croydon Harriers at Bedford 2010. Keith Mayhew photo.

Kelly Holmes with Loulou Rowlands. MF photo.

Katerina Thompson. MF photo.

Ned Quiney breaks the 5m barrier at Crystal Palace 2010. MF photo.

David Barrington beats computer results! photo.

The fair and knowledgeable Jeanne Coker. MF photo.

The Magnificent Arthur Wint. 440yds start at Motspur Park 1946. Getty Image.

Carolyn Franks discussing finer points of javelin throwing with Wilf Paish. MF photo.

Linda Harrison enjoying her athletics! MF photo.

Dedicated Derek Hayward on ESAA duty. MF photo.

Valiant team manager Matthew Kiernan prepares plunge in pursuit of points. Martin Rowe photo.

The "Chippy and the Pedagogue" Terry Lapins and Paul Weston with their England Athletics Officiating and coaching Awards. MF photo.

"Grass Roots" multi-tasker Peter Radford. MF photo.

Achilles Relays "Anchor Man" Mark Steed centre at Iffley Road with John De'ath, and fellow blue Alan Sexton. MF photos.

Bannister First Sub 4 minute mile Anniversary Achilles Relays Programme.

Tommy Thomas long time South London Harriers secretary photographer Ed Lacey Centre. Alan Black Photo.

Don Turner presents Surrey gold to Shirin Irving, one of Britain's brightest multi event hopes. MF photo.

The dedicated Don on duty while awaiting a hip Replacement. MF photo.

Jessica Ennis at full stretch in Long Jump. MF photo.

Jenny Meadows and Mike after Barcelona medal ceremony 2010. NF photo.

Jenny 6 Paris 2011.

The London Olympic Stadium nearing completion, spring 2011. NF photo.

Heart washed and modelled by mother, Beryl Fleet at age 96. MF photo.

Happy CRY Moment after Lexus Croydon 10k. Philippa Stanyard and Scottish cricketer Neil McCallum, now Mr and Mrs Neil McCallum with Martyn Rooney 2007. MF photo.

Cecilia Barriga in Surrey Schools action. MF photo.

CRY Logo.

Index

257

T

Cardiac Risk in the Young (CRY)

See Figures 142 – 145

Dear Reader

In the hope that you have enjoyed this book, and like me consider yourself to have been fortunate in life, I ask you to spare a thought for the many young people who suffer from, or have succumbed to heart disease, and their families.

Several years ago, but still fresh in Croydon athletics memory, was the sudden death of Cecilia Barriga, our girls' captain and promising middle distance runner. It was an awful blow to her family and to everyone who knew her.

CRY was able to give her family much needed support at that very difficult time, as it continues to do for many others. CRY also crucially helps young people suffering from heart conditions, to be given the best treatment as quickly as possible.

I raise funds for CRY by seeking donations for my action photos, and additionally in alongside "I Also Ran by Mike Who?" I will be donating all profits from personally signed and illustrated celebrity "Split Time (book) Markers". I take this opportunity to thank the fifty plus sports stars, who have taken the time and trouble to support the cause on this way.

Good fund running!

Best wishes

Mike Fleet

CRY,
Unit 7, Epsom Downs Metro Centre, Waterfield,
Tadworth, Surrey, KT20 5LR

What the Reviewers Said

"A great read in Mike's inimitable style. Both humorous and insightful, it covers the highs and lows of an athletic career on the track and then his efforts to give back to the sport after competitive retirement. Meticulously researched, Mike's love for the sport shines through on every page"

Ian Hodge, UKA Director of Development, National Union of Track Statisticians

"A humorous and readable inside story of the life of a competitive runner that displays a great affection for the sport"

Andy Dunn, Editor Runners World

"Many people in athletics will know Mike Fleet for being an 'ever-present' at domestic grassroots meetings, but few will be aware of his tremendous history in the sport and the fact that he once topped the UK 800m rankings and rubbed shoulders with legends like Steve Ovett. This is a delightful jog down memory lane from a man who has truly devoted a lifetime to his sport"

Jason Henderson, Editor Athletics Weekly

...and taken, please, with a pinch of salt!

"I simply lapped up 'I ALSO RAN BY MIKE WHO?' Can't wait for next round. This carousel of competition and charm simply left my head spinning with enthusiasm."

Aidan Marathon, Runners Whirled

"Having read this book, I now feel sufficiently strengthened to jump to it and throw myself wholeheartedly into the great sport of athletics. My heart is racing."

Ann Enthusiast, Athletics Weakling

"Far more than the bare essentials were uncovered when I ploughed happily through "I Also Ran by Mike Who?" Many a shining athletics gem is revealed."

Miles Skinner, Ploughboy Magazine

"A lot of blooming sport, but having dug in, the fruits of an outdoor career are clear to see."

I. V. Beanarunner, Gardenerd's World

"Happy memories of emotive TV commentator, the one and only David Coleman are evoked! Precied Surrey Half-Mile Championships coverage. 1959. Who cared who was third? 1960 Who cared who was third? 1961 Who cared who was third? 1962 who cared who was second? 1963 Who cared who was second? 1964 Who cared who was second? 1965 Who cared who was fourth? 1966 Who cared who was eliminated? 1967 WHO WON? MIKE FLEET did!"

A.Ballsup, Privet Eye

"A must for all Masters. The large sprint edition is recommended in the long run. Mike what's his name's book is one I'll never remember... If you can't see and are hard of hearing, have a shot at the shouting book version."

Y. E. Annie Olderunne, Gaga Magazine

"This is the finish. Mike has now run out of words."

Peter Sout, Stop Press